Households and Financialization in Europe

Households and Financialization in Europe develops a processual, relational and critical transdisciplinary approach to household financialization in Europe, utilizing a range of national and local case studies. It does so by drawing on debates in Marxist, feminist and radical IPE, anthropology and other fields.

The book explores the household as simultaneously a micro-level social institution specializing in social reproduction, distribution and other activities; a building bloc of larger economic and social structures; and an object of multiple systems of power/knowledge. Putting this conceptualization to use in original research, the authors identify geographically and historically situated ways in which financialization transforms households and their relationships with the wider economy and society. The book traces these transformations in case studies of variegated financialization in Eastern and Southern European (semi-) peripheries where households have faced particularly severe financial issues since the global financial crisis, such as over-indebtedness and asset devaluation. Key themes recurring throughout the book include: the key role of housing in household financialization, the co-constitutive relationship between financialization and social and spatial inequalities, specific patterns in the relations of financial actors and households in semi-peripheries, and the implications of semi-peripheral forms of real and financial accumulation for household financialization.

With its transdisciplinary approach, this book will be of great interest to students and scholars of finance, financialization, household economics, international and global political economy, uneven development, economic anthropology, and economic sociology.

Marek Mikuš is Head of Research Group at the Max Planck Institute for Social Anthropology in Halle, Germany. He is a social anthropologist engaging with work in heterodox economics, geography and sociology. His research has focussed on civil society, the state, public policy, social transformation and private and public finance in Eastern Europe. He currently heads Emmy Noether Research Group "Peripheral Debt: Money, Risk and Politics in Eastern Europe", which studies household indebtedness in Croatia, Hungary, Poland and Slovakia.

Petra Rodik was a member of the Department of Sociology at the Faculty of Humanities and Social Sciences at the University of Zagreb, Croatia, from 2002 to 2020. She recently left a tenure-track position to become an independent researcher and data scientist. Her research interests include financialization of housing, household debt and advances in research methods.

RIPE Series in Global Political Economy

Series Editors: James Brassett (University of Warwick, UK), Susanne Soederberg (Queen's University, Canada) and Eleni Tsingou (Copenhagen Business School, Denmark).

The RIPE Series published by Routledge is an essential forum for cutting-edge scholarship in International Political Economy. The series brings together new and established scholars working in critical, cultural and constructivist political economy. Books in the RIPE Series typically combine an innovative contribution to theoretical debates with rigorous empirical analysis.

The RIPE Series seeks to cultivate:

- Field-defining theoretical advances in International Political Economy
- Novel treatments of key issue areas, both historical and contemporary, such as global finance, trade, and production
- Analyses that explore the political economic dimensions of relatively neglected topics, such as the environment, gender relations, and migration
- Accessible work that will inspire advanced undergraduates and graduate students in International Political Economy.

The *RIPE Series in Global Political Economy* aims to address the needs of students and teachers.

Urban Displacements
Governing Surplus and Survival in Global Capitalism
Susanne Soederberg

Households and Financialization in Europe
Mapping Variegated Patterns in Semi-Peripheries
Edited by Marek Mikuš and Petra Rodik

For more information about this series, please visit: www.routledge.com/RIPE-Series-in-Global-Political-Economy/book-series/RIPE

Households and Financialization in Europe

Mapping Variegated Patterns in Semi-Peripheries

Edited by
Marek Mikuš and Petra Rodik

Routledge
Taylor & Francis Group
LONDON AND NEW YORK

First published 2021
by Routledge
2 Park Square, Milton Park, Abingdon, Oxon OX14 4RN

and by Routledge
605 Third Avenue, New York, NY 10158

Routledge is an imprint of the Taylor & Francis Group, an informa business

British Library Cataloguing-in-Publication Data
A catalogue record for this book is available from the British Library

Library of Congress Cataloging-in-Publication Data
A catalog record has been requested for this book

ISBN: 978-0-367-46455-4 (hbk)
ISBN: 978-0-367-69237-7 (pbk)
ISBN: 978-1-003-02885-7 (ebk)

Typeset in Times New Roman
by codeMantra

Contents

Figures

Figures

Acknowledgements

This collection started as a workshop on "Households and Peripheral Financialisation in Europe", which we organized at the Max Planck Institute for Social Anthropology in Halle, Germany on 22–23 February 2018. Early versions of the introduction and four of the chapters were presented at the workshop; Tomáš Hoření Samec, Jeanne Lazarus and Aimee Placas joined this project later. Chris Hann, Director of the Department of "Resilience and Transformation in Eurasia" and co-director of the "Financialisation" Research Group at the Max Planck Institute, made the workshop possible with his generous support, while Bettina Mann, Anett Kirchhof, Kristin Magnucki, Anke Meyer, Michaela Rittmeyer, Ingrid Schüller, Stefan Schwendtner and Berit Westwood have been involved in various organizational aspects. We wish to thank all participants in the workshop: Manuel Aalbers, Jane Guyer (who could not attend in person), Mateusz Halawa, Deborah James, Mikołaj Lewicki, Marcin Serafin and Andreas Streinzer for their inspiring papers and other contributions; Tristam Barrett, Ger Duijzings, James Carrier, Don Kalb, Dimitra Kofti and Hadas Weiss for acting as discussants and chairs; and Daniela Elena Ana, Sara Bencekovič, Alicja Bobek, Hugo Valenzuela García, Ingo Schröder, Martin Sokol and all others who took part. We further thank the editors of the RIPE Series in Global Political Economy, in particular Susanne Soederberg, for their support for this project as well as the three anonymous reviewers for their helpful comments on the book proposal and a draft of the introduction and one of the chapters. Iva Marčetić also read a draft of the introduction and offered useful feedback. Jessica Holmes, Hannah Rich and Emily Ross at Taylor & Francis Group have provided professional editorial and managerial support. Marek Mikuš has worked on this collection as Research Fellow in the "Financialisation" Research Group; Research Fellow in the GEOFIN ("Western Banks in Eastern Europe: New Geographies of Financialisation") project at the Trinity College Dublin; and Head of Emmy Noether Research Group "Peripheral Debt: Money, Risk and Politics in Eastern Europe", funded by the German Research Foundation and hosted by the Max Planck Institute for Social Anthropology. He is thankful for all these opportunities. Petra Rodik would like to thank the Department of Sociology at the Faculty of Humanities and Social Sciences, University of Zagreb, for supporting her prolonged research leaves, during which she conducted a three-month stay at the Max Planck Institute for Social Anthropology in Halle and worked as Research Fellow in the GEOFIN project at the Trinity College Dublin. She would especially like to thank Chris Hann for making her research visit to the Max Planck Institute for Social Anthropology possible. For her, this was a cornerstone for many significant developments, one of which is this volume.

Notes on contributors

Natalia Buier is a Research Associate at the Max Planck Institute for Social Anthropology, Germany, and François Chevalier Fellow at the Madrid Institute for Advanced Study, Spain. Her current research interests include financialization of infrastructure and connections between capitalist social formations and ecological crises.

Ágnes Gagyi is a Researcher at the University of Gothenburg, Sweden, and member of the Working Group for Public Sociology Helyzet in Budapest, Hungary. Her work focusses on Eastern European politics and social movements in the context of the region's long-term global economic and geopolitical integration.

Tomáš Hoření Samec works at the Institute of Sociology of the Czech Academy of Sciences. He is interested in critical housing studies, urban studies and analysis of discourses on housing debt and financialization.

Csaba Jelinek is a Research Fellow at the Centre for Economic and Regional Studies at the Hungarian Academy of Sciences and a co-founder of the Periféria Policy and Research Center, Hungary. He is currently doing research on infrastructure developments, housing policy and housing cooperatives.

Jeanne Lazarus is CNRS (Centre national de la recherche scientifique) Research Fellow at the Center for the Sociology of Organizations at Sciences Po, Paris, France. Her research has focussed on relationships between bankers and customers in French retail banks. She studies how public policy structures household finance and conceives of the protection of populations deemed to be at risk of financial insecurity due to precarious employment and the withdrawal of social welfare provisions. She is particularly interested in the making of a "responsible" financial market for individuals.

Zaira T. Lofranco is a social anthropologist and Adjunct Professor at the State University of Milan, Italy. She been a member of the Eastbordnet network and a fellow of the EU-funded research project Anticorruption

Polices Revisited (ANTICORRP). Her research interests include political economy, corruption, financialization of household economies, housing and credit and debt relations.

Marek Mikuš is Head of Research Group at the Max Planck Institute for Social Anthropology in Halle, Germany. He is a social anthropologist engaging with work in heterodox economics, geography and sociology. His research has focussed on civil society, the state, public policy, social transformation and private and public finance in Eastern Europe. He currently heads Emmy Noether Research Group "Peripheral Debt: Money, Risk and Politics in Eastern Europe", which studies household indebtedness in Croatia, Hungary, Poland and Slovakia.

Aimee Placas is a faculty member of the College Year in Athens programme run by the International Center for Hellenic and Mediterranean Studies (ΔΙΚΕΜΕΣ) in Athens, Greece. Her research interests include consumption, debt and bankruptcy, the effect of the economic crisis on over-indebted households and everyday economic life in Greece.

Zsuzsanna Pósfai is a founding member of the Periféria Policy and Research Center based in Budapest, Hungary. Her research focusses on the financialization of housing in Hungary, households' indebtedness and potential new forms of progressive housing finance.

Petra Rodik was a member of the Department of Sociology at the Faculty of Humanities and Social Sciences at the University of Zagreb, Croatia, from 2002 to 2020. She recently left a tenure-track position to become an independent researcher and data scientist. Her research interests include financialization of housing, household debt and advances in research methods.

Irene Sabaté Muriel is a social anthropologist and a Lecturer at the Universitat de Barcelona, Spain, where she is a member of the Reciprocity Studies Group (GER) and teaches economic and urban anthropology. Her research interests include political economy, reciprocity, provisioning, work and social reproduction, housing, debt and credit relations, and financialization.

András Vigvári is a social anthropologist working at the Centre for Economic and Regional Studies at the Hungarian Academy of Sciences. His research examines peri-urbanization, displacement and informal housing in the context of housing financialization in Hungary.

Introduction

Households and peripheral financialization in Eastern and Southern Europe

Marek Mikuš and Petra Rodik

Introduction

The past 20-something years have seen a rapid growth of multidisciplinary literature on financialization – a concept that encompasses the manifold economic, political and social transformations driven by the increasing power, pervasiveness and complexity of finance in recent decades. If initially less prominently, much of this scholarship underscored the deepening imbrication of non-elite individuals with finance. Some scholars grasped this as a process of the financialization of households – "financial motives, rationales, and measures becoming increasingly dominant, both in the way individuals and households are being evaluated and approached, and in how they come to make decisions in life" (Aalbers 2017: 3). While this formulation stresses ideational and ideological aspects, scholars engaged also with the core material mechanisms of the financialization of households – in particular, the massive increase in their financial liabilities and holdings of financial assets (Gonzalez 2015).

However, despite the increasing scope and sophistication of this literature, we argue that its understanding of households suffers from two important weaknesses that this volume seeks to address. First, authors tended to approach the household as an internally undifferentiated and opaque "black box", "a pass-through mechanism for flows of goods and services in the macro-economy" (Montgomerie and Tepe-Belfrage 2017: 656). They tended to abstract households from their social contexts and make conclusions about "average statistical households" based on survey data and presumptions about the social content of their conduct (Gonzalez 2015: 783, 785–786). Second, most existing scholarship on household financialization adhered to the dominant geographic focus in the financialization literature and focussed on the Anglo-Saxon cores rather than peripheries and semi-peripheries at multiple spatial scales (Gonzalez 2015: 783; Lai and Tan 2015: 76; Murphy and Scott 2014: 73).

Most of the existing literature on the financialization of households gravitates to two broad analytical approaches.[1] First, scholars working in multiple traditions of comparative and international political economy, such as Marxist, feminist or "British social accounting", focussed on structural causes and outcomes of household financialization (e.g. Erturk et al. 2007; Froud et al. 1997; Fuller 2016; Lapavitsas 2013; LeBaron 2010; Montgomerie 2006a, 2006b, 2009, 2013; Roberts 2013, 2016; Soederberg 2014). They linked the process to major shifts in political economy and regulation, such as changing profit-making and accumulation strategies, stagnation of real wages, and neoliberal policies of financial liberalization, welfare-state retrenchment and "asset-based welfare" centred on housing and pension finance. In turn, the economy at large came to depend on the sustained capacity of households to service their debts, provide collateral backing financial assets and act as "shock absorbers of the last resort" (Bryan et al. 2009; Bryan and Rafferty 2017; Montgomerie 2016). Focussing on trends in the financial conduct of households in global and national political economies, these contributions tended to privilege macro over meso and micro levels of analysis and reproduce a narrow vision of the "economic" in their treatment of households (Roberts 2013: 22, 24). This can be partly attributed to the uncritical use of existing statistical data on finance of private individuals, which resulted in a lack of distinction between the household as a unit of measurement and an object of analysis (Montgomerie and Tepe-Belfrage 2017: 656). Some Marxist scholars seemed to over-identify households with reproduction of labour power and treat them as a proxy for labour at the expense of their other aspects (Bryan et al. 2009; Lapavitsas 2013: 38–39).

Second, a heterogeneous group of economic sociologists, geographers and political economists drawing on poststructuralist and constructivist theories developed an approach known as the "financialization of daily life" (e.g. Aitken 2007; Coppock 2013; Fligstein and Goldstein 2015; Langley 2006, 2007; Langley and Leyshon 2012; Martin 2002; Türken et al. 2015). This literature is distinguished by its preoccupation with how financialization penetrates everyday life, that is, the micro level of analysis. Compared to the former body of scholarship, it is more interested in a new financialized culture that invites a widening public to embrace financial risk. This corresponds to a more prominent focus on issues of discourse, ideology, subjectification and the role of households as investors, in addition to those of debtors and consumers (Gonzalez 2015: 785; van der Zwan 2014: 111). However, these scholars too tended to avoid a clear conceptualization of the household and substitute a close-up study of actual households with analyses of statistical data and public policies and narratives. For example, Paul Langley's (2008) well-cited book discusses extensively the changing financial behaviour of households, but this seems to be inferred from secondary data and interviews with professionals. There is no attempt to define the household and clarify its relationship with the individual, another major subject of Langley's monograph that seems more aligned with his Foucauldian framework.

This collection aims to deepen the engagement with the household in the financialization literature by rethinking it as an analytical concept moving towards a close-up, processual and relational study of actual households. In doing so, we wish to contribute to the discussion about how contemporary finance shapes the ways of thinking about, forming and acting upon contemporary households (DeLuca 2017a). Our second key objective is to balance the dominant focus on the cores of the global economy with an enquiry into the financialization of households in Eastern and Southern European semi-peripheries where, as we will argue, it tended to take specific forms. In the next section of this introduction, we therefore review the existing scholarship on variegated financialization and core-periphery relations and explain how we approach this problematic in the context of household financialization. The third section unpacks the way in which the household figures in current feminist analyses of household financialization, which focus on its implications for social reproduction as a key process in the household. We also trace a longer trajectory of debates and critiques of the analytical concept of the household in anthropology. In the fourth section, we build on these sources to conceptualize the household as a micro-level social institution oriented to a characteristic set of activities (including, but not limited to, social reproduction) as well as an artefact of various forms of knowledge and a subject of social norms and public discourse. The fifth section reviews the existing literature on the financialization of households and, building on the insights of the earlier sections, explains our overall approach to household financialization in semi-peripheral settings. We also present some preliminary observations about the specificities of recent household financialization in European semi-peripheries. An outline of the collection concludes this introduction.

Variegated financialization and core-periphery relations

Recognizing that processes of financialization develop in distinctive forms in different settings, political economists recently presented multiple accounts of what could be summarized as variegated financialization (Becker et al. 2010; Bohle 2018; Lapavitsas 2013; Lapavitsas and Powell 2013; Radošević and Cvijanović 2015; Rodrigues et al. 2016). Their contributions were influenced mainly by the scholarly traditions of comparative institutionalism (Engelen and Konings 2010), Varieties of Capitalism (VoC; see Hall and Soskice 2001) and Marxist political economy (Fine 2013), including in the latter rubric especially dependency theory and world-systems theory (WST). Our empirical focus necessitates an engagement with the existing scholarship on peripheral financialization at the macro level. However, this is complicated by discrepancies in the ways in which authors theorized such forms of financialization.[2] In this introduction, we therefore tease out the key arguments (and inconsistencies) of these contributions to explain our own approach to financialization in European semi-peripheries.

Costas Lapavitsas (2013: 200) differentiated "mature" financialization in "developed" countries from "subordinate" financialization in "developing" countries. The label subordinate is intended to highlight the neo-imperialistic, hierarchical and exploitative nature of relations that these forms of financialization reproduce. The rise of speculative capital flows since the 1970s, the resulting current account surpluses and inflation-targeting policies led central banks in many developing countries to accumulate world money (US dollar) reserves, thereby creating a monetary basis for subordinate financialization (Lapavitsas 2013: 245–255). The latter was further intensified by the expansion of foreign banks to peripheries. Lapavitsas (2013: 288–300) discussed also core-periphery relations in the eurozone with a focus on the dependence of Southern European countries on capital inflows from core countries, resulting in their rising current account deficits and the accumulation of external and internal debt in the 2000s. Notably, Eastern Europe has been exposed to a broadly similar financialization dynamic (Gabor 2010). However, Lapavitsas did not explain the implications of these European core-periphery relations for his notion of subordinated financialization. If the euro is a newly created world money that challenges the hegemony of the dollar (Lapavitsas 2013: 289), what is the relationship between the eurozone and the dollar-based world-system? Are core-periphery relationships of the eurozone totally subordinated to the world-system or do they possess a degree of autonomy? A fleeting reference to "internal" and "external" eurozone peripheries (Lapavitsas 2013: 291, n. 49) hints at the latter option.

Joachim Becker and co-authors similarly distinguished two forms of financialization: one based on fictitious capital, which relies on highly developed financial markets and prevails in the core, and the other based on interest-bearing capital, more common in the periphery where higher interest rates attract foreign capital inflows (Becker et al. 2010: 228–231; see also Becker and Ćetković 2015: 71–72). While peripheries share this dependence on capital inflows ("extraversion"), there are considerable socio-economic differences between them. Those countries that "either achieved partial industrialization or have developed a significant financial sector responsible for specialized services" (Becker et al. 2010: 226) should be considered semi-peripheral rather than peripheral. According to the authors, the heterogeneity of peripheries should be grasped with a regulationist typology accounting for modes of regulation – arrangements of legal, institutional and policy frameworks and social norms. This takes the form of binary classifications of accumulation regimes, such as productive/financialized, intensive/extensive and introverted/extraverted (Becker et al. 2010: 227), or forms of financialization, such as based on fictitious capital/interest-bearing capital and elite/mass-based.

João Rodrigues, Ana C. Santos and Nuno Teles (2016) theorized semi-peripheral financialization based on the case study of Portugal. However, its defining features, such as the critical role of international financial integration, external agents and bank loanable capital (rather than capital markets; Rodrigues et al. 2016: 505), fail to clearly distinguish semi-peripheral from peripheral financialization as conceptualized by Becker et al. (2010). The account of the Portuguese case therefore does not yield a sufficiently distinctive model of semi-peripheral financialization. It is rather an analysis of financialization in a (particular) semi-periphery, which is suggested also by the classification of Portugal as a semi-periphery on the basis of arguments about its position in relations of real accumulation rather than those of financial accumulation (Rodrigues et al. 2016: 486).

In their monograph on varieties of capitalism in Eastern Europe, Dorothee Bohle and Béla Greskovits (2012) split the region into semi-core (the Visegrád group and Slovenia), semi-periphery (Baltic countries, Bulgaria and Romania) and periphery (ex-Soviet bloc countries) (Bohle and Greskovits 2012: 44–47). These terms demarcate different patterns of international economic integration, measured by indicators of real accumulation with an emphasis on development of complex industries (Bohle and Greskovits 2012: 44–45). It is argued that financialization has been most pronounced in the semi-peripheral group of countries and "reinforced their specific weaknesses in terms of global competitiveness" (Bohle and Greskovits 2012: 93). In a more recent paper on housing financialization, however, Bohle (2018) lumped states previously distinguished as semi-core (Hungary) and semi-periphery (Latvia) into a single Eastern European periphery, compared with a North-Western European periphery represented by Ireland and Iceland. All four cases are framed as a single "Europe's periphery" with a broadly similar pattern of housing financialization characterized by: high demand for housing; the reliance of banks (main originators of credit booms) on external sources of funding; and the countries' lack of a reserve currency, with the latter two features making them particularly vulnerable to sudden reversals of capital flows (Bohle 2018: 212–214).

To summarize, authors have so far used the terminology of dependency and world-system theories to discuss (semi-) peripheral financialization in a rather inconsistent manner. In our view, a theoretically consistent conceptualization of *(semi-) peripheral financialization* should refer to core-periphery relations reproduced by processes of financial accumulation and maintain an analytical distinction between them and core-periphery relations of real accumulation, which the WST understands as the hierarchical division of labour in commodity chains of production processes (Chase-Dunn 1989; Wallerstein 1979). The two sets of relations obviously intersect, but they are not mutually reducible; it follows that a spatial node or zone may be differently positioned along the two continua. Such approach is approximated by Becker et al. (2010) and Lapavitsas (2013) with their models of peripheral (or subordinate) financialization that emphasize asymmetrical capital flows and the central roles of interest-bearing capital and world money. By contrast, it is theoretically inconsistent to label financialization as (semi-) peripheral simply because it occurs in a (semi-) peripheral setting in terms of real accumulation (cf. Rodrigues et al. 2016). In such cases, it is preferable to speak more loosely of *financialization in the (semi-) periphery*. Our empirical focus implies the need to describe how peripheral financialization impacted households in the particular case of Eastern and Southern peripheries (both "internal" and "external")[3] of the eurozone (Celi et al. 2018: 234–240; Lapavitsas 2013: 288–300; Sepos 2016), which is itself embedded in the global hierarchies of world money and financial centres and an unequal world economy more broadly. Engaging more closely and qualitatively than has so far been the case with the effects of such large-scale patterns on households could contribute to the further development and nuancing of the models of peripheral financialization. At the same time, we must recognize that households tend to be embedded in both financial and real accumulation relations. From this perspective, the looser idea of financialization in the (semi-) periphery has the advantage of making room for a consideration of the interplay between peripheral financialization and wider economic peripherality.

With this in mind, both we and our contributors have chosen to adopt the concept of semi-periphery to characterize the intermediate position of Eastern and Southern Europe in the world-system of real accumulation relations. This, together with an awareness of their peripherality within European productive and financial capitalism, serves to highlight the common characteristics of the two regions, typically compartmentalized in separate bodies of scholarship, as a basis for comparative analysis. Although both regions achieved a considerable degree of industrialization (Becker et al. 2010: 226), their economies still occupy subordinate and dependent positions vis-à-vis core zones. The two regions share a legacy of late industrialization and dependence on foreign capital, technology and innovation. Southern Europe has undergone a process of re-peripheralization due to eurozone integration, resulting in reduced competitiveness, declining manufacturing and reliance on Northern European financial capital as the driver of a hypertrophic expansion of non-tradable sectors such as construction, real estate and tourism (Gambarotto and Solari 2015; López and Rodríguez 2011; Rhodes 2015; Rodrigues et al. 2016). After early postsocialist de-industrialization, much of Eastern Europe has experienced extensive re-industrialization driven by foreign investments, but the new industries are in foreign (mainly Western European) ownership and marked by lower levels of autonomy and added value than their counterparts in cores (Bohle and Greskovits 2012: 40–48; Shields 2009). This economic profile, and its accompanying neoliberalized state forms, have crucial consequences for households: persistently lower wages than in cores; deregulated, "flexibilized" labour markets; meagre public provision of welfare and housing; and increased exposure of livelihoods to capital flow reversals and credit and assets busts (Allen 2006; Bohle 2014, 2018; Bohle and Greskovits 2012). The belated, but all the more rapid development of extraverted financial sectors (e.g. Rodrigues et al. 2016: 487–490) has exacerbated the latter tendency by channelling foreign interest-bearing capital to household credit and housing – in other words, by fuelling peripheral financialization.

We further seek to contribute to a better understanding of how core-periphery relations structure financialization by developing multiple levels of analysis. First, we agree with the need to move the discussion of variegated financialization beyond static country groupings and to recognize idiosyncratic developments in particular countries (Fernandez and Aalbers 2016).

Thus, our contributors note some specificities of the patterns of financialization in the countries they study, such as the presence of mortgage securitization in Spain, a feature associated rather with "mature" financialization (Sabaté, this volume), or the limited carry-trade activity resulting in an absence of foreign-currency lending to households in the Czech Republic, unlike in much of Eastern Europe (Hoření Samec, this volume). The notion of semi-peripheral financialization could be perhaps used more rigorously to describe such intermediate cases, as well as those when capital inflows into the domestic financial sector were combined with the sector's outward expansion (as seen in Spain or Greece). A narrower notion of peripheral financialization would then describe cases such as the one of Bosnia and Herzegovina, which was only on the receiving side of financial capital flows and was subjected to financial extraction through speculative operations based on informal euroization and currency carry-trade of the type common across Eastern Europe (Gabor 2010). Second, the chapters in Section II go beyond the nation-state to the meso level of analysis by tracing how financialization operates through, and further exacerbates, sub-national geographies of uneven development and the consequences this has for households and their reproductive strategies.

Genealogies of the concept of the household

We opened this introduction by arguing that the household is a prominent but ill-defined and in fact pre-theoretical concept in much of the literature on financialization. In a rare contribution engaging with this problem, Johnna Montgomerie and Daniela Tepe-Belfrage (2017) criticized the treatment of the household as a "black box" and presented their own "household economy" framing to make the household visible both as a unit and an object of analysis.

> [T]he household economy provides the basis of the national economy by serving as the site where productive and reproductive labour coalesce … [H]ouseholds are not simply a unit of measurement.… Rather, the household is a heuristic for capturing a fluid social structure that is not only more complex than a collection of individual behaviours and preferences but also more unequal and differentiated than the 'household sector' as explained through macroeconomic trends.
>
> (Montgomerie and Tepe-Belfrage 2017: 656)

The authors' concept of household economy draws on the substantial body of work on social reproduction in feminist, radical and WST scholarship, much of which focussed on its transformations in the context of globalization and neoliberalization (Bakker and Gill 2003; Bakker and Silvey 2008; Dunaway 2001; Elias and Gunawardana 2013; Peterson 2010; Safri and Graham 2010). Feminist analysts of household financialization generally draw on ideas about social reproduction originating from this literature (Elson 2013; LeBaron 2010; Roberts 2013, 2016). Accordingly, they grasped household financialization as co-constitutive with the commodification, individualization and privatization of social reproduction that the wider feminist literature associated with the neoliberal restructuring of recent decades. Social reproduction is understood as a composite of three key processes: biological reproduction, reproduction of labour power and reproduction of provisioning and caring needs (Bakker 2003: 77–78; Roberts 2013: 24).

Feminist scholars developed two key arguments about the recent articulation of financialization and social reproduction. First, they argued that households in Canada, the UK and the US, in particular low-income, middle-class, female-headed and/or minority households, turned to what Gonzalez (2015) described as a logic of "defensive consumption", that is, borrowing to maintain consumption standards (and associated social status) in the face of stagnant incomes and an erosion of welfare entitlements and public services (LeBaron 2010: 902–906; Montgomerie 2009, 2013; Montgomerie and Tepe-Belfrage 2017: 663–664; Roberts 2016). Susanne Soederberg (2014: 60–64) developed a related concept of "debtfarism" to describe a rhetorical and regulatory tendency of extending ("democratizing") access to credit to the poor such as to mitigate and depoliticize social conflicts, buoy consumption and discipline the poor in more effective ways. The second feminist argument about the financialization of social reproduction draws on the ideas of "privatized Keynesianism" (Crouch 2009) and "asset-based welfare" (Dewilde and De Decker 2016; Doling and Ronald 2010). This argument draws attention to mutually reinforcing relationships between the privatization of housing and pension systems and policies that promote debt-based homeownership as a "fix" for the lack of public provision and encourage individuals to adopt a speculative outlook (Allon 2014, 2015). Feminist scholars analysed relevant policies (mainly in core countries), their assumptions and limits in practice, and their gendered and distributionally regressive effects (Montgomerie and Büdenbender 2015; Roberts 2013; Young 2003). Both sets of contributions point out the unsustainable nature of consumption and mortgage finance as solutions to tensions produced by neoliberalization and their tendency to ultimately intensify the ongoing crisis of social reproduction (Fraser 2016; Roberts 2016).

This literature and our own approach to households share the emphasis on social reproduction as key to understanding households. We also share its concern with the ways in which various systems of inequality, including gender, operate across households and structure their relationships with other actors and domains. At the same time, we believe that the engagement with households in this feminist work has not entirely overcome some of the epistemological and methodological limitations of most financialization scholarship. In particular, inasmuch as it continues to focus on relations between households and macro-structures and tendencies of financialized capitalism and mostly relies on statistical data and institutional analysis to do so, it still assumes households as monolithic, internally undifferentiated units that follow a single rationality abstracted from highly varied experiences of actual households: for example the one of defensive consumption. Some explicit definitions of the household (e.g. as a site of the reproduction of labour power) as well as some arguments about the causes of its financialization (e.g. as an outcome of debtfarism) are somewhat functionalist and determinist. Despite the stated interest of many scholars in daily life, we have still learnt relatively little about practices and experiences of actually existing households, which tend to be messier and more ambiguous than elegant analytical narratives. Even in feminist work, the relevance of gender, race, class and so on has been documented mostly in terms of differential outcomes for categories of households, not intra-household processes (cf. Montgomerie and Tepe-Belfrage 2017). In addition, as Felipe Gonzalez (2015: 786) noted, the thesis of defensive consumption seems to be in tune with the dominant focus of financialization scholarship on Anglo-America where wage stagnation and a decline of middle classes have been indeed topical. Thus, while sharing key concerns and ideas with the feminist work on financialization of social reproduction, we propose a transdisciplinary approach enriched by an engagement with anthropology, a discipline with a decent track record of thinking about and studying households in qualitative, intimate and reflexive ways. In the rest of this section, we therefore revisit rich anthropological debates about the household, which have been rarely, if ever, noted in scholarship on financialization.

Anthropologists did not put much emphasis on the household as an analytical concept before around 1960. It was rather the concept of the family that guided their analyses of social organization (e.g. Lowie 1920; Murdock 1949). Nineteenth-century evolutionist accounts ordered family types in speculative sequences of stages. In mid-twentieth century, functionalist sociologists explained the modern nuclear family as a perfect adaptation to the needs of the industrial urban society (Netting et al. 1984: xv). Structural functionalist anthropologists developed static typologies of descent systems that they assumed to govern the life of non-state societies. Descent groups such as lineages were accordingly theorized as their primary social, political and economic units (Guyer 1981: 87, 89–91). Formation of domestic groups was presumed to normally follow from kinship-based rules of residence, which made the household somewhat of a residual category "to take up the slack between ideal family types and the actual groups of people observed in ethnographic situations" (Wilk and Netting 1984: 2).

In the 1960s, anthropologists such as Paul Bohannan (1963) and Donald Bender (1967) explicitly codified the seemingly straightforward distinction between the household as a social group defined by co-residence and the family as a group rooted in kinship. At that time, increasingly common fieldwork in Latin American and Western settings led anthropologists to start to recognize the household as an important locus of economic decision-making (Chibnik 2011: 131). There has also been a shift from the tendency to explain local forms purely by local conditions to a consideration of their relations with larger structures, which reflected advancing urbanization and the consolidation of capitalism and states in traditional areas of anthropological research. As a classical concept of peasant studies, the household carried with it a recognition of a "local social structure and tradition of life within a wider stratified political and economic system" (Guyer 1981: 87). At the same time, an important assumption originating in peasant studies was that the household was a highly self-contained production and consumption unit within the wider monetized economy. The influential model of the peasant economy developed by Alexander Chayanov (1966) in the 1920s assumed that production in peasant households pursued a single goal: satisfying the locally homogeneous standard of consumption. Work effort in each household thus varied during its lifetime according to what Chayanov modelled as a universal, biologically grounded cycle of household development. The idea of the developmental cycle of domestic groups was later elaborated by anthropologists such as Fortes (1949, 1958) and Goody (1958) who added a recognition of variations due to non-demographic factors. However, the idea of the autarchic household continued to inform influential takes on the concept in and beyond anthropology. Marshall Sahlins (1973) retained the main assumptions of Chayanov's model in his theory of domestic mode of production, which he applied to a wide range of pre-industrial economies. Marxist anthropologist Claude Meillassoux (1981: 6–7, 87, 91–98) argued that this mode of production did not exist in its pure form anymore, but its social relations lived on within households that remained sites of the reproduction of labour power outside of the sphere of capitalist production. Finally, Gary Becker's (1981) New Home Economics presented a neoclassical variation on the concept of the household as a production and consumption unit in modern capitalist society.

Critiques of these established notions of the household were on the rise in anthropology since the 1970s. In the field, anthropologists often found that resource pooling did not follow co-residence and household membership was fluid (Chibnik 2011: 132; Guyer 1981: 98–99). By the end of the decade, Sylvia Yanagisako (1979: 164) observed that defining the household by co-residence had not made the usage of the term consistent. This was the case because it had been defined implicitly also by so-called "domestic" activities, "usually related to food production and consumption or sexual reproduction and childrearing" (Yanagisako 1979: 165). While some anthropologists produced lists of such "domestic functions" (Bender 1967; Gonzalez 1969), it turned out impossible to find a single functional criterion (or a set of criteria) that would apply to all households in all settings (Wilk and Netting 1984: 4). Redefining the household in terms of domestic functions rather than co-residence also did not correct the lack of attention to relationships within households and between households and the wider society.

Several lines of critique developed in response. One targeted the functionalist notion of the household as a unit performing a supposedly universal set of domestic functions. Yanagisako (1979: 187–189) argued that such understanding accepted uncritically the conceptual separation of domestic (private) and politico-jural (public) domains, together with the assumption that biological reproduction is necessarily the primary activity in the former. Such assumptions constituted domestic groups as natural units, standing somehow in separation from, or even opposition to, the society (Harris 1981). Yanagisako (1979: 199–200) called for a recognition that households were just as much part of political and economic structures as they were reproductive units, and, accordingly, met many functions beyond procreation and socialization. There was nothing wrong with functional analysis of domestic groups in itself, but this needed to start from categories and practices of each society (see also Yanagisako 1984). A related critique came from feminist scholars who challenged the notion of the household as a unitary decision-making unit headed by an adult male. Anthropologists documented a more complex reality of multiple gendered forms of authority in the household (Clark 1989; Lockwood 1989; Yanagisako 1979: 190–191). Building on such ethnographic insights, Jane Guyer (1981: 100) brought forward a more individual-oriented view of the household as "constituted by a series of implicit or explicit contracts, not by total subsumption of the members into a solidary unit". Taken together, these critiques imply that analysis of domestic social organization should go beyond households as units to encompass internal decision-making, relationships crosscutting households (e.g. gender, generational) and relationships of inequality between households (Guyer 1981: 97–104). Agreeing with Yanagisako (1979: 200) that the household and the family should be seen as little more than descriptive terms, Guyer (1981: 104–105) concluded that they "indicate problems to be explored and not analytical concepts to be applied in a rigid fashion". In economics, Becker's (1981) model of the household as a firm was rejected on both theoretical and empirical grounds and replaced by collective household models based on bargaining between members, with feminist economists stressing gendered dimensions of such processes (e.g. Folbre 1986; Hart 1992).

Rethinking the household as an analytical concept

In our view, these debates offer two major lessons for critical thinking about the household. First, there is no single morphological or functional definition of the household that would be applicable to domestic social organization in all contexts. A conceptualization of the household therefore needs to be sufficiently flexible to allow for variation on the ground, while the latter needs to be systematically accounted for when the household is used as an instrument of comparative analysis. Second, since there is no reason to assume that units identified as households will be the only means of satisfying "domestic functions", additional concepts will be inevitably required to analyse such processes in their full scope and complexity.

At the same time, there are several strong arguments in favour of retaining the household as an analytical concept rather than just a loose descriptive label (cf. Guyer 1981: 104–105; Yanagisako 1979: 200). First, there is the recognition that something like households with a relatively stable set of attributes can be identified, and is highly common, in most societies:

> [M]ost people in most societies at most times live in households, membership in which is usually based on kin relationships of marriage and descent, which are simultaneously a combination of dwelling unit, a unit of economic cooperation (at least in distribution and consumption), and the unit within which most reproduction and early childhood socialization takes place.
>
> (Kunstadter 1984: 300; see also Chibnik 2011: 132)

In other words, in most societies, households are extremely important social units in the sense of being "more than groups of dyadic pairs" and "more than the sum of their parts" (Netting et al. 1984: xxii). Crucially for our focus, many economic decisions are made and strategies followed at the level of the household (Chibnik 2011: 134, 141). The problem with the non-universality of the household is reduced in our case since variation is inevitably reduced within contemporary Europe compared to the more diverse range of societies considered in comparative analyses of anthropologists. Second, the idea of the financialization of the household implies its transformation, which can be only assessed if we can compare households in various points in time. This necessitates an analytical concept of the household that is sufficiently robust to support such comparisons. Third, the household will almost certainly remain an important category of quantitative disciplines, and as such it could be one of the media of a more intensive dialogue between disciplines with a shared interest in financialization. This does not mean ignoring the significant differences between the ways in which, for example, anthropologists and statisticians conceptualize the household. But qualitative social science should not avoid a careful use of quantitative data while quantitative disciplines could benefit from its more reflexive and fine-grained perspective on the household.

Our starting point for rethinking the analytical concept of the household is its already mentioned definition as a task- or activity-oriented social institution, in contrast to the more structural concept of the family. In one of the most explicit elaborations of this approach, Wilk and Netting (1984: 3) argued that describing what households do is logically prior to describing their morphology (size and structure). They listed five "activity groups" usually performed by households: *production*, *distribution*, *transmission* (of good and rights, especially through inheritance), *reproduction* and *co-residence* (Wilk and Netting 1984: 5–6). While they subsumed *consumption* under distribution, which in the household context corresponds to resource pooling and redistribution, we consider it as sufficiently important in the context of financialization to warrant its separate consideration. Following Guyer (1997), we further distinguish *investment*, understood as acquisition and maintenance of assets, as a household activity that grows in importance under financialization (Fligstein and Goldstein 2015; Guyer 2017; Lai 2016;

Langley 2006, 2008; Weiss 2016). Rather than being a classical investment in production, in household economics it plays the role of saving and insurance (Guyer 1997: 118–119), which public policy under financialization may seek to promote as "asset-based welfare" (see above).

At the same time, building on the above anthropological and feminist critiques, we see households as always embedded in, and their forms and practices as shaped by, wider social relationships and institutions, cultural and legal norms, and ideational and ideological frameworks. Two crucial guidelines for a relational study of households are that "activities carried out by any one 'household' unit cannot be fully understood or explained without investigating the links and transfers among units" and that "units analytically designated as households have to be understood as part of broader processes and structured hierarchies that cut *across* and *through* those units" (Guyer and Peters 1987: 211, their emphasis). This includes the hierarchies of gender, age, class, race and rural/urban residence as well as network relations (Wong 1984). Relations with financial institutions are part of this social embeddedness of households. They emerge in a dynamic interrelationship with hierarchies cutting across households as financial institutions develop and tailor their "products" to specific, often hierarchically ordered categories of households, leading to an uneven distribution of risks and benefits (Burton 2017; Ducourant 2014; Dymski et al. 2013; Fourcade and Healy 2013; Mikuš 2019; Wyly et al. 2009; Gagyi et al., and Sabaté, this volume).

With this wider embeddedness in mind, we conceptualize the household as a micro-level social institution that is the site of (some combination of) reproduction, consumption, distribution, production, transmission and investment. Although we share the central concern of feminist and radical political economists with social reproduction, we believe that our activity-oriented approach to the household offers a richer and more nuanced typology of key socio-economic processes that take place in or involve households. This is important for understanding not only what individual households do and is done to them but also the embeddedness of their localized practices in meso- and macro-level circuits of social reproduction, consumption, production and so on. In this regard, our activity-oriented approach to the household is in line with the French tradition of research on credit and banking that builds on the work of Pierre Bourdieu (Lacan and Lazarus 2015). While the extent and forms of these activities vary between communities and individual households as well as in time, social groups combining most of these activities are likely to be identifiable and common in all societies (and are certainly so in contemporary European societies). Paying attention to groups in which such processes take place (not necessarily only households) is complementary with studying how they also unfold through networks (Lofranco, Placas and Sabaté, this volume; cf. Wong 1984). These are two analytical categories of empirical phenomena that are both valid objects of study best explored in their interrelationships, as individuals connected by a network are likely to be also members of multiple relatively discrete groups.

Our conceptualization of the household includes one additional crucial component that has been foregrounded by recent anthropological contributions on the subject. This is a recognition of the fact that, in addition to being a social institution and a concept of its scholarly analysis, the household is also a category of various other systems of knowledge and discourse (Hoření Samec, and Placas, this volume). At least two aspects can be differentiated. On the one hand, there is the aspect of expertise and governance: the implicit and explicit categories of the household, which Guyer (2017: 324) described as one of the "oldest components of administrative infrastructure", in law, administration, policy and, indeed, finance (see also DeLuca 2017a, 2017b; Zaloom 2017). Particularly relevant for our focus are questions about whether and how financial institutions consider and operationalize the households which their individual clients are members of, for example for the purposes of credit scoring and defining the group of people sharing the liability. On the other hand, there is the more ideological and political aspect of the household as a "scale of social and political life" that may be articulated and contested through political discourse and enacted in everyday life (DeLuca 2017b). For example, particular forms of households may be promoted as modern or, on the contrary, appropriately "traditional" while other forms may be stigmatized. In both cases, then, it is crucial to attend to the dynamic interrelationships between household models (norms that may be codified, promoted and enforced) and actual social practices.

Synthesis: mapping household financialization in Eastern and Southern Europe

Our activity-oriented approach to households makes questions about whether and how household activities are being transformed central in the study of household financialization. The typology of activities, while non-exhaustive and intended to be applied flexibly, can be used as a heuristic tool to map existing theoretical and empirical knowledge and its blind spots. This is facilitated by the fact that many contributions have already studied the financialization of households as a process mediated by their typical practices, such as taking out and repaying mortgages, using bank services, using public utilities, or planning and saving for retirement. In this section, we review existing work on household financialization through the prism of the activity-oriented conceptualization of the household and then build on this to formulate our overall analytical approach to household financialization in semi-peripheral settings in Eastern and Southern Europe.

Relationships between finance and households' involvement in *production* have been assessed from different angles. Some authors analysed the deepening indebtedness of households as a mechanism that intensifies labour discipline and subordination (LeBaron 2014; Saiag 2020) and seemingly compensates for stagnant wages and the proliferation of low-paid and precarious jobs under neoliberalization, which serves to stabilize the status quo (Soedeberg 2014). Other studies explored more indirect implications of financialization for the participation of households in production, such as through its impact on labour markets and workers' collective bargaining positions (Santos et al. 2017), employment and income stability (Lazarus 2017; Mattioli 2020) and quality of jobs (Floro and Messier 2011). Anthropologists explored also the effects of financial penetration on pastoral and agricultural communities (Dudley 2000; Shipton 2009; Sneath 2012) and on small-scale entrepreneurship, in particular through microfinance (Elyachar 2005; Harriss-White 2014; Kar 2018; Schuster 2015), mostly stressing the tendency of finance to introduce additional risk and exploitation instead of driving economic development.

A well-documented channel of household financialization is the proliferation of new forms of *investment*, especially in financial and financialized (real estate) assets as supposed guarantees of one's own future social security. The already noted concepts of privatized Keynesianism and asset-based welfare were developed to theorize emergent (or hypothetical) welfare regimes based on the private use of various financial products, such as pension funds, equity-release mortgages and so on (Borgeraas et al. 2016; Dewilde and De Decker 2016; Lowe et al. 2012; Montgomerie and Büdenbender 2015). The financialization of pension systems in particular has received much attention (Begim 2018; Langley 2004, 2006, 2008; Wainwright and Kibler 2014; Weiss 2015). A closely related issue of the creation of investment subjects was one of the key topics of the literature on the financialization of daily life (Aitken 2007; Langley 2008; Martin 2002). Although this approach was initially developed with Anglo-American contexts in mind, more recently it has informed analyses in a range of other settings: for example Singapore (Lai 2016), France (Lazarus 2017) or Israel (Weiss 2015). It was used in comparative qualitative (Poppe et al. 2016) and quantitative studies (Wood 2018) based on empirical research in the UK, the US and Nordic countries, as well as in work on migrants as a particular kind of newly financialized subjects (Palomera 2014a, 2014b; Zapata 2013).

Studies of the implications of financialization for *reproduction* in households focussed especially on mortgaged homeownership as a means of accessing housing as the key material basis of reproduction (Aalbers 2008, 2016; Bourdieu 2005; García-Lamarca and Kaika 2016; Palomera 2014a, 2014b; Poppe et al. 2016; Roberts 2013, 2016). With housing policies abandoning the Fordist norm of affordable state-supported housing, mortgages have become the only means of accessing acceptable housing for younger generations and especially those living in countries without developed rental markets (Aalbers 2016: 74). As Gonzalez (2015) further reminds us in his contribution on the Chilean middle class, buying mortgaged real estate is only the beginning of the process of creating a home, which requires additional projects of refurbishing, acquiring the furniture and appliances and so on. While households in Chile and elsewhere commonly use consumer credit for such purposes, Borgeraas et al. (2016) showed that Norwegian households increasingly rely on the highly financialized practice of mortgage equity withdrawal to fund refurbishment as well as purchases of cars and additional real estate. In both cases, households' reliance on debt becomes normalized and their quotidian processes exposed to market volatilities. Tristam Barrett (2020a) has demonstrated the impact of financialization on social reproduction in Azerbaijan by documenting the prominent association between debt and life-cycle events, especially weddings that increasingly become occasions for getting indebted and means of pooling resources for repayment. However, the effects of financialization on some other crucial aspects of reproduction, such as childrearing, care and emotional and relational labour, remains less developed in the literature (Halawa and Olcoń-Kubicka 2018; Han 2012; James 2015; Montgomerie and Tepe-Belfrage 2017).

The financialization of *consumption*, an activity that is intimately entangled with reproduction, was addressed mainly through the lens of the defensive consumption thesis. As noted, contributions subscribing to this view suggest that households incurred increasing debts in recent decades to compensate for declining or stagnating real wages and maintain their consumption standards, lifestyles and social status (Eroğlu 2014; Fligstein and Goldstein 2015; LeBaron 2010; Montgomerie 2007, 2009; Schor 1998). This argument therefore focusses on how finance mediates an increasingly troubled relationship between households' participation in production and consumption. However, as noted, it has limited applicability in semi-peripheral contexts where household financialization is associated rather with consumptive and status aspirations of emergent, if highly insecure, middle classes as well as newly "banked" working classes (Gonzalez 2015; Halawa 2015; Han 2012; James 2015; Saiag 2020).

Although it is analytically useful to differentiate the types of tasks performed by households, in reality they are entangled and often conflicting. Deborah James's (2015) research on the role of debt in the emergence of a new black middle class in post-apartheid South Africa documents the tensions of upward mobility when both the "quest for things" needed for middle-class lifestyle (consumptive aspirations) and the "quest for care" in the form of traditional obligations towards kin (distributive expectations) are realized through credit. The very fact of successfully acquiring a middle-class status may produce new claims from the extended family, which, in turn, provokes a reconsideration of the scope of familial redistribution and a push toward nuclearization of the family. Jaime Palomera (2014a, 2014b) addresses similar issues in his account of Latin American migrants in Spain who took out subprime mortgages during the credit boom. When instalments subsequently soared, the new homeowners started to sublet rooms informally to be able to keep up with repayment – often to their kin who followed them to Spain. The latter reciprocated for affordable and safe accommodation by acts of care and help with running the landlords' small businesses. However, the imperative of regular monetary repayment also introduced a logic of commodification and hierarchical patron-client dynamics to these relationships of reciprocity (as well as those with kin back home to whom migrants previously sent the bulk of their income) and hence new tensions.

These and many other studies on financialization speak also to the embeddedness of households in wider social relations, institutions and formations. Relations between financialization and class, or social stratification and inequalities more broadly, have been addressed through quantitative (Dewilde and De Decker 2016; Floro and Messier 2011; Montgomerie 2011; Santos et al. 2017), mixed (Rodik 2015, 2019; Rodik and Žitko 2015) and qualitative methods (Gonzalez 2015; James 2015; Palomera 2014a, 2014b). Several studies contributed to a better understanding of households' network relations, such as those with kin (Barrett 2020a; James 2015; Kofti 2020; Sabaté 2016), financial advisers (Lai 2016) and banking professionals (Vargha 2011). Socio-spatial aspects of household financialization recently received substantial attention in human geography, particularly in the financial ecologies approach (Coppock 2013; French et al. 2011; Lai 2016) and case studies on a variety of urban and rural localities (Murphy and Scott 2014; Waldron 2016). Contributions to urban political economy addressed the nexus between household financialization, social stratification and urban restructuring (Floro and Messier 2011; Loftus et al. 2016; Woodworth and Ulfstjerne 2016).

Blind spots in the literature on household financialization are evident especially regarding implications for *distribution* and *transmission* in and between households. Relevant observations about shifting patterns of distribution (pooling and redistribution) are present in particular in ethnographies (e.g. Barrett 2020a; Han 2012; Kofti 2020; Palomera 2014b), though they have been rarely analysed in those explicit terms (cf. James 2015: 23–24, 27). The lack of explicit treatments of the relationship between financialization and transmission of resources (cf. Kofti 2020: 268–271) is striking, especially considering the importance of inheritance and more generally intergenerational and intra-familial transmission of resources for access to housing and, hence, by implication, the terms under which households engage with (or avoid) mortgage finance. Several studies suggest that established familial models of shared ownership and wealth transmission in Eastern and Southern European contexts mediate the commodification and financialization of housing in specific ways (Aalbers 2009; Allen 2006; Allen et al. 2004; Cirman 2008; Lux et al. 2018; Stephens et al. 2015).

These and many other empirical contributions are an indispensable source of data on various aspects of household financialization in a range of geographic and social settings, thereby serving also as a potential basis for comparative analysis. However, one can get easily lost in the wealth of complex and not-so-easily-comparable insights generated by widely divergent foci and frameworks. While attention to detail, complexity and ambiguity is indispensable in research on daily life, it should not discourage us from efforts to identify the most important tendencies in transformations of various household processes and their overall articulation in both internal and external household relations. The thesis of defensive consumption is one attempt at such parsimonious argument, but as we already argued, it has limited relevance for semi-peripheral contexts. As for the theses of privatized Keynesianism, asset-based welfare and debtfarism, they focus on the logic of public policy, to which they attribute a purposeful character, and tend to deduce household practices from the former as its consequences.

As an alternative, we propose a set of general arguments that highlight key transformations in basic household practices and their mutual articulation under financialization, and trace these transformations to shifts in foundational capitalist social relations (Lapavitsas 2013: 3–4, 36) rather than designs of ruling elites assumed to be highly calculated and effective. We find inspiring the argument of Bryan and co-authors (2009: 460–464) that under financialization, reproduction of labour power in the household takes on characteristics of the circuit of capital. Since it now starts with credit (to buy commodity inputs for the household), a portion of wages earned must accrue as interest payments on the money capital advanced to the household. Reproduction of labour power thus becomes itself a source of surplus value in the form of interest and "[f]rom the perspective of capital, the post-interest wage starts to appear as labor's surplus" (Bryan et al. 2009: 463). The wage residual is now subject to a competitive calculation of what part is required for subsistence and what part is available for debt service (Bryan et al. 2009: 464). This represents a new competitive pressure on households and pushes them to offer more workers to the market who will be willing to work harder, longer and under worse conditions than would have been the case otherwise (Bryan et al. 2009: 470; LeBaron 2014; Saiag 2020; Soederberg 2014). Financialization thus changes the ways in which households engage in production and balance this with other activities by intensifying their proletarianization – reliance on wage income at the expense of other productive and reproductive activities.

While this parsimonious argument usefully identifies key structural shifts in fundamental social relations in which households are implicated, our approach necessitates going beyond the tendency in some Marxist and other scholarship to reduce households to their roles in production and reproduction of labour power. Consistently with the aforementioned feminist arguments, we may therefore further note that financialization is likely to contribute to the wider ongoing commodification and marketization of social reproduction: for example through neo-conservative state housing policies that make government mortgage subsidies conditional upon childbearing (see Gagyi et al., this volume) or the practice of relying on private nannies to free up time for wage labour. These processes likely have major implications also for distribution in and beyond the household, but these are not uniform. On the one hand, financialization strains the capacity of the members of the household to provide care and reciprocity to each other and may ultimately result in its disintegration (Montgomerie and Tepe-Belfrage 2017; Rodik 2015), thus also affecting co-residence. On the other hand, increased debt service steps up the requirements for resource pooling within or beyond the household and may even lead to the establishment of new households and inter-household networks as resource-pooling units (Barrett 2020a; Kofti 2020; Palomera 2014b; Lofranco, Placas, and Sabaté, this volume). Expanded access to credit may increase, at least temporarily, the ability of households to distribute resources to members and non-members and/or expectations of such distribution (James 2015). The increased reliance on credit further affects consumption practices: not only through the need to balance consumption and debt servicing but also through the increased influence of finance on who is able to consume what and under which terms, in particular through the metrics of creditworthiness (Fourcade and Healy 2013). The expansion and diversification of household holdings of financial and non-financial assets reflects the growing role of investment in the portfolio of household activities, as highlighted in the literature on investor subjects (Lai 2016; Lai and Tan 2015; Langley 2006, 2007; Loftus et al. 2016). This is a potentially contradictory tendency in relation to proletarianization since it sets up worker households as rentiers (Palomera 2014b). However, it is best understood as a parallel mechanism of the financialization of households, inasmuch as accessing basic necessities of life such as shelter or pension becomes framed as a financial investment and mediated by financial markets. The ever-more important decisions about such investments (and loans needed to make them) condition the incursion of financial calculation, monitoring and planning into the household (Bryan et al. 2009: 461–462; Halawa and Olcoń-Kubicka 2018).

How do core-periphery relations refract these systemic tendencies of the financialization of households? As we already noted, households are embedded in two types of core-periphery relations under financialization: those of real (productive) accumulation and those of financial accumulation. Scholars working in the WST tradition formulated some useful arguments about the position of households in the first set of relations. Namely, households involved in relatively peripheral activities within commodity chains of production rely on income from wage labour for their reproduction to a lesser degree than those involved in core-like activities. This is due to persistent wage differentials such as those between Southern and Eastern Europe, on the one hand, and North-Western Europe, on the other. The resulting "semiproletarian households" in peripheries combine their insufficient wage incomes with subsistence production and self-provisioning (see also Meillassoux 1981). Such pooling of diverse resources is facilitated also by more extensive household structures and inter-household networks. Cyclical rhythms and secular trends of the global economy create similar variations between households, as periods of expansion push households towards proletarianization and less extensive (nuclear) structures, and periods of contractions in the opposite direction (Dunaway 2001; Smith et al. 1984; Wallerstein and Smith 1992a, 1992b). In terms of our conceptualization of households as activity-oriented groups, this suggests that households in peripheries and semi-peripheries, compared to those in cores, are likely to be involved in more diverse forms of production, more intensive distribution in and beyond the household, and less commodified and marketized forms of reproduction. Most chapters in this collection pinpoint some of these tendencies and their layered, potentially contradictory implications for household financialization in European semi-peripheries: they enable households to avoid or limit their exposure to financialization and improve their resilience vis-à-vis its effects, but they also provide additional opportunities for value extraction from households. This is another reason to nuance the above thesis about proletarianization as an outcome of household financialization, in particular in peripheries and semi-peripheries.

Regarding core-periphery relations of financial accumulation, we need to identify the ways in which financial actors adapt their strategies of extraction to different settings in which they operate. Income levels, asset prices, employment structures, institutional and legal frameworks, and characteristics of retail credit markets are some of the relevant considerations. The arguments against methodological nationalism and in favour of analysing finance at multiple scales (French et al. 2011) highlight that while financial institutions operate in international financial markets, their retail branches function at sub-national and local levels and target various niches of the aggregate "household sector" (Langley 2008; Montgomerie 2011). At the same time, relevant institutional and legislative frameworks exist mainly at the country level while being harmonized at the supranational level through frameworks such as the Basel Accords. The many possible combinations of financing sources, regulatory frameworks and market niches result in a wide range of financial products for households that are assembled in different ways and carry different forms and levels of risk. In the context of household lending, risks usually stem from excessive debt, variable interest rates or indexing to foreign currencies, but other aspects of contracting such as the use of co-debtors and guarantors as well as aspects of bankruptcy and enforcement laws may produce additional risks, as the chapters by Hoření Samec, Lofranco and Sabaté demonstrate. Comparative overviews and case studies of legal frameworks and practices in household lending and debt collection detail some of the relevant variations (Barrett 2020b; Deville 2015; Drudi et al. 2009: 26–27; Micklitz and Domurath 2009; Mikuš 2020; Niemi et al. 2009). Such insights need to be integrated more closely into comparative analyses of household financialization, most of which have prioritized aggregate indicators of household indebtedness and income or broad institutionalist comparisons of "regimes".

To reorient the focus, we propose that if the relation between the core and the periphery is an important source of profit for financial companies operating internationally, then our task is to research the key sources of profitability generated by relations of the same financial companies and households in semi-peripheries. That is, we need to extend the same relational approach to meso and micro levels of analysis and ask questions such as: in what ways do banks and other financial institutions establish profit-making relations with households in specific semi-peripheral contexts?

Which strategies do they follow to exploit the vulnerabilities of households as manifested in their practices and internal and external relations? And how do the macro-level dynamics reviewed in the second section of this introduction relate to households?

We propose two general observations that appear to be relevant for practices of financial institutions vis-à-vis households across Eastern and Southern European semi-peripheries. First, household financialization took place in the context of rapid and locally unprecedented credit and housing booms (and successive busts), which calls for careful historicization. It could be argued that the proliferation of financial products on offer simply responded to a pre-existing demand. But it has itself boosted demand, for example through its impact on house prices, thus driving households towards an ever-deeper imbrication with financial networks. These booms were part of distinctively peripheral patterns of financialization and as such were to a great extent driven by inflows of foreign interest-bearing capital, accompanied by a rapid development of the financial industry (branch networks, IT solutions etc.), which also contributed to the expansion of lending to households in settings in which it was previously limited. This type of dynamic had at least two important implications: many households were engaging intensively with financial products and services that had been previously non-existent or rare, and therefore unfamiliar, in their local contexts; and they often found themselves exposed to highly volatile credit and housing markets as a result.

Second, banks' intermediary positions between interbank money markets and domestic retail banking markets (Mikuš 2019: 301; Rodik 2019: 57–70), the liberalization of cross-border financial capital flows and the lack of adequate legal protection of households combined to create conditions for highly profitable lending on a mass scale. If we distinguish "selling risky loans to risky borrowers (*sub-prime lending*) [and] selling exploitative loans to all exploitable borrowers (*predatory lending*)" (Aalbers 2016: 52, added emphasis), it is the latter aspect that has been particularly important in Eastern and Southern European semi-peripheries and manifested in what Mikuš (2019: 297, 307–308) described as a "mainstreaming of predatory lending" – its targeting of all categories of debtors. Exploitative contracting exists in core countries too, but we argue that banks in European semi-peripheries explored and exploited even broader set of possibilities stemming from the under-regulation of consumer lending (Bohle 2014, 2018; Burton 2017; Rodik and Žitko 2015). They designed credit products with features such as floating interest rates, foreign-currency indexation or high fees and penalties, often in combinations, thereby expanding the extraction of value and transfer of risk to debtors. In addition to under-regulation, specific national legal and institutional frameworks also boosted the position of lenders and options of expropriation available to them. For example, enforcement laws in some countries (e.g. Spain and Croatia) enabled banks to claim outstanding debts from households even after the foreclosure of their real estate. We may tentatively conclude that practices of financial institutions vis-à-vis households in European semi-peripheries have so far, compared to cores, drawn in smaller cross-sections of the society due to the later onset of financialization (Rodrigues et al. 2016: 497–501), but have done so more rapidly and often in ways that intensified value extraction and risk transfer to households, leading overall to more uneven and potentially more intensive impacts on households.

Outline of the collection

In various ways, all chapters of this collection document the co-constitution of variegated household financialization by financial actors and households interacting in more or less peripheral locations in relations of real and financial accumulation. The two chapters in Section I: Collateralization of Social Ties focus on the interplay between financialization and the robust distributive role of households and inter-household networks, especially familial and quasi-familial, in semi-peripheries. Both contributions argue that financial institutions harnessed these networks underpinned by moral obligations of reciprocity and solidarity as a form of "social collateral" – a concept associated so far mainly with microfinance in developing countries (e.g. Schuster 2015). In both cases, they have done so mainly through the contractual technique of guarantorship that served to make additional persons, typically relatives and friends of the primary debtor, liable for the debts. The similarities are all the more striking considering that the two chapters discuss different categories of credit in very different contexts. Irene Sabaté focusses on mortgage borrowing in Barcelona, Spain, in particular among low-income transnational migrants, while Zaira Lofranco looks at consumer loans among generally impoverished urban population in Sarajevo, Bosnia and Herzegovina. The collateralization of social ties, sometimes enhanced by outright irregular practices such as "cross-guarantorship" in Spain, has served the purpose of increasing the creditworthiness of these vulnerable categories of borrowers, substitute for other forms of collateral that were found inadequate or less convenient (such as real estate in Bosnia), and ultimately enable predatory financial over-inclusion.

The rampant over-indebtedness in the context of the recession after the 2007–2008 Global Financial Crisis revealed how these techniques enabled creditors to expand the scope of value extraction beyond primary debtors and their co-resident households. From the perspective of debtors (and their guarantors), financialized social ties played a double-edged role. On the one hand, they were a source of resilience as their distributive role was reaffirmed and financial and in-kind assistance was channelled to those who needed it most. In particular in the Barcelonan case study, this often took the form of changed patterns of co-residence as debtors moved in together with relatives, especially parents, sometimes after a disintegration of their own nuclear family household due to the financial pressure. On the other hand, the spreading of financial extraction along these networks produced tensions and potentially narrowed the scope of inter-household distribution.

Sabaté identifies a "centripetal" tendency of some households to deal with their indebtedness solely with their own internal resources in order to avoid such tensions and potential loss of autonomy and dignity. Lofranco identifies a tendency to "privatize risk" through a more selective involvement (both one's own and others') in guarantorship relations or opting for insurance policies as an alternative, albeit costlier, form of repayment insurance. Overall, then, by harnessing inter-household networks of distribution and co-operation, financialization puts them under increasing strain that may trigger their truncation and/or redrawing.

The two chapters in Section II: Spaces of Financialized Housing and Reproduction shift the analytical focus from distribution and inter-household networks to housing financialization and its impact on social reproduction in households and its variegation in space and time. Both chapters place housing financialization in the context of "infrastructural, spatial and social hierarchies through which the present phase of financialization is articulated" (Gagyi et al., p. 83). More specifically, they focus on patterns of spatial development characteristic of the peripheries of capital cities – Budapest, Hungary and Madrid, Spain, respectively – that have experienced intensive credit-based urban development in the boom phase, and equally drastic collapse of house prices after the crash. In doing so, they extend the analysis of core-periphery relations of financialization to the sub-national level to explore what Ágnes Gagyi and her co-authors theorize as "intermediate spaces" of uneven development in Hungary, itself embedded in transnational and longue-durée processes of capitalist development.

In the bust phase of the credit cycle, the trajectories of the two settings diverged to some extent. Gagyi and co-authors pinpoint a process of socio-spatial segregation in peri-urban areas. Some areas attract new cohorts of investors while other areas attract people experiencing what Natalia Buier terms "mobilities of disadvantage". The latter is illustrated by the case study of an informal settlement in a former allotment garden inhabited by defaulted mortgagors, people priced out from central areas of Budapest and those who deliberately avoid mortgage borrowing. By fashioning informal housing solutions on the urban fringe of Budapest, they compensate for their direct or indirect losses due to housing financialization through enhanced reproductive labour in the household while maintaining access to the metropolitan labour market. Such "semiproletarian" strategies point to the capacity of households to moderate the pressure towards proletarianization. However, the authors argue that such strategies could be seen as providing "bottom-up subsidies to capital" by facilitating the exclusion of the costs of social reproduction from circuits of capital and their internationalization by households in the bust stage of the financialized cycle.

Buier takes a similarly place-oriented approach to a large-scale housing development project on the fringes of the metropolitan region of Madrid. This is a paradigmatic example of failed speculative urban development – an entire new town built around the promise of high-speed rail link to Madrid, which has hardly materialized, and affected by the bankruptcy of the developer that has resulted in a halt to construction, missing public infrastructure and a collapse of house prices. Unlike Gagyi et al., Buier shows how this results in housing pathways of two generations of residents crossing within the same space. The affluent first generation of residents, who bought their homes at inflated pre-crash prices, persists in the financialized mindset of homeownership as investment and wants to restore the pre-crisis housing bloom. Being in control of local politics, they seek to keep alive the original branding of the town as a safe suburban haven for middle-class nuclear families. The poorer second generation of residents, similarly to the Hungarian allotment dwellers, have been attracted by the post-boom property prices that enabled them to become owners of otherwise unaffordable property while staying in a proximity of Madrid. The co-habitation of these two groups leads to paradoxes and tensions. While the arrival of the second-generation residents has the potential to actually revitalize the local housing market, the prevalence of working-class and "non-normal" (single-parent, retired etc.) households among them threatens the town's image desired by the first generation. As a result, their needs and even their very presence are "airbrushed" from local politics. In both cases, then, elites (more affluent residents and investors in housing) and state policies articulate projects that promote an ongoing financialization of households and housing as well as neo-conservative visions of "normal" families and households.

The interrelationships between financialization and normative household models is the dominant theme of Section III: Financialized Households in Public Discourse and Culture. The two chapters analyse the ways in which politicians and public institutions articulated normative concepts of households and individual financial subjects within debates about the introduction of new legislation on lending and debt collection from households. Revealingly, in Greece and the Czech Republic alike, such supposedly protective legislation has been adopted only after the credit boom, in response to a spike in over-indebtedness and debt collection. Both chapters connect consumer lending by individuals and households to their attempts to pursue various aspects of social reproduction, such as setting up neolocal nuclear family households (with their intense cultural valorization in Greece) or simply getting by, in semi-peripheral settings of chronically insufficient wages and public welfare and dramatically expanded credit supply. Public debates and the associated legal reforms in both contexts display two strikingly similar features. First, they have a strong disciplinary, "paternalistic" (Hoření Samec) and "pedagogical" (Placas) character, sharply distinguishing between morally good and bad uses of debt. While enhancing debtor protection to some extent, these discourses and laws also promote the neoliberal ethos of individual responsibility as the solution for negative consequences of financialization.

Second, while administrative (statistical) definitions of the household are clear-cut, in practice political elites and state institutions take advantage of the ambivalent and blurred connotations of the notions of household, family and consumer in popular and public nature. On the one hand, they craft and apply legislation in a manner that enables, or at least does not prevent, the "familial" extractive practices of collecting debt from wider familial networks identified in Section I. Aimee Placas describes a particularly emblematic example of this in the shape of Greek judges who encourage applicants for protective personal bankruptcy to mobilize financial support from relatives beyond their household, only to criticize them if they themselves provide such support to others. On the other hand, their discourse advocates individual responsibility and solutions such as financial literacy, even in cases when they recognize the embeddedness of individual subjects in familial networks of obligations. In the Czech case, Tomáš Hoření Samec describes this as a discursive construction of the household as a hybrid, simultaneously unitary and compound, actor – one that is composed of individuals who nevertheless need to co-operate for their corporate good, with individual responsibility and conservative family models as dual guidelines. Thus, both cases point to relational and culturally embedded everyday practices as the material building blocks of financialization. They also show how the norms of prudent and responsible individuals and households are discursively constructed and pragmatically mobilized to naturalize a vision of tamed, controlled financialization – an ideological vision detached from realities of everyday life.

Notes

1 Our review of the literature is similar but not identical to the one provided by Gonzalez (2015).
2 This is not surprising, given that the concepts of periphery and semi-periphery themselves tend to be used in varied ways in international political economy and other disciplines (Fischer-Tahir and Naumann 2013; Worth and Moore 2009).
3 We consider as external eurozone peripheries those European countries (both members and non-members of the EU) that have not adopted the euro but depend on capital inflows from the eurozone. Examples in our collection are Bosnia and Herzegovina, the Czech Republic and Hungary.

References

Aalbers, M. B. (2008) The financialization of home and the mortgage market crisis. *Competition & Change* 12(2): 148–166. doi: 10.1179/102452908x289802.
Aalbers, M. B. (2009) Residential capitalism in Italy and the Netherlands. In: Seabrooke, L. & Schwartz, H. (eds.) *The politics of housing booms and busts*. London: Palgrave Macmillan, pp. 146–169. doi: 10.1057/9780230280441_7.
Aalbers, M. B. (2016) *The financialization of housing: a political economy approach*. Abingdon: Routledge.
Aalbers, M. B. (2017) Corporate financialization. In: Richardson, D., Castree, N., Goodchild, M. F., Kobayashi, A., Liu, W. & Marston, R. A. (eds.) *The international encyclopedia of geography: people, the earth, environment, and technology*. doi: 10.1002/9781118786352.wbieg0598.
Aitken, R. (2007) *Performing capital: toward a cultural economy of popular and global finance*. New York: Palgrave Macmillan.

Allen, J. (2006) Welfare regimes, welfare systems and housing in Southern Europe. *International Journal of Housing Policy* 6(3): 251–277. doi: 10.1080/14616710600973102.

Allen, J., Barlow, J., Leal, J., Maloutas, T. & Padovani, L., eds. (2004) *Housing and welfare in Southern Europe*. Oxford: Blackwell.

Allon, F. (2014) The feminisation of finance: gender, labour and the limits of inclusion. *Australian Feminist Studies* 29(79): 12–30. doi: 10.1080/08164649.2014.901279.

Allon, F. (2015) Everyday leverage, or leveraging the everyday. *Cultural Studies* 29(5–6): 687–706. doi 10.1080/09502386.2015.1017140.

Bakker, I. (2003) Neo-liberal governance and the reprivatization of social reproduction: social provisioning and shifting gender orders. In: Bakker, I. & Gill, S. (eds.) *Power, production and social reproduction: human in/security in the global political economy*. Basingstoke: Palgrave Macmillan, pp. 66–82. doi: 10.1057/9780230522404_4.

Bakker, I. & Gill, S., eds. (2003) *Power, production and social reproduction: human in/security in the global political economy*. Basingstoke: Palgrave Macmillan. doi: 10.1057/9780230522404.

Bakker, I. & Silvey, R., eds. (2008) *Beyond states and markets: the challenges of social reproduction*. Abingdon: Routledge.

Barrett, T. (2020a) Financialization and reproduction in Baku, Azerbaijan. In: Hann, C. & Kalb, D. (eds.) *Financialization: relational approaches*. New York: Berghahn Books, pp. 136–156.

Barrett, T. (2020b) "Your debts are our problem": the politicization of debt in Azerbaijan. *Focaal—Journal of Global and Historical Anthropology* 87: 1–15. doi: 10.3167/fcl.2020.012801.

Becker, G. S. (1981) *A treatise on the family*. Cambridge: Harvard University Press.

Becker, J. & Ćetković, P. (2015) Patterns of financialisation in Southeast European and Visegrád countries. In: Radošević, D. & Cvijanović, V. (eds.) *Financialisation and financial crisis in South-Eastern European countries*. Frankfurt am Main: Peter Lang, pp. 71–90.

Becker, J., Jäger, J., Leubolt, B. & Weissenbacher, R. (2010) Peripheral financialization and vulnerability to crisis: a regulationist perspective. *Competition & Change* 14(3–4): 225–247. doi: 10.1179/102452910X12837703615337.

Begim, A. (2018) How to retire like a Soviet person: informality, household finances, and kinship in financialized Kazakhstan. *Journal of the Royal Anthropological Institute* 24(4): 767–785. doi: 10.1111/1467-9655.12916.

Bender, D. R. (1967) A refinement of the concept of household: families, co-residence, and domestic functions. *American Anthropologist* 69(5): 493–504. doi: 10.1525/aa.1967.69.5.02a00050.

Bohannan, P. (1963) *Social anthropology*. New York: Holt, Rinehart & Winston.

Bohle, D. (2014) Post-socialist housing meets transnational finance: foreign banks, mortgage lending, and the privatization of welfare in Hungary and Estonia. *Review of International Political Economy* 21(4): 913–948. doi: 10.1080/09692290.2013.801022.

Bohle, D. (2018) Mortgaging Europe's periphery. *Studies in Comparative International Development* 53: 196–217. doi: 10.1007/s12116-018-9260-7.

Bohle, D. & Greskovits, B. (2012) *Capitalist diversity on Europe's periphery*. Ithaca: Cornell University Press.

Borgeraas, E., Poppe, C. & Lavik, R. (2016) Consuming the home: walking the thin line between welfare and catastrophe. *Italian Sociological Review* 6(1): 87–111.

Bourdieu, P. (2005) *The social structures of the economy*. Cambridge: Polity.

Bryan, D., Martin, R. & Rafferty, M. (2009) Financialization and Marx: giving labor and capital a financial makeover. *Review of Radical Political Economics* 41(4): 458–472. doi: 10.1177/0486613409341368.

Bryan, D. & Rafferty, M. (2017) Reframing austerity: financial morality, savings and securitization. *Journal of Cultural Economy* 10(4): 339–355. doi: 10.1080/17530350.2017.1287764.

Burton, D. (2017) Credit inclusion and the home credit market in post-communist member states of the European Union. *Critical Social Policy* 37(3): 444–463. doi: 10.1177/0261018316672991.

Celi, G., Ginzburg, A., Guarascio, D. & Simonazzi, A. (2018) *Crisis in the European Monetary Union: a core-periphery perspective*. Abingdon: Routledge.

Chase-Dunn, C. (1989) *Global formation: structures of the global economy*. Cambridge: Blackwell.

Chayanov, A. V. (1966) *The theory of the peasant economy*. Homewood: Richard Irwin.

Chibnik, M. (2011) *Anthropology, economics, and choice*. Austin: Texas University Press.

Cirman, A. (2008) Intergenerational transfers as a response to changes in the housing market in Slovenia. *European Journal of Housing Policy* 8(3): 303–315. doi: 10.1080/14616710802256710.

Clark, G. (1989) Separation between trading and home for Asante women in Kumasi Central Market, Ghana. In: Wilk, R. R. (ed.) *The household economy: reconsidering the domestic mode of production*. Boulder: Westview, pp. 91–118.

Coppock, S. (2013) The everyday geographies of financialisation: impacts, subjects and alternatives. *Cambridge Journal of Regions, Economy & Society* 6(3): 479–500. doi: 10.1093/cjres/rst012.

Crouch, C. (2009) Privatised Keynesianism: an unacknowledged policy regime. *The British Journal of Politics and International Relations* 11(3): 382–399. doi: 10.1111/j.1467-856X.2009.00377.x.

DeLuca, E. (2017a) The household. *Cultural Anthropology* website, August 4. Available from: https://culanth.org/fieldsights/1125-the-household [Accessed 20 November 2020].

DeLuca, E. (2017b) Transition. *Cultural Anthropology* website, August 14. Available from: https://culanth.org/fieldsights/1164-transition [Accessed 20 November 2020].

Deville, J. (2015) *Lived economies of default: consumer credit, debt collection and the capture of affect*. New York: Routledge.

Dewilde, C. & De Decker, P. (2016) Changing inequalities in housing outcomes across Western Europe. *Housing, Theory and Society* 33(2): 121–161. doi: 10.1080/14036096.2015.1109545.

Doling, J. & Ronald, R. (2010) Home ownership and asset-based welfare. *Journal of Housing and the Built Environment* 25(2): 165–173. doi: 10.1007/s10901-009-9177-6.

Drudi, F. et al. (2009) Housing finance in the euro area. ECB Occasional Paper No. 101. Available from: https://papers.ssrn.com/sol3/papers.cfm?abstract_id=1325202 [Accessed 20 November 2020].

Ducourant, H. (2014) Why do the poor pay more for their credit? A French case study. In: Guérin, I., Morvant-Roux, S. & Villarreal, M. (eds.) *Microfinance, debt and over-indebtedness: juggling with money*. Abingdon: Routledge, pp. 24–45.

Dudley, K. M. (2000) *Debt and dispossession: farm loss in America's heartland*. Chicago: University of Chicago Press.

Dunaway, W. A. (2001) The double register of history: situating the forgotten woman and her household in capitalist commodity chains. *Journal of World-Systems Research* 7(1): 2–29. doi: 10.5195/jwsr.2001.182.

Dymski, G., Hernandez, J. & Mohanty, L. (2013) Race, gender, power, and the US subprime mortgage and foreclosure crisis: a meso analysis. *Feminist Economics* 19(3): 124–151. doi: 10.1080/13545701.2013.791401.

Elias, J. & Gunawardana, S. J., eds. (2013) *The global political economy of the household in Asia*. Basingstoke: Palgrave Macmillan. doi: 10.1057/9781137338907.

Elson, D. (2013) Economic crises from the 1980s to the 2010s: a gender analysis. In: Rai, S. M. & Waylen, G. (eds.) *New frontiers in feminist political economy*. London: Routledge, pp. 189–212.

Elyachar, J. (2005) *Markets of dispossession: NGOs, economic development, and the state in Cairo*. Durham: Duke University Press.

Engelen, E. & Konings, M. (2010) Financial capitalism resurgent: comparative institutionalism and the challenges of financialization. In: Morgan, G., Campbell, J. L., Crouch, C., Pedersen, O. K. & Whitley, R. (eds.) *The Oxford handbook of comparative institutional analysis*. Oxford: Oxford University Press, pp. 601–624.

Eroğlu, E. (2014) Financialisation of capitalism: expansion of indebtedness from global level to household level in Turkey. *Yönetim Bilimleri Dergisi* 12(24): 101–129.

Erturk, I., Froud, J., Johal, S., Leaver, A. & Williams, K. (2007) The democratization of finance? Promises, outcomes and conditions. *Review of International Political Economy* 14(4): 553–575. doi: 10.1080/09692290701475312.

Fernandez, R. & Aalbers, M. B. (2016) Financialization and housing: between globalization and varieties of capitalism. *Competition & Change* 20(2): 71–88. doi: 10.1177/1024529415623916.

Fine, B. (2013) Financialization from a Marxist perspective. *International Journal of Political Economy* 42(4): 47–66. doi: 10.2753/IJP0891-1916420403.

Fischer-Tahir, A. & Naumann, M., eds. (2013) *Peripheralization: the making of spatial dependencies and social injustice*. Wiesbaden: Springer.

Fligstein, N. & Goldstein, A. (2015) The emergence of a finance culture in American households, 1989–2007. *Socio-Economic Review* 13(3): 575–601. doi: 10.1093/ser/mwu035.

Floro, M. S. & Messier, J. (2011) Is there a link between quality of employment and indebtedness? The case of urban low-income households in Ecuador. *Cambridge Journal of Economics* 35(3): 499–526. doi: 10.1093/cje/beq034.

Folbre, N. (1986) Hearts and spades: paradigms of household economics. *World Development* 14(2): 245–255. doi: 10.1016/0305-750X(86)90056-2.

Fortes, M. (1949) *Time and social structure: an Ashanti case study*. Indianapolis: Bobbs-Merrill.

Fortes, M. (1958) Introduction. In: Goody, J. (ed.) *The developmental cycle in domestic groups*. Cambridge: Cambridge University Press, pp. 1–14.

Fourcade, M. & Healy, K. (2013) Classification situations: life-chances in the neoliberal era. *Accounting, Organizations and Society* 38(8): 559–572. doi: 10.1016/j.aos.2013.11.002.

Fraser, N. (2016) Contradictions of capital and care. *New Left Review* 100: 99–117.

French, S., Leyshon, A. & Wainwright, T. (2011) Financializing space, spacing financialization. *Progress in Human Geography* 35(6): 798–819. doi: 10.1177/0309132510396749.

Froud, J., Haslam, C., Johal, S., Williams, J. & Williams, K. (1997) From social settlement to household lottery. *Economy and Society* 26(3): 340–372. doi: 10.1080/03085149700000018.

Fuller, G. W. (2016) *The great debt transformation: households, financialization, and policy responses.* Basingstoke: Palgrave Macmillan.

Gabor, D. (2010) (De) financialization and crisis in Eastern Europe. *Competition & Change* 14(3–4): 248–270. doi: 10.1179/102452910X12837703615373.

Gambarotto, F. & Solari, S. (2015) The peripheralization of Southern European capitalism within the EMU. *Review of International Political Economy* 22(4): 788–812. doi: 10.1080/09692290.2014.955518.

García-Lamarca, M. & Kaika, M. (2016) "Mortgaged lives": the biopolitics of debt and housing financialisation. *Transactions of the Institute of British Geographers* 41(3): 313–327. doi: 10.1111/tran.12126.

Gonzalez, F. (2015) Where are the consumers? "Real households" and the financialization of consumption. *Cultural Studies* 29(5–6): 781–806. doi: 10.1080/09502386.2015.1017144.

Gonzalez, N. L. S. (1969) *Black Carib household structure: a study of migration and modernization.* Seattle: University of Washington Press.

Goody, J. (1958) The fission of domestic groups among the LoGaba. In: Goody, J. (eds.) *The developmental cycle in domestic groups.* Cambridge: Cambridge University Press, pp. 53–91.

Guyer, J. I. (1981) Household and community in African studies. *African Studies Review* 24(2/3): 87–137. doi: 10.2307/523903.

Guyer, J. I. (1997) Endowments and assets: the anthropology of wealth and the economics of intrahousehold allocation. In: Haddad, L., Hoddinott, J. & Alderman, H. (eds.) *Intrahousehold resource allocation in developing countries: models, methods, and policy.* Baltimore: John Hopkins University Press, pp. 112–125.

Guyer, J. I. (2017) Survivals as infrastructure: twenty-first-century struggles with household and family in formal computations. In: Harvey, P., Jensen, C. B. & Morita, A. (eds.) *Infrastructures and social complexity: a companion.* Abingdon: Routledge, pp. 323–334.

Guyer, J. I. & Peters, P. E. (1987) Introduction. *Development and Change* 18(2): 197–214. doi: 10.1111/j.1467-7660.1987.tb00269.x.

Halawa, M. (2015) In new Warsaw: mortgage credit and the unfolding of space and time. *Cultural Studies* 29(5–6): 707–732. doi: 10.1080/09502386.2015.1017141.

Halawa, M. & Olcoń-Kubicka, M. (2018) Digital householding: calculating and moralizing domestic life through homemade spreadsheets. *Journal of Cultural Economy* 11(6): 514–534. doi: 10.1080/17530350.2018.1486728.

Hall, P. A. & Soskice, D. W. (2001) *Varieties of capitalism: the institutional foundations of comparative advantage.* Oxford: Oxford University Press.

Han, C. (2012) *Life in debt: times of care and violence in neoliberal Chile.* Berkeley: University of California Press.

Harris, O. (1981) Households as natural units. In: Young, K., Wolkowitz, C. & McCullagh, R. (eds.) *Of marriage and the market: women's subordination in international perspective.* London: CSE Books, pp. 49–68.

Harriss-White, B. (2014) Debt, credit and contractual synchrony in a South Indian market town. In: Guérin, I., Morvant-Roux, S. & Villarreal, M. (eds.) *Microfinance, debt and over-indebtedness: juggling with money.* Abingdon: Routledge, pp. 103–124.

Hart, G. (1992) Imagined unities: constructions of "the household" in economic theory. In: Ortiz, S. & Lees, S. (eds.) *Understanding economic process*. Lanham: University Press of America, pp. 112–129.

James, D. (2015) *Money from nothing: indebtedness and aspiration in South Africa*. Stanford: Stanford University Press.

Kar, S. (2018) *Financializing poverty: labor and risk in Indian microfinance*. Stanford: Stanford University Press.

Kofti, D. (2020) Financialized kinship and challenges for the Greek *oikos*. In: Hann, C. & Kalb, D. (eds.) *Financialization: relational approaches*. New York: Berghahn Books, pp. 266–285.

Kunstadter, P. (1984) Cultural ideals, socioeconomic change, and household composition: Karen, Lua', Hmong, and Thai in Northwestern Thailand. In: Netting, R. M., Wilk, R. R. & Arnauld, E. J. (eds.) *Households: comparative and historical studies of the domestic group*. Berkeley: University of California Press, pp. 299–329.

Lacan, L. & Lazarus, J. (2015) A relationship and a practice: on the French sociology of credit. MaxPo Discussion Paper 15/1.

Lai, K. P. Y. (2016) Financial advisors, financial ecologies and the variegated financialisation of everyday investors. *Transactions of the Institute of British Geographers* 41(1): 27–40. doi: 10.1111/tran.12101.

Lai, K. P. Y. & Tan, C. H. (2015) "Neighbours first, bankers second": mobilising financial citizenship in Singapore. *Geoforum* 64: 65–77. doi: 10.1016/j.geoforum.2015.05.023.

Langley, P. (2004) In the eye of the "perfect storm": the final salary pensions crisis and financialisation of Anglo-American capitalism. *New Political Economy* 9(4): 539–558. doi: 10.1080/1356346042000311164.

Langley, P. (2006) The making of investor subjects in Anglo-American pensions. *Environment and Planning D: Society and Space* 24(6): 919–934. doi: 10.1068/d405t.

Langley, P. (2007) Uncertain subjects of Anglo-American financialization. *Cultural Critique* 65: 67–91.

Langley, P. (2008) *The everyday life of global finance: saving and borrowing in Anglo-America*. Oxford: Oxford University Press.

Langley, P. & Leyshon, A. (2012) Guest editors' introduction: financial subjects: culture and materiality. *Journal of Cultural Economy* 5(4): 369–373. doi: 10.1080/17530350.2012.703146.

Lapavitsas, C. (2013) *Profiting without producing: how finance exploits us all*. London: Verso.

Lapavitsas, C. & Powell, J. (2013) Financialisation varied: a comparative analysis of advanced economies. *Cambridge Journal of Regions, Economy & Society* 6(3): 359–379. doi: 10.1093/cjres/rst019.

Lazarus, J. (2017) About the universality of a concept: is there a financialization of daily life in France? *Civitas - Revista de Ciências Sociais* 17(1): 26–42. doi: 10.15448/1984-7289.2017.1.25942.

LeBaron, G. (2010) The political economy of the household: neoliberal restructuring, enclosures, and daily life. *Review of International Political Economy* 17(5): 889–912. doi: 10.1080/09692290903573914.

LeBaron, G. (2014) Reconceptualizing debt bondage: debt as a class-based form of labor discipline. *Critical Sociology* 40(5): 763–780. doi: 10.1177/0896920513512695.

Lockwood, V. (1989) Tubuai women potato planters and the political economy of intra-household gender relations. In: Wilk, R. R. (ed.) *The household economy: reconsidering the domestic mode of production*. Boulder: Westview, pp. 197–220.

Loftus, A., March, H. & Nash, F. (2016) Water infrastructure and the making of financial subjects in the South East of England. *Water Alternatives* 9(2): 319–335.

López, I. & Rodríguez, E. (2011) The Spanish model. *New Left Review* 69: 5–29.

Lowe, S. G., Searle, B. A. & Smith, S. J. (2012) From housing wealth to mortgage debt: the emergence of Britain's asset-shaped welfare state. *Social Policy and Society* 11(1): 105–116. doi: 10.1017/S1474746411000455.

Lowie, R. H. (1920) *Primitive society*. New York: Boni and Loveright.

Lux, M., Samec, T., Bartos, V. et al. (2018) Who actually decides? Parental influence on the housing tenure choice of their children. *Urban Studies* 55(2): 406–426. doi: 10.1177/0042098016646665.

Martin, R. (2002) *Financialization of daily Life*. Philadelphia: Temple University Press.

Mattioli, F. (2020) *Dark finance: illiquidity and authoritarianism at the margins of Europe*. Stanford: Stanford University Press.

Meillassoux, C. (1981) *Maidens, meal and money: capitalism and the domestic community*. Cambridge: Cambridge University Press.

Micklitz, H.-W. & Domurath, I., eds. (2015) *Consumer debt and social exclusion in Europe*. Farnham: Ashgate.

Mikuš, M. (2019) Contesting household debt in Croatia: the double movement of financialization and the fetishism of money in Eastern European peripheries. *Dialectical Anthropology* 43: 295–315. doi: 10.1007/s10624-019-09551-8.

Mikuš, M. (2020) Making debt work: devising and debating debt collection in Croatia. In: Hann, C. & Kalb, D. (eds.) *Financialization: relational approaches*. New York: Berghahn Books, pp. 241–265.

Montgomerie, J. (2006a) Giving credit where it's due: public policy and household debt in the United States, the United Kingdom and Canada. *Policy and Society* 25(3): 109–141. doi: 10.1016/S1449-4035(06)70085-6.

Montgomerie, J. (2006b) The financialization of the American credit card industry. *Competition & Change* 10(3): 301–319. doi: 10.1179/102452906X114393.

Montgomerie, J. (2007) The logic of neo-liberalism and the political economy of consumer debt-led growth. In: Lee, S. & McBride, S. (eds.) *Neo-liberalism, state power and global governance*. Dordrecht: Springer, pp. 157–172. doi: 10.1007/978-1-4020-6220-9_10.

Montgomerie, J. (2009) The pursuit of (past) happiness? Middle-class indebtedness and American financialisation. *New Political Economy* 14(1): 1–24. doi: 10.1080/13563460802671196.

Montgomerie, J. (2011) The age of insecurity: indebtedness and the politics of abandonment. CRESC Working Paper 92. University of Manchester.

Montgomerie, J. (2013) America's debt safety-net. *Public Administration* 91(4): 871–888. doi: 10.1111/j.1467-9299.2012.02094.x.

Montgomerie, J. (2016) Austerity and the household: the politics of economic storytelling. *British Politics* 11(4): 418–437. doi: 10.1057/s41293-016-0039-z.

Montgomerie, J. & Büdenbender, M. (2015) Round the houses: homeownership and failures of asset-based welfare in the United Kingdom. *New Political Economy* 20(3): 386–405. doi: 10.1080/13563467.2014.951429.

Montgomerie, J. & Tepe-Belfrage, D. (2017) Caring for debts: how the household economy exposes the limits of financialisation. *Critical Sociology* 43(4–5): 653–668. doi: 10.1177/0896920516664962.

Murdock, G. P. (1949) *Social structure*. New York: Macmillan.

Murphy, E. & Scott, M. (2014) Household vulnerability in rural areas: results of an index applied during a housing crash, economic crisis and under austerity conditions. *Geoforum* 51: 75–86. doi: 10.1016/j.geoforum.2013.10.001.

Netting, R. M., Wilk, R. R. & Arnauld, E. J. (1984) Introduction. In: Netting, R. M., Wilk, R. R. & Arnauld, E. J. (eds.) *Households: comparative and historical studies of the domestic group.* Berkeley: University of California Press, pp. xiii–xxxviii.

Niemi, J., Ramsay, I. & Whitford, W. C., eds. (2009) *Consumer credit, debt and bankruptcy: comparative and international perspectives.* Oxford: Hart.

Palomera, J. (2014a) How did finance capital infiltrate the world of the urban poor? Homeownership and social fragmentation in a Spanish neighborhood. *International Journal of Urban and Regional Research* 38(1): 218–235. doi: 10.1111/1468-2427.12055.

Palomera, J. (2014b) Reciprocity, commodification, and poverty in the era of financialization. *Current Anthropology* 55(S9): S105–S115. doi: 10.1086/676420.

Peterson, V. S. (2010) Global householding amid global crises. *Politics & Gender* 6(2): 271–281. doi: 10.1017/S1743923X10000073

Poppe, C., Collard, S. & Jakobsen, T. B. (2016) What has debt got to do with it? The valuation of homeownership in the era of financialization. *Housing, Theory and Society* 33(1): 59–76. doi: 10.1080/14036096.2015.1089934.

Radošević, D. & Cvijanović, V., eds. (2015) *Financialisation and financial crisis in South-Eastern European countries.* Frankfurt: Peter Lang. doi: 10.37260/978-3-653-05862-8.

Rhodes, M. (2015) Southern Europe in social science: a "Southern European model"? In: Baumeister, M. & Sala, R. (eds.) *Southern Europe? Italy, Spain, Portugal, and Greece from the 1950s to the present day.* Frankfurt: Campus Verlag, pp. 51–76.

Roberts, A. (2013) Financing social reproduction: the gendered relations of debt and mortgage finance in twenty-first-century America. *New Political Economy* 18(1): 21–42. doi: 10.1080/13563467.2012.662951.

Roberts, A. (2016) Household debt and the financialization of social reproduction: theorizing the UK housing and hunger crises. In: Soederberg, S. (ed.) *Risking capitalism. Research in Political Economy*, Vol. 31. Emerald, pp. 135–164. doi: 10.1108/S0161-723020160000031009.

Rodik, P. (2015) The impact of the Swiss franc loans crisis on Croatian households. In: Değirmencioğlu, S. M. & Walker, C. (eds.) *Social and psychological dimensions of personal debt and the debt industry.* Basingstoke: Palgrave Macmillan, pp. 61–83. doi: 10.1057/9781137407795_4.

Rodik, P. (2019) *Pre(zaduženi): društveni aspekti zaduženosti kućanstava u Hrvatskoj.* Zagreb: Naklada Jesenski & Turk.

Rodik, P. & Žitko, M. (2015) Financialization, household debt and new vulnerabilities in post-socialist societies. In: Radošević, D. & Cvijanović, V. (eds.) *Financialisation and financial crisis in South-Eastern European countries.* Frankfurt: Peter Lang, pp. 49–70. doi: 10.3726/978-3-653-05862-8.

Rodrigues, J., Santos, A. C. & Teles, N. (2016) Semi-peripheral financialisation: the case of Portugal. *Review of International Political Economy* 23(3): 480–510. doi: 10.1080/09692290.2016.1143381.

Sabaté, I. (2016) The Spanish mortgage crisis and the re-emergence of moral economies in uncertain times. *History and Anthropology* 27(1): 107–120. doi: 10.1080/02757206.2015.1111882.

Safri, M. & Graham, J. (2010) The global household: toward a feminist postcapitalist international political economy. *Signs: Journal of Women in Culture and Society* 36(1): 99–125. doi: 10.1086/652913.

Sahlins, M. (1973) *Stone age economics*. Chicago: Aldine.

Saiag, H. (2020) Financialization from the margins: notes on the incorporation of Argentina's subproletariat into consumer credit (2009–2015). *Focaal—Journal of Global and Historical Anthropology* 87 (2020): 16–32. doi: 10.3167/fcl.2020.012804.

Santos, A. C., Lopes, C. A. & Betzelt, S. (2017) Financialisation and work in the EU: inequality, debt and labour market segmentation. *Revista de economía mundial* 46: 91–116.

Schor, J. B. (1998) *The overspent American: upscaling, downshifting and the new consumer*. New York: Basic Books.

Schuster, C. E. (2015) *Social collateral: women and microfinance in Paraguay's smuggling economy*. Oakland: University of California Press.

Sepos, A. (2016) The centre–periphery divide in the Eurocrisis: a theoretical approach. In: Magone, J. M., Laffan, B. & Schweiger, C. (eds.) *Core-periphery relations in the European Union: power and conflict in a dualist political economy*. New York: Routledge, pp. 35–55.

Shields, S. (2009) CEE as a new semi-periphery: transnational social forces and Poland's transition. In: Worth, O. & Moore, P. (eds.) *Globalization and the "new" semi-peripheries*. Basingstoke: Palgrave Macmillan, pp. 159–176. doi: 10.1057/9780230245167_10.

Shipton, P. (2009) *Mortgaging the ancestors: ideologies of attachment in Africa*. New Haven: Yale University Press.

Smith, J., Wallerstein, I. & Evens, H.-D., eds. (1984) *Households and the world-economy*. Beverly Hills: Sage.

Sneath, D. (2012) The "age of the market" and the regime of debt: the role of credit in the transformation of pastoral Mongolia. *Social Anthropology* 20(4): 458–473. doi: 10.1111/j.1469-8676.2012.00223.x.

Soederberg, S. (2014) *Debtfare states and the poverty industry: money, discipline and the surplus population*. Abingdon: Routledge.

Stephens, M., Lux, M. & Sunega, P. (2015) Post-socialist housing systems in Europe: housing welfare regimes by default? *Housing Studies* 30(8): 1210–1234. doi: 10.1080/02673037.2015.1013090.

Türken, S., Carlquist, E. & Allen, H. (2015) Chasing happiness through personal debt: an example of neoliberal influence in Norwegian society. In: Değirmencioğlu, S. M. & Walker, C. (eds.) *Social and psychological dimensions of personal debt and the debt industry*. Basingstoke: Palgrave Macmillan, pp. 160–179. doi: 10.1057/9781137407795_9.

Van der Zwan, N. (2014) Making sense of financialization. *Socio-Economic Review* 12(1): 99–129. doi: 10.1093/ser/mwt020.

Vargha, Z. (2011) From long-term savings to instant mortgages: financial demonstration and the role of interaction in markets. *Organization* 18(2): 215–235. doi: 10.1177/1350508410392100.

Wainwright, T. & Kibler, E. (2014) Beyond financialization: older entrepreneurship and retirement planning. *Journal of Economic Geography* 14(4): 849–864. doi: 10.1093/jeg/lbt023.

Waldron, R. (2013) The "unrevealed casualties" of the Irish mortgage crisis: analysing the broader impacts of mortgage market financialisation. *Geoforum* 69: 53–66. doi: 10.1016/j.geoforum.2015.11.005.

Wallerstein, I. (1979) *The capitalist world-economy*. Cambridge: Cambridge University Press.

Wallerstein, I. & Smith, J. (1992a) Core-periphery and household structures. In: Smith, J. & Wallerstein, I. (coord.) *Creating and transforming households: constraints of the world economy*. Cambridge: Cambridge University Press, pp. 253–262.

Wallerstein, I. & Smith, J. (1992b) Households as an institution of the world-economy. In: Smith, J. & Wallerstein, I. (coord.) *Creating and transforming households: constraints of the world economy*. Cambridge: Cambridge University Press, pp. 3–23.

Weiss, H. (2015) Financialization and its discontents: Israelis negotiating pensions. *American Anthropologist* 117(3): 506–518. doi: 10.1111/aman.12283.

Weiss, H. (2016) Contesting the value of household property. *Dialectical Anthropology* 40(3): 287–303. doi: 10.1007/s10624-016-9428-3.

Wilk, R. R. & Netting, R. M. (1984) Households: changing form and function. In: Netting, R. M., Wilk, R. R. & Arnauld, E. J. (eds.) *Households: comparative and historical studies of the domestic group*. Berkeley: University of California Press, pp. 1–28.

Wong, D. (1984) The limits of using the household as a unit of analysis. In: Smith, J., Wallerstein, I. & Evens, H.-D. (eds.) *Households and the world-economy*. Beverly Hills: Sage, pp. 56–63.

Wood, J. D. G. (2018) The integrating role of private homeownership and mortgage credit in British neoliberalism. *Housing Studies* 33(7): 993–1013. doi: 10.1080/02673037.2017.1414159.

Woodworth, M. D. & Ulfstjerne, M. (2016) Taking part: the social experience of informal finance in Ordos, Inner Mongolia. *The Journal of Asian Studies* 75(3): 649–672. doi: 10.1017/S0021911816000504.

Worth, O. & Moore, P. eds. (2009) *Globalization and the "new" semi-peripheries*. Basingstoke: Palgrave Macmillan. doi: 10.1057/9780230245167.

Wyly, E., Moos, M., Hammel, D. & Kabahizi, E. (2009) Cartographies of race and class: mapping the class-monopoly rents of American subprime mortgage capital. *International Journal of Urban and Regional Research* 33(2): 332–354. doi: 10.1111/j.1468-2427.2009.00870.x.

Yanagisako, S. J. (1979) Family and household: the analysis of domestic groups. *Annual Review of Anthropology* 8: 161–205. doi: 10.1146/annurev.an.08.100179.001113.

Yanagisako, S. J. (1984) Explicating residence: a cultural analysis of changing households among Japanese-Americans. In: Netting, R. M., Wilk, R. R. & Arnauld, E. J. (eds.) *Households: comparative and historical studies of the domestic group*. Berkeley: University of California Press, pp. 330–352.

Young, B. (2003) Financial crises and social reproduction: Asia, Argentina and Brazil. In: Bakker, I. & Gill, S. (eds.) *Power, production and social reproduction: human in/security in the global political economy*. Basingstoke: Palgrave Macmillan, pp. 103–123. doi: 10.1057/9780230522404_6.

Zaloom, C. (2017) Finance. *Cultural Anthropology* website, August 7. Available from: https://culanth.org/fieldsights/1163-finance [Accessed 27 November 2020].

Zapata, G. P. (2013) The migration–development nexus: rendering migrants as transnational financial subjects through housing. *Geoforum* 47: 93–102. doi: 10.1016/j.geoforum.2013.03.010.

Section I

Collateralization of social ties

1 Within and beyond the household

Spanish mortgage debtors' tactics to cope with financialization in a semi-periphery

Irene Sabaté Muriel

Introduction: financialized household economies in Spain

Mortgage finance is one of the arenas in which financialization has been most salient in recent years (Aalbers 2008; Rolnik 2013), reflecting the basic human need for shelter. But despite the universality of this need, the financialization of housing shows a geographically uneven, path-dependent pattern (Aalbers 2009). In Southern European countries, characterized as semi-peripheral economies affected by financialization (Santos et al. 2017), the weakness of policies aiming at a partial de-commodification of housing through public subsidies or direct provision paved the way for the irruption of financial mechanisms in the field of housing provision, particularly through the incentivization of homeownership and mortgage borrowing. This has been the case also for those segments of society that would have been entitled to rental social housing under other welfare regimes (Esping-Andersen 1990). In Spain, they were forced into indebtedness by the lack of a sufficient social housing stock and the disadvantages encountered by tenants in the private rental market. Indeed, scholars have highlighted timid public housing provision and the role of family support in accessing owner-occupation – the predominant and preferred form of tenure – as the main features of Southern European housing regimes, including the Spanish one (Allen et al. 2004; Leal 2005; López and Rodríguez 2010). Beyond Southern Europe, such familial housing regimes are typical also for Eastern and North Western European peripheries, likely due to their shared legacies of late industrialization and weak state capacity. While literature on financialization duly noted this association (e.g. Bohle 2018), it did not explore whether and how familialism in housing and social life in general shaped financialization processes in these spaces.

In this chapter, I focus on the role of kinship-based and other inter-household relations in the expansion of mortgage finance in Spain in 1997–2007 as well as the subsequent wave of mortgage defaults and home repossessions in order to understand the distinct forms of financialization – of both housing and households – in a national context widely described as a semi-periphery of global capitalism. Although a certain level of industrialization was attained in the second half of the twentieth century, the semi-peripherality of Spanish economy persisted, as seen from its import dependency, low rates of productivity and competitiveness, and low wages that stagnated or fell in recent decades (López and Rodríguez 2010, 2011). Despite its integration into the eurozone, Spain remains peripheral within it, as highlighted by the derogatory PIIGS label applied to the five member states[1] hardest hit by the post-2009 European debt crises. Besides its dependency on foreign technologies and investment (Charnock et al. 2014), the Spanish economy relies heavily on capital accumulation during speculative cycles in labour-intensive sectors such as construction or tourism. These two sectors are, in turn, intimately linked to the housing regime that has been the basis for the expansion of mortgage finance in Spain (Naredo and Montiel 2011) in the framework of a deregulation of financial activities and dependence on foreign financial capital and operations taking place in global markets (Méndez 2019).

Both governments and economic elites in real estate and finance systematically discouraged forms of tenure other than homeownership. They achieved considerable success: by 2016, 77.1% of Spanish households were homeowners (Instituto Nacional de Estadística 2016). Since the Francoist period, historical, political and economic factors have built up the widespread aspiration to this form of tenure among the population (Allen et al. 2004; Di Feliciantonio and Aalbers 2018; Leal 2005; López and Rodríguez 2010, 2011), including the working classes (Aramburu 2015), to the extent that it has become commonplace to talk about a "culture of homeownership". However, this label does not hold up to an analysis from a political economy perspective (Palomera 2014) since identifiable political decisions, rather than cultural traits or preferences, are in fact at the roots of the predominance of this form of tenure. As several authors have shown, since the 1950s, housing policies, regulations of access to credit, land use laws and subsidies to the construction sector have been put in place with the aim of expanding homeownership and creating a "homeowners' society" (*sociedad de propietarios*). At the same time, working classes went through a process of de-proletarization and disciplining (López and Rodríguez 2010: 239; Naredo and Montiel 2011: 31) that prevented them from claiming higher wages and improved welfare and housing provision, and denied them the entitlements and material living standards enjoyed by citizens in core countries of the EU.

The chief financial product that enabled the expanded acquisition of owned-occupied properties during the 1997–2007 housing bubble were mortgage loans (Naredo 2009; Rodríguez and Espinoza 2017). Granting them became the main source of profits for Spanish banks, particularly savings banks, in that period, while the state incentivized their use by tax reductions. As Leal (2005) and Allen et al. (2004) have pointed out, similar structural conditions became the key drivers of the proliferation of mortgage lending under Southern European familial welfare regimes where, given the timid intervention of the state in housing provision, much of the support – and the social pressure – for accessing housing comes from relatives. In a setting of macroeconomic growth and euphoria, triumphalist discourses about the country's new prosperity – an alleged "Spanish miracle" – were extended to domestic economies. Banks and real estate agencies welcomed mortgage applications even from the most precarious segments of society, including first-generation immigrants (Terrones 2013).[2] The deregulation of land use and financial markets through policies and legislative changes adopted since the early 1990s (Coq-Huelva 2013; Vives and Rullán 2014) resulted in a steep increase in residential construction and an influx of loanable capital into the sector, which, in turn, encouraged banks to relax their creditworthiness criteria to a dubious extent (Charnock et al. 2014: 94; Nasarre 2011; Sabaté 2020; Zunzunegui 2013). The unprecedented availability of credit was derived from the plentiful loanable capital that Spanish banks obtained by selling mortgage-covered bonds (*cédulas hipotecarias*) in international financial markets (Charnock et al. 2014: 91) as well as through short-term interbank loans (Méndez 2019: 81), with German banks playing a particularly salient role as lenders (Charnock et al. 2014: 83). This inflow of loanable capital was enabled by economic and regulatory conditions set up by Spain's accession to the EU in 1986 and the European Monetary Union in 1999 (Méndez 2019). The adoption of the euro, coupled with a closer integration of Spanish banks into European and global financial markets in which control over credit money has been progressively loosened, enabled a huge decrease of interest rates and extension of loan repayment periods in Spain (Naredo and Montiel 2011: 51). These factors account for a hypertrophy of credit (Méndez 2019: 79)[3] that resulted in a pervasive indebtedness of both households buying properties and developers building them.

This expansion of credit availability for Spanish households was celebrated at that time as a means of "financial inclusion" or even "democratization of finance" (van der Zwan 2014) and therefore as an opportunity for upward social mobility. However, it would reveal itself as catastrophic a few years later, after the bubble burst and millions of jobs were lost to a deep and long economic crisis. Indeed, domestic economies were fragile already during the years of ephemeral prosperity: incomes were contingent and dependent on temporary jobs and overtime work, while the deepening indebtedness entailed an assumption of significant risks by individuals. Besides, neither solid public welfare provision nor a legal framework for personal bankruptcy existed. Nevertheless, these risks were systematically downplayed in hegemonic narratives and macroeconomic accounts. A vast number of working- and middle-class households thus became trapped in mortgage default, subjected to home repossession processes,[4] and threatened by homelessness and perpetual indebtedness (Figure 1.1).[5]

In their efforts to avoid or redress such situations, defaulting debtors prioritized the repayment of their mortgage loans over other expenses, including the most basic ones (Sabaté 2018). As the incomes of households

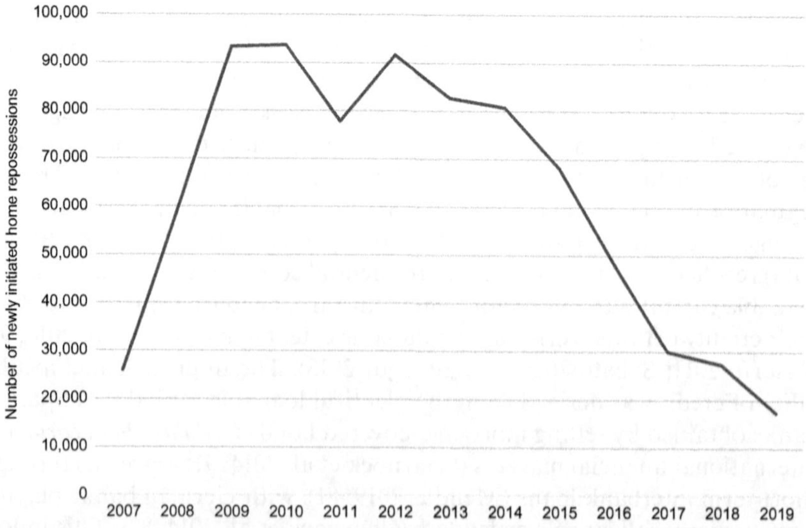

Figure 1.1 Newly initiated home repossessions, Spain, 2007–2019.
Source: Drawn on the basis of data from CGPJ (2020).

were shrinking, they were soon forced to seek the support of their social networks in order to meet their repayments. Debtors' strategies to avoid default transcended the boundaries of co-residence by involving a variety of non-co-resident actors, especially members of their extended families.[6] Moral obligations underlying informal social bonds were entangled with the legal obligations of those who appeared as guarantors or even co-mortgagors in loan contracts – often parents or siblings of principal debtors – and thereby assumed formal liability for the loan with their own income and assets. Through these relations, creditors not only seized the wealth of debtors but also gained access to much of their social environment. The effects of financial expropriation through debt were thus aggravated and amplified, transcending its definition by Lapavitsas (2009: 114, added emphasis) as "the extraction of financial profits directly out of *personal* income". As this chapter contends, what is at stake here is not only debtors' personal income or even the total income of their co-resident households but the wealth of their entire social networks. Of course, this entails a particularly lucrative scenario for creditors who might have been well aware of the opportunities offered by the Spanish mortgage market right from the beginning: not only as a result of the deregulation of financial products, the building boom and people's eagerness to become homeowners, but also as a result of the welfare role that kin networks play in the Spanish society. This would help explain predatory lending practices targeting vulnerable customers that almost inadvertently involved their inter-household networks from the moment that mortgage loans were taken out. Formal and informal arrangements and obligations allowed creditors to squeeze the network's resources both when difficulties with repayment appeared and after default.

In view of this observation, I will argue for a need to transcend the narrow focus on the household as a co-resident group and taken-for-granted unit of analysis[7] in order to understand the Spanish mortgage crisis. Following the anthropological tradition of social network research (Lomnitz 1976; Stack 1974), the weight of economic strategies based on inter-domestic networks at different stages of mortgage borrowing, repayment and default needs to be brought in. Such an enlargement of analysis is essential for a rigorous account of financialization in semi-peripheral settings. Building on ethnographic data collected in the metropolitan area of Barcelona between 2012 and 2015 among mortgage debtors and other actors[8] involved in the mortgage crisis, including two local assemblies of the anti-repossession movement PAH (Platform for People Affected by Mortgages),[9] I show that households, rather than being discrete and static subjects of decision-making and action in their pursuit of social reproduction, exhibit shifting boundaries as they adapt to dynamic economic environments.

Households, social networks and financial obligations

This section will present ethnographic data on the experiences of debtors at risk of or already facing home repossession as a result of mortgage indebtedness. Already during the housing bubble, when working- and middle-class domestic economies seemed to thrive and their apparent prosperity was materializing in the purchase of housing, financial decision-making was not confined to the boundaries of centripetal, well-defined co-resident households – typically equated with nuclear families – but instead strongly depended on external influences. Prospective debtors took into account opinions and interests of non-co-residents and/or non-relatives, sometimes even on a transnational scale, in order to decide about the next step to be taken. Subsequently, as a result of economic hardship and, in some cases, the loss of the home, the boundaries of the household were often transformed, thus reshaping co-residence patterns. These decisions, practices and strategies are part of what we can call "householding", understood as the "ongoing process of creating and maintaining a household as a basic unit of social reproduction, which covers all stages of individual and household life cycle" (Douglass 2006: 423). The two particular aspects of householding to be illustrated in the following sub-sections are, first, the role of social networks in the mortgage process, both in the stage of taking out the loan and during the period of repayment, and, second, the relationship of mortgage indebtedness and default with practices of co-residence. This data is intended to back the idea that debt-related obligations and responsibilities both transcend and shape the boundaries of co-resident households, a contention that will be taken up again in the conclusion.

Role of the extended family and other networks in the mortgage process

In order to analyse the weight of inter-domestic networks as vehicles for mobilizing financial resources to meet mortgage repayments, we need to stop at each stage of the mortgage process. First of all, such networks were already at play before debtors accessed homeownership, as their members actively encouraged and rewarded the decision to take out a mortgage, often by providing material resources. The ideal of homeownership as the best form of tenure and the wisest strategy for planning one's future was implicit in social norms and expectations and explicit in advice from relatives and friends, triggering emulation practices. In doing so, they contributed to "recruit[ing] the household into financial markets" (DeLuca 2017).

Cecilia, who came to Barcelona from Bolivia in 1993 alongside five of her siblings, had always been a tenant until, in 2006, all her brothers and sisters had already purchased their flats and she was the only one still resisting doing so. Her elderly mother was about to come to visit from Bolivia, and Cecilia was somewhat ashamed to be the only child who could not show off some material success despite having married a Spanish man. Then one of her sisters told her about credit offers of her bank, and Cecilia finally gave in to the pressure and decided to buy a small flat. One of her brothers would act as a guarantor of the contract, further complicating the intricate net of crossed guarantees[10] among the siblings that would lead all of them to default in a few years' time. Many of my informants reported that their extended family members, often parents or siblings, as well as friends and acquaintances in the case of migrants, agreed to be included as guarantors in mortgage loan contracts, thus taking on risks that, in most cases, they were hardly aware of.

Nelson's case likewise illustrates the quest for stability and inclusion underlying migrants' turn to homeownership. After several years of sharing rental flats with fellow Ecuadorians, he applied for family reunification with his wife and three children. The rental market was prohibitive, and he had heard that being a homeowner would increase the chances of having his application accepted and accelerate the process of bringing his family to Barcelona. He then met an acquaintance, Álvaro. Although the initial plan was merely to share a rented apartment, Nelson and Álvaro ended up as co-owners of two apartments and therefore shared a common fate of vulnerable mortgagors. Even though he ended up buying an over-priced flat in a very bad condition and a stigmatized location, Nelson experienced that moment as a big step towards the attainment of well-being for his family. His decision to buy a flat was intimately linked to his wish to provide future stability to his family in the absence of other sources of welfare. And, in his determination to do so, Nelson agreed to form a legal tie with a fellow Ecuadorian who was no more than a semi-stranger to him. Even though they never co-resided and, in fact, lost contact with each other after the purchases, they were reminded about their mutual liability years later when Álvaro went into arrears and dragged Nelson to default as well. They thus discovered that, for the creditors' purposes, they were trapped in family-like ties. This example illustrates the flexible adaptations of migrants' householding strategies, in this case on a global scale (Douglass 2006).

Expectations and pressures from kin played an important role also for non-migrant mortgage debtors. That was the case for Marimar, a computer engineer who had been sharing a rented flat with several workmates. After a few years, when she was in her mid-30s, her parents sold a small peri-urban plot where they used to keep a vegetable garden in order to offer her money for a down payment for a flat. That fact, together with the maturity of her bank savings plan that provided considerable tax advantages, led her to make a quick decision to take out a mortgage in order to buy a small apartment in a residential area not far from her workplace.

In the second stage of the process, some households started to struggle to keep up the repayment, typically as a result of job loss but also other circumstances affecting their domestic economies, such as under-employment or unavailability of overtime work, illness or disability, the exhaustion of public benefits after months of unemployment, or marital breakup. At that moment, resorting to kin financial support was a widespread practice. For example, Esmeralda, an unemployed hairdresser in her late 40s, told me about the first months of hardship after her husband lost his job and she could not work due to illness. As they were confident that new job opportunities would emerge, the first month they asked her father for support, then her parents-in-law, then her brother and so forth. By the time it became clear that their situation was a long-lasting one, they have "squeezed the whole family dry".

In other cases, economic support was not required for the specific purpose of repaying the mortgage, at least not in the beginning. However, as the pressure on debtors' domestic economies increased and expenses other than the mortgage could not be faced, some relatives provided support in kind to satisfy basic needs. That was, for instance, the case of Mayte and Juan, who had three children and, during several years of prosperity, obtained sufficient incomes from their jobs as a supermarket checker and a construction worker. Now that Juan was unemployed, the whole family ate one daily meal at Juan's mother's, which enabled considerable savings and guaranteed some variety in their diet. Also, as one of the children got sick and needed to be seen by a private doctor, it was the grandparents who paid for it. In another case of in-kind parental support, the parents of Sonia, a divorced mother of one who was unemployed and at risk of repossession, volunteered to take care of the little girl until she turned three and could enter a public school free of charge. This enabled Sonia to save the money that she would otherwise have to pay for her daughter's nursery school while she was looking for a job. Similarly, Mónica, a mother of two who faced repossession after breaking up with her batterer partner, has also received material support from her parents in the form of food, a new washing machine when the old one broke down, candles when she got her electricity cut due to unpaid bills and so on.

Economic support from kin, either as cash for repayments or in kind, was not free of tensions and conflict. Rather, it was often provided alongside some degree of recrimination, even in situations where support was unconditional, like in Mayte's case, whose mother and parents-in-law periodically reminded her and her husband that "things would have been different" if they had resisted their wish to move to a bigger flat. But tensions could be much stronger in the cases where three generations were forced to live together. For instance, Vanessa, a divorced mother of two teenagers who had lost her job as a security guard, had been supported by her parents throughout the whole foreclosure process, but she was hiding the situation from her sister out of concern that she would react with anger, particularly given the fact that their parents' home was also under threat. Esteban, an electrician who could no longer work due to a heart illness, described his and his wife's determination to keep their problem within the limits of their own nuclear family. To cope with the situation, they only considered using resources available to them directly: her wage as a part-time worker, his minimal disability pension and the sporadic earnings he got from informal jobs. This seems as a very centripetal, inward-oriented understanding of family solidarities limited to the boundaries of the co-resident nuclear family, which is ideologically constructed as a self-standing economic unit among wide sectors of contemporary Western societies. Indeed, especially prominently in Esteban's case but to various degrees also in many others, the striving to first keep on repaying, and then, after default, solve one's problem without external intervention was attached to notions of honour, dignity and self-respect, in contrast to the acceptance of failure necessary to ask for external support. In line with this, some debtors talked about their reluctance to tell relatives about their situation as a strategy to avoid being the object of criticism and, in addition, being forced to accept assistance from someone with whom they did not entertain a good relationship.

In the third stage of the mortgage process, in which the home was lost to repossession, the most urgent need, that is for a substitute shelter, was often satisfied by the extended family. For instance, after their eviction, Hernán and Vicky first moved to Argentina, Hernán's country of origin, and then came back to Spain, relying on their respective extended families in both countries throughout. Eventually, however, having verified that their former flat remained vacant, they decided to squat it. With that move, they aspired to more autonomy from relatives following years of strong dependence on them. Likewise, Máximo and his family, after fighting for a solution to their situation within the PAH assembly for two years and learning that they were expecting a third child, decided to go back to Ecuador where one of Máximo's brothers offered him a job – ironically in real estate business.

One must take into account the fact that when relatives acted as guarantors, which made them liable for any outstanding debt after repossession, their incomes and assets too could be seized by creditors. This was stipulated in mortgage loan contracts but rarely taken seriously by those willing to help their kin to access homeownership. Typically, it was elderly parents who found themselves at risk of losing their already repaid flats as their children went into arrears and lost their properties, which public opinion perceives as the most unfair impact of the mortgage crisis. That was the case for Salvador, an unemployed security guard and a father of one. His parents-in-law had supported him and his wife by acting as their guarantors and, after the younger couple ran into problems with repayment, risked losing their own flat, already repaid years ago. In his negotiations with the bank, Salvador prioritized that aspect over any other consideration: he wanted to free his relatives from the burden of his own debt. However, banks were eager to seize not only the collateral of the mortgage but also property owned by guarantors: housing units as well as other items such as cars. Vanessa likewise feared this outcome – her parents' flat, where they now all lived together, was also at risk of repossession. In such situations, the impact of mortgage default was amplified along family ties, blurring the boundaries of the household in the most dramatic manner. Financial pressure was also put on Mayte's mother, a pensioner of very modest means, as not only Mayte but also another of her daughters – two out of three – went into arrears with her mortgage and needed her support. By channelling material resources, inter-household bonds reinforced a sense of solidarity in the face of hardship, but they also spread the risk of repossession and general impoverishment in the social networks of defaulting mortgagors.

Finally, it is also pertinent to mention here that the accounts of informants involved in the anti-repossession movement, the PAH, pointed at a recreation of family-like ties among active members of the assemblies. This could be noticed also in the discursive and graphic production of the movement that emphasized solidarities among activists: for example by using the neologism "PAH-milia" (a contraction of the words PAH and *familia*, "family") to highlight the warmth and affection provided to debtors in hardship by fellow members. In this vein, Sonia reported the unconditional acceptance[11] she had received from the assembly after a dark period in her life when she felt socially isolated and unable to find a way out of over-indebtedness. Indeed, the methodology promoted by the PAH, based on collective provision of advice aimed at the empowerment of debtors (Colau and Alemany 2012; Mangot 2013; Mir et al. 2013), triggered a circulation of information and knowledge on legal and practical aspects of repossession processes. Also, from a material viewpoint, social bonds within the PAH allowed for a circulation of a wide range of resources, from food to childcare, clothes, furniture or help during relocations. Many participants in PAH assemblies experienced a considerable extension of social networks to which they could resort for support. For some PAH members, like Mayte, these newly created networks did not replace but were added to previous kin bonds and therefore might receive a different consideration, while for others, like Mayte's neighbour who was a migrant from Morocco, they were the only resource available, apart from public social services and charitable institutions, to obtain some material support.

Practices of co-residence in the face of (over-) indebtedness and repossessions

This section will illustrate the interrelationships between practices of co-residence, which may include processes of fission and fusion of co-resident groups, and the experiences of mortgage borrowing, repayment, default and, eventually, home repossessions. In many cases, the emergency situation caused by an eviction leads households to seek alternative shelter in relatives' homes. This was the experience of Vanessa and her two daughters: they moved to her parents' flat where they cohabited in a small space and within narrow norms imposed by the hosts. Although the situation was tense and conflicts escalated, Vanessa asked her girls for patience time after time, as they had no alternative shelter for the moment. In Sonia's case, she and her partner and daughter had moved to her parents' even before the eviction occurred, as that location provided them with an easier access to public facilities, transportation and childcare.

Another way in which mortgage borrowing reshaped practices of co-residence, mainly in the case of migrants but also to some extent younger autochthonous mortgagors, was the strategy of subletting rooms. This could be so right from the moment of the purchase, a move that was often calculated on the basis of the availability of people ready to sub-rent rooms, as has been already recognized in some ethnographic accounts of how migrants and other members of the working class accessed homeownership during the housing bubble (Palomera 2014; Terrones 2013). In those cases, several households shared the same dwelling, and, as a result, the boundaries of co-resident groups were wider than those of the household as a unit of social reproduction, while previous examples mainly presented the opposite scenario. Cecilia recalled how, when she bought her apartment, she did not plan to move in immediately, as she was staying with her husband in a rented flat nearer their workplaces. As the owner of an apartment she was not inhabiting, she decided to rent the rooms to cover the monthly mortgage repayments. The apartment was thus home to several other households until, some years later, Cecilia decided to end a stormy marital relationship and move into her own property, which she would then lose to repossession.

The strategy of renting out a whole property or subletting parts of it to cope with mortgage repayment, either when financial troubles emerged or right from the moment of the purchase, was well known and even encouraged by mortgage lenders as a way to widen their reach into the poorest strata of potential mortgagors. As Palomera (2014) has illustrated, it sometimes resulted in overcrowding and tensions among co-residents, and it promoted the exploitation of the most vulnerable dwellers by those who, having succeeded in accessing a mortgage, started off from a stronger position but were also exposed to considerable financial risks as their repayment increased and income decreased.

As another kind of effect of mortgage indebtedness on household boundaries, some informants described how, when they started to find themselves in trouble, and especially when they went into arrears, strong pressures towards the disintegration of co-resident households were experienced. This was the result of tensions and disputes among household members that prevented them from making common decisions and following agreed-upon strategies. Both Mónica and Sonia experienced marital breakup during the repossession crisis. The negotiation of responsibility for the repayment and the entitlement to stay in the mortgaged property resulted in different outcomes in the two cases. In Mónica's story, domestic violence did not end when her husband moved away but rather took an economic form as he stopped repaying his part without warning Mónica. Six months later, she realized that the mortgage was in default, and therefore she and her two children were at serious risk of eviction.[12] From that moment on, it has been Mónica's father who took the initiative to bring his daughter's case to the PAH assembly. As for Sonia, her nuclear family – her partner, her baby daughter and herself – moved into her parents' home when their financial situation became unsustainable. They were both unemployed, and their monthly mortgage repayment was rising. The apartment they purchased was located outside Barcelona, near Sonia's former workplace but too far from the neighbourhood where she grew up. Now that she was unemployed, living with her parents allowed her and her partner to cut expenses on food and energy bills. It also provided them with support in the form of childcare. However, after several months, Sonia saw no other option than to stop the repayment. Shortly after she did, her partner, who disagreed with the decision, left her. From that moment, even if he remained involved in the upbringing of their daughter, he no longer supported her or Sonia economically, which he justified by his lack of employment. As a result, Sonia and her daughter cohabited with and depended on her parents' pensions for several years while the mortgaged property remained vacant.

Debtors' stories are full of situations when marital breakup and disagreements about the best way to provide for children were added to their financial concerns. But the order of events could also be the opposite, with economic hardship appearing after household disintegration. That was, for instance, Luis's case: after he broke up with his wife, she continued to live with their child. Soon afterwards, she lost her job and entered a long period of financial instability, during which Luis, who had moved into his father's home and managed to preserve his job as a cook, assumed responsibility for the mortgage repayment and the bills for almost four years until the situation became unsustainable for him too and they went into arrears. As his ex-wife got sick and could not look after their son, he also led the negotiations with the bank and took care of the son for most of the time. Fortunately, as he was no longer a co-owner of the property nor a party to the loan contract, the bank could not seize his wage. Still, the moral obligation to care for his son, and in another sense to assist his sick ex-wife, made him channel a great part of his earnings to the financial institution. Of course, this did not happen without conflict, namely regarding the mother's lack of initiative in seeking solutions, as it was Luis who joined the anti-repossession movement where he got empowered and acquired the necessary knowledge to cope with the creditor's pressures.

In contrast to these experiences of reshaped households, Esteban's story illustrates a reinforcement of his co-resident household's internal cohesion as well as its external boundaries, linked to his and his wife's strong determination to get out of financial hardship by themselves and protect their two daughters from its adverse effects. After they had gotten into trouble as a result of Esteban's heart condition and inability to keep working, they have tried to safeguard their own well-being as well as their children's future prospects, especially by prioritizing continued investments in their education. Instead of entering employment, the adult daughter remained at home and unemployed and continued her university studies, while her teenage sister was only allowed to do some baby-sitting in order to not neglect her duties at school. The four-member household has been thus perpetuated throughout several years of hardship.[13]

Social connectedness and the exposure to financial expropriation

Financial capitalism extracts value from households (Zaloom 2017) just as different regimes of accumulation have done in the past. Indeed, anthropologists and feminist scholars have been contending for decades that capitalist accumulation does not rely only on individuals selling their workforce in the job market but also on households where unpaid reproductive work is carried out – often in an invisible manner that needs to be exposed (Benería 1979; Federici 2012; Himmelweit and Mohun 1977). Accordingly, I departed from the assumption that just as households were the basis for surplus extraction under industrial capitalism, they continue to be so in the era of financial capitalism, which can be deduced from the penetration of financial mechanisms into their everyday practices (van der Zwan 2014). However, ethnographic accounts of local communities have shown that in many cases, inter-domestic networks, rather than discrete households composed of nuclear families, are the most significant unit of analysis of social reproduction (Lomnitz 1976; Stack 1974). An excessive stress on households as discrete, self-contained entities – an idea already criticized by Guyer (1981) or Yanagisako (2001) – may obscure the whole picture of how financialization is deployed, particularly among vulnerable populations for whom the practice of reciprocity, founded on mutual obligations, is essential to get by on a daily basis.

In this chapter, the focus has been on the fact that financial responsibilities entailed by mortgage indebtedness have the ability to both transcend and shape the boundaries of the household as a result of the entanglement of formal relations, such as loan guarantees and co-ownership, and informal bonds, notably kinship. In my case study, households exhibit very shifting boundaries and are connected to inter-household networks that are flexible enough to ensure adaptation to the quick changes brought about by macroeconomic cycles, crises and adverse life circumstances. Although it may, at first sight, seem that the individual holder of a mortgage loan is the only person liable for repayment, thus confirming the "fictional individual of the financial contract" (Zaloom 2017), an element of complexity is added if we take into account that, in nearly all cases I encountered in the field, banks imposed the addition of co-debtors and guarantors to the loan agreement in order to safeguard their interests in the event of default. Moreover, beyond these formal liabilities and regardless of the specificities of contracts, the ethnography reveals that debtors' wider social networks end up taking responsibility for mortgage repayments. The construction and attribution of such responsibilities is highly contingent and case-specific, as they are directly related to the nature of the underlying social relations, and vary greatly among different categories of debtors affected by default and repossession, such as migrants and non-migrants (Lundsteen and Sabaté 2018). Responsibilities may be differently attributed and accepted by members and non-members of co-resident households, emancipated and non-emancipated adult children, relatives who are also in financial trouble and those who are not, and so on. As a result, the process of financial extraction displays variable features as it leeches resources off social networks that vary in their ability to mobilize resources, their extent and number of members, their geographical scale, their degree of cohesion, their endurance in the face of conflicts and so on.

At the same time, my data has shown that the enactment of reciprocal obligations within social networks is often experienced as an excessive, unsustainable burden both by defaulting debtors and by kin members – a burden that may lead to serious tensions. In line with this, in some PAH assemblies, an apparent paradox emerged when debtors with restricted kin networks, or with no kin at all, were congratulated on having more bargaining power vis-à-vis creditors as they tried to have their debts written off. In contrast, debtors who could rely on kin support were told to hide that fact from creditors in order to prevent them from putting their whole networks under pressure. I also described situations when defaulting households kept their problem to themselves. They might have done so in an effort not only to protect their networks from harassment by creditors but also to preserve their independence as individuals or households from potential demands for compensation entailed in reciprocity. Similarly, debtors who were parents consistently displayed a strong determination not to damage their children's future through inherited debt. This aspiration seems to be based on the awareness that indebtedness and financial hardship is a transmissible condition, something that spreads and perpetuates poverty both synchronically and diachronically.

The evidence collected during my fieldwork suggests that creditors were aware of the welfare role that kin and kin-like networks play in Southern European societies, in which the insufficient reach of public welfare systems is counteracted by the strong reciprocal bonds shaping their familial welfare regimes and specifically in the context of mortgage lending. Lenders systematically identified intergenerational kinship bonds and turned them into formal guarantees as a strategy to reduce risk. For instance, a bank branch director explained to me how having relatives act as guarantors reassured creditors, implying that solidarity that could be expected from other types of relations – friends or acquaintances – was far less reliable than the one expected from kin.[14]

In the case of the most precarious customers, bank employees and mortgage brokers displayed awareness also of the material support that could be channelled through social networks based on principles other than kinship. This was particularly so for borrowers with a migrant background: in a country where first-generation immigrants were accessing homeownership on a mass scale, which was a peculiarity of the Spanish housing bubble, having people with a common national origin acting as guarantors for each other was a frequent practice aimed at securing repayment on the basis of mutual support among compatriots.[15]

Indeed, predatory lending practices identified in the Spanish mortgage market (Nasarre 2011; Sabaté 2020; Zunzunegui 2013), including the issuance of subprime loans to vulnerable customers, can be explained in part by the fact that creditors saw their customers' social networks as forms of repayment insurance or collateral, that is to say, they envisioned accessing resources through such networks in the event of default.[16] In this sense, the efficacy of social networks as vehicles of material support is double-edged. They do reduce the risk of default and partly alleviate the material scarcity caused by the prioritization of mortgage repayment over other expenses. But also, once debtors have gone into arrears, they may facilitate and amplify the extraction of resources from people other than debtors themselves. As a result, well-connected debtors are in a weaker position to negotiate debt forbearance or cancellation, while members of their social networks, even those who are not acting as formal guarantors, experience the coercion of informal obligations to take responsibility for debts. Debtors' social capital, understood as their ability to mobilize resources through social connections (Bourdieu 1980), is thus monetized and becomes a vehicle of extended financial expropriation (Lapavitsas 2009).

Finally, deeper reflection is needed in order to determine whether the interdependence of households and kin networks as described in this chapter is some peculiarity of indebtedness and financialization in peripheral or semi-peripheral locations, or whether, on the contrary, it is a more universal feature of how everyday financial obligations are coped with in capitalist societies, especially by their most vulnerable members. On the one hand, to take but one striking example, Zaloom's (2017) insights on student debt in the US, where extra-domestic bonds also play a crucial role – though one rendered invisible – for middle-class families intending to send their children to college, speak in favour of the latter assertion, as such families are by no means "peripheral": they are located right in the centre of global capitalism. On the other hand, the opposite conclusion is supported by the fact that reliance on inter-household, including intergenerational solidarity and support to purchase a home and keep up the mortgage repayment, has been identified – by both scholars and creditors – as a shared feature of housing regimes across European peripheries with familial welfare regimes (Bohle 2018). In any case, a greater comparative effort is needed in order to verify or discard a direct association between the role of households, the weight of social networks and uneven geographies of financialization.

Acknowledgements

This work was supported by the Wenner Gren Foundation under a Post-PhD Grant 2014; the Catalan Government under grants 2014SGR1284 and 2017 SGR01307; and the Spanish Ministry for Economy and Competition, and the European Fund for Regional Development, under grant CSO2015-67368-P. The author also wishes to thank the organizers of the workshop "Households and Peripheral Financialisation in Europe" that took place at the Max Planck Institute for Social Anthropology in February 2018 for the initial inspiration, as well as the editors of this collection for their careful reading of previous drafts of this chapter.

Notes

1 Portugal, Italy, Ireland, Greece and Spain.
2 More than half a million of international migrants arrived annually in Spain between 2001 and 2008. This phenomenon was more intense in Spain than in any other European country (Charnock et al. 2014: 96) and entailed a historical shift from a long tradition of economic emigration to a situation where foreign workers were attracted to the country by job opportunities, mostly in the construction and domestic work sectors as well as in agriculture, often with a high degree of informality. In 2008, just after the burst of the housing bubble, the largest foreign community was the Romanian one, followed by the Moroccan community and then several Latin American nationalities, of which Ecuadorians were most numerous. The latter would be particularly hard hit by the spate of home repossessions (Pereda et al. 2008).
3 The total volume of capital lent in the form of mortgage loans increased by almost 20% a year on average in the 2000–2007 period (Méndez 2019: 79).
4 In Spain, more than 800,000 home repossessions were initiated between 2007 and the first quarter of 2020 (Consejo General del Poder Judicial 2020).

5 The effects of a home repossession may go beyond the loss of the home as, due to the peculiarities of the Spanish Mortgage Act, the evicted debtor may still owe the difference between the outstanding amount of the loan and the property's auction price.

6 An involvement that, as Mikuš and Rodik point out in the introduction to this volume, supports the critique of the unreflected identification of the scale of the household with a co-resident group.

7 This narrow focus is typical of statistical data collection and of sociological and economic reports guiding policymaking. Among the many examples, see, for instance, the European Commission report proposing a "common operational European definition of over-indebtedness" (EC 2008: 5), or the study of the Spanish case by Gutiérrez de Cabiedes and Cantero (2014) included in a comparative working paper on consumer over-indebtedness in six EU member states. Works like these routinely fail to problematize household boundaries or criticize their necessary correspondence with co-residence, while ethnographic data seriously call these assumptions into question.

8 Including activists, judges, lawyers, real estate agents, bank employees, financial brokers, civil servants, municipal social workers, volunteers at charities and third sector organizations acting as debt advisers and mediators, high school teachers, one notary public and one priest. Throughout this chapter, pseudonyms are used to refer to participants in my research.

9 We will not focus here on the literature that has explored the organization, strategies and goals of the anti-repossession movement. For an account by two of the first PAH leaders, see Colau and Alemany (2012).

10 As a bank employee in a mortgage department explained to me in an interview, this strategy consisted of simultaneously applying for mortgage loans in two different banks, with one person acting as the borrower and the other as the guarantor in one case and exchanging their roles in the other. Both creditors granted the loans after checking the solvency of each applicant with the Banco de España. This authority would not match the data until several weeks later. As a result, both borrowers were liable for both loans and became over-indebted. Financial middlemen and real estate agents participated in this irregular practice as a means for issuing mortgage loans to customers with very precarious domestic economies (Sabaté 2020).

11 This does not mean that Sonia's experience can be generalized: certain criteria needed to be met to be accepted as a member deserving the assembly's support (Sabaté forthcoming). Also, not all of the newly created bonds among those affected by evictions were necessarily unconditional or long-lasting. On the contrary, Bereményi and Montero (2019) have also identified the importance of "disposable ties" (Desmond 2012) in the stories of PAH members. We could also notice this quality in Nelson's and Álvaro's relationship that faded away completely after their respective evictions.

12 The entanglement between domestic violence and households' coping strategies in the face of mortgage default emerges in several of my informants' accounts. It motivated the creation of a special Gender Committee within the PAH assembly in Barcelona and is an aspect in need of further exploration.

13 Esteban and his wife were also determined to remain in their neighbourhood where the family was deeply rooted and embedded in social networks, despite strong gentrification pressures.

14 "When guarantors were asked for, people usually relied on their parents. The loan applicant was asked 'who would pay if you could not?' and that tended to be the answer. If they suggested a friend instead, we were suspicious…" [Roger, director of a savings bank branch].

15 "There were lots of Pakistani people in that neighborhood. We did not have default problems back then; they were very good payers [...]. Normally, two relatives or friends started by buying a flat, many people moved in and paid rent, and that's how they repaid the loan. Then they would act as guarantors for each other" [Josep, a savings bank employee].

16 Another important factor in predatory lending, mortgage securitization, has been tackled elsewhere (Sabaté 2016).

References

Aalbers, M. B. (2008) The financialization of home and the mortgage market crisis. *Competition & Change* 12(2): 148–166. doi: 10.1179/102452908X289802.

Aalbers, M. B. (2009) Geographies of the financial crisis. *Area* 41(1): 34–42. doi: 10.1111/j.1475-4762.2008.00877.x.

Allen, J., Barlow, J., Leal, J., Maloutas, T. & Padovani, L. (2004) *Housing and welfare in Southern Europe.* Oxford: Blackwell.

Aramburu, M. (2015) Rental as a taste of freedom: the decline of home ownership amongst working-class youth in Spain during times of crisis. *International Journal of Urban and Regional Research* 39(6): 1172–1190. doi: 10.1111/1468-2427.12218.

Benería, L. (1979) Reproduction, production and the sexual division of labour. *Cambridge Journal of Economics* 3(3): 203–225.

Bereményi, B. Á. & Montero, E. (2019) Crisis hipotecaria, capital social y empoderamiento: una exploración a partir del caso de la PAH. *Arbor* 195(793): 1–12. doi: 10.3989/arbor.2019.793n3006.

Bohle, D. (2018) Mortgaging Europe's periphery. *Studies in Comparative International Development* 53: 196–217. doi: 10.1007/s12116-018-9260-7.

Bourdieu, P. (1980) Le capital social: notes provisoires. *Actes de la recherche en sciences sociales* 31: 2–3.

CGPJ (2020) Ejecuciones hipotecarias presentadas por Tribunal Superior de Justicia. In dataset: Datos sobre el efecto de la crisis sobre los órganos judiciales (until 2Q 2020). Madrid: Consejo General del Poder Judicial. Available from: http://www.poderjudicial.es/stfls/ESTADISTICA/FICHEROS/Crisis/Datos%20sobre%20el%20efecto%20de%20la%20crisis%20en%20los%20organos%20judiciales%20TSJ.xlsx [Accessed 25 November 2020].

Charnock, G., Purcell, T. & Ribera-Fumaz, R. (2014) *The limits to capital in Spain: crisis and revolt in the European south.* Basingstoke: Palgrave Macmillan.

Colau, A. & Alemany, A. (2012) *Vides hipotecades: de la bombolla immobiliària al dret a l'habitatge.* Barcelona: Angle Editorial.

Coq-Huelva, D. (2013) Urbanisation and financialisation in the context of a rescaling state: the case of Spain. *Antipode* 45(5): 1213–1231. doi: 10.1111/anti.12011.

DeLuca, E. (2017) The household. *Cultural Anthropology* website, August 4. Available from: https://culanth.org/fieldsights/1125-the-household [Accessed 27 January 2020].

Desmond, M. (2012) Disposable ties and the urban poor. *American Journal of Sociology* 117(5): 1295–1335. doi: 10.1086/663574.

Di Feliciantonio, C. & Aalbers, M. B. (2018) The prehistories of neoliberal housing policies in Italy and Spain and their reification in times of crisis. *Housing Policy Debate* 28(1): 135–151. doi: 10.1080/10511482.2016.1276468.

Douglass, M. (2006) Global householding in Pacific Asia. *International Development Planning Review* 28(4): 421–446. doi: 10.3828/idpr.28.4.1.

EC (2008) Towards a common operational European definition of over-indebtedness. Brussels: European Commission, Directorate-General for Employment, Social Affairs and Equal Opportunities. Available from: http://www.oee.fr/files/study_overindebtedness_en.pdf [Accessed 1 September 2020].

Esping-Andersen, G. (1990) *The three worlds of welfare capitalism*. Princeton: Princeton University Press.

Federici, S. (2012) *Revolution at point zero: housework, reproduction, and feminist struggle*. Oakland: PM Press.

Gutiérrez de Cabiedes, P. & Cantero, M. (2014) Spain. In: Domurath, I., Comparato, G. & Micklitz, H.-W. (eds.) *The over-indebtedness of European consumers: a view from six countries*. EUI Working Paper LAW 2014/10, pp. 108–161. Available from: https://cadmus.eui.eu/handle/1814/32451 [Accessed 1 September 2020].

Guyer, J. I. (1981) Household and community in African studies. *African Studies Review* 24(2/3): 87–137. doi: 10.2307/523903.

Himmelweit, S. & Mohun, S. (1977) Domestic labour and capital. *Cambridge Journal of Economics* 1(1): 15–31.

Instituto Nacional de Estadística (2016) Encuesta de Condiciones de Vida. Available from: https://www.ine.es/jaxiT3/Tabla.htm?t=4566 [Accessed 1 September 2020].

Lapavitsas, C. (2009) Financialised capitalism: crisis and financial expropriation. *Historical Materialism* 17(2): 114–148. doi: 10.1163/156920609X436153.

Leal, J. (2005) La política de vivienda en España. *Documentación Social* 138: 63–80.

Lomnitz, L. (1976) *Cómo sobreviven los marginados*. Ciudad de México: Siglo XXI Editores.

López, I. & Rodríguez, E. (2010) *Fin de ciclo: financiarización, territorio y sociedad de propietarios en la onda larga del capitalismo hispano (1959–2010)*. Madrid: Traficantes de Sueños.

López, I. & Rodríguez, E. (2011) The Spanish model. *New Left Review* 69: 5–29.

Lundsteen, M. & Sabaté, I. (2018) The social articulation of the crisis and political mobilisation in Spain: some reflections on the shortcomings of the new social movements. In: Fedyuk, O. & Stewart, P. (eds.) *Inclusion and exclusion in Europe: migration, work and employment perspectives*. London: Rowman & Littlefield, pp. 197–220.

Mangot, L. (2013) La Plataforma de Afectados por la Hipoteca: de la crisis a la estafa: del Prozac al empoderamiento. *Clivatge* 2: 56–88.

Méndez, R. (2019) *Ciudades en venta: estrategias financieras y nuevo ciclo inmobiliario en España*. València: Publicacions de la Universitat de València.

Mir, J., França, J. & Macías, C. (2013) Fundamentos de la Plataforma de Afectados por la Hipoteca: activismo, asesoramiento colectivo y desobediencia civil no violenta. *Educación Social* 55: 52–61.

Naredo, J. M. (2009) La cara oculta de la crisis: el fin del boom inmobiliario y sus consecuencias. *Revista de Economía Crítica* 7: 118–133.

Naredo, J. M. & Montiel, A. (2011) *El modelo inmobiliario español y su culminación en el caso valenciano*. Barcelona: Icaria.

Nasarre, S. (2011) Malas prácticas bancarias en la actividad hipotecaria. *Revista Crítica de Derecho Inmobiliario* 727: 2665–2737.

Palomera, J. (2014) How did finance infiltrate the world of the urban poor? Homeownership and social fragmentation in a Spanish neighbourhood. *International Journal of Urban and Regional Research* 38(1): 218–235. doi: 10.1111/1468-2427.12055.

Pereda, C., Actis, W. & De Prada, M. A. (2008) Dimensiones de la inmigración en España: impactos y desafíos. *Papeles* 103: 95–104.

Rodríguez, R. & Espinoza, M. (2017) *De la especulación al derecho a la vivienda: más allá de las contradicciones del modelo inmobiliario español.* Madrid: Traficantes de Sueños.

Rolnik, R. (2013) Late neoliberalism: the financialisation of homeownership and housing rights. *International Journal of Urban and Regional Research* 37(3): 1058–1066. doi: 10.1111/1468-2427.12062.

Sabaté, I. (2016) Mortgage indebtedness and home repossessions as symptoms of the financialisation of housing provisioning in Spain. *Critique of Anthropology* 36(2): 197–211. doi: 10.1177/0308275X15614636.

Sabaté, I. (2018) To repay or not to repay: financial vulnerability among mortgage debtors in Spain. *Etnográfica* 22(1): 5–26. doi: 10.4000/etnografica.5130.

Sabaté, I. (2020) Mortgage lending and economic wrongdoing during the Spanish housing bubble. *Research in Economic Anthropology* 40: 91–107. doi: 10.1108/S0190-128120200000040007.

Sabaté, I. (forthcoming) Do mortgagors in hardship deserve debt relief? Legitimising and challenging inequality during the Spanish home repossessions crisis. In: Tosic, J. & Streinzer, A. (eds.) *Deservingness – genealogies, struggles and ideologies.* New York: Berghahn Books.

Santos, A. C., Rodrigues, J. & Teles, N. (2017) Semi-peripheral financialisation and social reproduction: the case of Portugal. *New Political Economy* 23(4): 475–494. doi: 10.1080/13563467.2017.1371126.

Stack, C. (1974) *All our kin: strategies for survival in a black community.* New York: Harper & Row.

Terrones, A. (2013) Segregation, housing market segmentation and the origin of over-indebtedness: the access to homeownership by foreign migrants based on over-indebtedness. Paper delivered at the 25th European Network for Housing Research Conference, June 2013, Tarragona, Spain.

Van der Zwan, N. (2014) Making sense of financialization. *Socio-Economic Review* 12(1): 99–129. doi: 10.1093/ser/mwt020.

Vives, S. & Rullán, O. (2014) La apropiación de las rentas del suelo en la ciudad neoliberal española. *Boletín de la Asociación de Geógrafos Españoles* 65: 387–408.

Yanagisako, S. J. (2001) Household in anthropology. In: Smelser, N. J. & Baltes, P. B. (eds.) *International encyclopedia of the social & behavioral sciences.* Pergamon, pp. 6930–6934. doi: 10.1016/B0-08-043076-7/00887-1.

Zaloom, C. (2017) Finance. *Cultural Anthropology* website, August 7. Available from: https://culanth.org/fieldsights/1163-finance [Accessed 27 January 2020].

Zunzunegui, F. (2013) Over-indebtedness and mortgage lending. *Revista de Derecho Bancario y Bursátil* 129: 35–76. doi: 10.2139/ssrn.2242428.

2 "I would not be a loan guarantor even for my blood brother"

Financialization of inter-household solidarity and the privatization of risk in Bosnia and Herzegovina

Zaira T. Lofranco

Introduction

Guarantors (*žiranti, jamciljemci*)[1] repaying debts of original borrowers have become a widely discussed topic in Bosnia and Herzegovina (BiH) after the 2007–2008 global financial crisis (GFC) when the number of non-performing loans (NPLs) started to increase steadily.[2] While statistics on the phenomenon has been contentious, official data of the Central Bank of Bosnia and Herzegovina (CBBiH) reveals a significant increase in the volume of loans repaid by guarantors starting in 2009. In 2010, 5,607 guarantors, which was 21.5% more than the year earlier, repaid a total of 18.1m KM (BiH convertible marks, ISO code: BAM),[3] up 98.6% compared with the previous year (CBBiH 2010: 29). In 2012, 4,391 guarantors still repaid 15.8m KM (CBBiH 2012: 39). In response to the phenomenon, the Association for the Protection of Guarantors in Bosnia and Hercegovina (Udruženje za zaštitu žiranata u Bosni i Hercegovini; Guarantors' Association from now on) had been founded in June 2009 in Šamac (Republika Srpska)[4] and soon after opened offices in Sarajevo, Mostar and several other municipalities. While the Association of Banks of Bosnia and Hercegovina (Udruženje banaka Bosne i Hercegovine; Banks' Association from now) downplayed the phenomenon, the Guarantors' Association reported significantly higher figures. According to its president, guarantors repaid 25m KM to credit institutions in 2012 alone, with each guarantor repaying 3,150 KM on average (FENA 2013).

In the years following the GFC and particularly in 2011–2013, the "guarantors' issue"[5] became the subject of heated debates in newspapers and on regional TV channels and social networks, often under the rubric of "deceived guarantors" (*prevareni žiranti*). This category encompasses a wide range of cases, including people whose documents were stolen, falsified or misused by their family members, acquaintances or even unknown persons to fulfil banks' demands for guarantors and access loans. In such cases, we deal with involuntary guarantors who only found out about their involvement when the credit institution started to collect debt not being repaid by the borrower. Another category of "deceived guarantors" is people who voluntarily accepted to act as guarantors for relatives, friends or colleagues. Despite their voluntary decision, these people too presented themselves to the media as victims of a fraud. In such cases, the media accused credit institutions of approving loans to clients with unverified creditworthiness, while blaming the borrowers for exploiting the guarantors' goodwill to access loans that they were unable to repay. Even after the adoption of the federal Law on Guarantor Protection in 2013,[6] which gradually reduced new cases, the CBBiH continued to consider the guarantors' issue a long-lasting burden for households that often had their own loans to repay as well (CBBiH 2015: 31).[7] My ethnographic data collected during fieldwork in late 2019[8] shows that daily struggles of primary borrowers and their guarantors to repay loans still impact the social reproduction of a significant number of households.

As a result of these individual and collective experiences, many Bosnians took up the habit of making bitter declarations such as "there are no friends anymore" and "I would not be a guarantor even for my blood brother" or, alternatively, "for my born son" (*mom rođenom sinu*). These statements articulate immediate frustrations of guarantors with incurred economic damage but also, more broadly, a disillusionment with "traditional" values of Bosnian inter-household solidarity rooted in an extended concept of kinship. It is precisely this solidarity extending beyond the nuclear family household that has been at the centre of the public debate about guarantors. The media repeatedly identified as the origin of the problem a familialistic behaviour of Bosnians who agreed to be guarantors without necessary information, armed only with a desire to fulfil their duty to cousins, *kumovi* (godparents), neighbours, friends and colleagues (see, for example, Al Jazeera Balkans 2013b). This interpretation has been further reinforced by post-crisis financial education programmes. In 2019, workers of an association providing free legal advice to indebted Bosnians explained to me that many of their interlocutors light-heartedly accepted guarantorship as an equivalent of *kumstvo* (godparenthood), a traditional form of symbolic kinship.

This chapter questions the culturalization of the over-indebtedness of Bosnian guarantors and the interpretation of their conduct as a simple transposition of "irrational" principles of popular moral economy – namely reliance on traditional models of extended family and inter-household solidarity – into the "rational" formal credit market. Acknowledging the importance of analysing the household as a relational rather than a self-contained unit (DeLuca 2017), this chapter will investigate how household financialization in BiH has tapped into existing familial and inter-household relations and associated moral values and transformed them as a result. Anthropologists have already identified and explored the mobilization of familial and other social ties in different contexts as "social collateral" for credit. Pioneering studies focussed on microfinance lenders who targeted poor and previously "unbankable" strata in developing countries and, in an absence of suitable material collateral, secured the loans with the social capital of debtors. By strategies such as organizing debtors into groups whose members depended on each other's steady repayment, lenders found a way of collateralizing the social relations and reputation of debtors (Guérin 2014; Kar 2017; Schuster 2015). In the post-crisis period, anthropologists noted similar patterns in post-industrial countries, including prominently in Southern European semi-peripheries such as Greece and Spain. These contributions, dealing mainly with housing loans issued by commercial banks, documented how social networks of both middle-class and poor borrowers (such as marginalized migrants) have been mobilized to access credit (including by using the institution of guarantorship) and to extract financial value when borrowers could not keep up repayment (Kofti 2020; Palomera 2014; Placas, and Sabaté, this volume).

This chapter adds to the former body of literature by analysing the specific case of social collateral in BiH as a postsocialist, post-war country affected by a process of peripheral financialization (Becker et al. 2010). This means taking into consideration a long-term trajectory of transformations of Bosnian inter-household relations in a setting of wartime deprivation and post-war austerity and dependence on foreign financial capital, which exposed the economy to exogenous financial shocks, such as the GFC. Through diachronic analysis, the chapter will account for transformations of the traditional model of extended family household while also acknowledging the renewed centrality of intra- and inter-household co-operation for coping with the enduring institutional and economic crisis in the postsocialist and post-war period. Drawing on ethnographic data collected in the Sarajevo area during and after the GFC, the chapter will show how the legal institution of guarantorship was (ab)used to satisfy the imperatives of wage-based creditworthiness and expand the base of financial value extraction through debt, harnessing kin and kin-like networks for a new, financialized kind of inter-household exchange. The inclusion of households in this exchange is obscured by the legal constitution of participants in borrower-guarantor relations as "fictional individual[s] of the financial contract" (Zaloom 2017). However, analysing practices of debt collection during the post-GFC recession, the chapter will contend that relations between borrowers and guarantors are far from being inter-*personal*. Instead, they involve wider inter-domestic networks held together by legal and moral obligations to endure value extraction by financial institutions. The chapter will conclude by examining households' resistance to these extractive practices through what I will describe as a privatization of risk.

The political economy of peripheral financialization and social collateral in BiH

The emergence of the guarantors' issue in the aftermath of the GFC revealed the impact of a process of peripheral financialization and expansion of household credit driven by inflows of foreign capital. The phenomenon has its origins in external financial liberalization and the subsequent expansion of transnational banking corporations across the entire postsocialist South-Eastern Europe. Since the passing of the 1998 Law on Foreign Direct Investment (FDI), banking has been one of the key sectors targeted by FDIs in BiH. In the immediate aftermath of the 1992–1995 Bosnian War, multilateral foreign donors capitalized domestic banks and incoming foreign banks in an effort to support post-conflict reconstruction through microloans with competitive interest rates (Bateman and Sinković 2017; van der Windt et al. 2011).[9] However, dominance on retail credit market was gradually achieved by newly privatized banks, capitalized by their mostly Western European-based mother companies. Foreign-owned banks held about 91% of total banking assets by 2005 (CBBiH 2009b: 22). The Bosnian economist Fikret Čausević (2012: 4) reported that in 2011 Austrian banks controlled 42% of the banking sector, Italian banks 23% and Slovenian 14%.

The foreign privatization of both banks and firms inaugurated a financialized political economy in the country. In a context of neoliberal restructuring, central banks in postsocialist Eastern Europe in general were barred from supporting productive economy. Post-war institutional fragmentation in BiH has further amplified this tendency. Since the 1995 Dayton Agreement, the country has not seen a common banking and industrial policy. The Central Bank of BiH has been solely responsible for monetary policy while the credit policy and the regulation of banking activities had been the duty of the two entities' banking agencies (Banking Agency of the Federation of Bosnia and Herzegovina – FBA, and Banking Agency of Republika Srpska – BARS). A major effect of foreign banking privatization and fragmentation of banking policy was a disinvestment in the industrial sector in a country in which warfare had destroyed nearly all of productive infrastructure (Becker and Ćetković 2015: 73). This resulted in a massive deindustrialization and an accelerated process of financialization led by foreign "impatient finance" (Gabor 2010, 2011). As in other South-Eastern European countries, financialization in BiH conformed to the peripheral model based on cross-border inflows of interest-bearing capital, mainly from the EU core, and expansion of credit especially to non-financial companies and households (Becker and Ćetković 2015: 72). From 2002 to 2007, claims on the household sector were the fastest-growing category of bank claims (CBBiH 2007: 28). After turning negative during the GFC (2008–2012), the growth rate of household loans has returned to positive values since 2013.[10] Since the early 2000s, these dynamics resulted in the increase of the GDP share of household debt from 13.7% in 2003 (Becker and Ćetković 2015: 75) to 31.1% in 2018 (CBBiH 2018: 32).

The growth of household lending was initially stifled by large spreads between active and passive interest rates due to the perceived increased risk of BiH as a post-war country. Average active interest rate on bank loans in 2000 was 30.5%, one of the highest among postsocialist countries in Europe (CBBiH 2009b: 14). The situation changed after 2004 as BiH's moderate economic recovery and increased competition in the banking sector enabled better lending conditions and faster expansion of bank portfolios. By 2006, average active interest rate on bank loans dropped to 8% (CBBiH 2009b: 14). Unlike in most other South-Eastern and especially East-Central European semi-peripheral economies, the structure of bank loans to households has been always dominated by small and mid-sized, long-term, unsecured consumer (general-purpose) loans rather than larger and more long-term housing loans secured by a mortgage. Only 24% of household loans were housing loans in 2008 while 69% were consumer loans, which further increased to 71% in 2012 (Becker and Ćetković 2015: 76). In 2017 consumer loans amounted to 78.3% of total loans to households, and they registered continuous growth up until the present (Figures 2.1 and 2.2).

Reasons for the prevalence of this form of lending were multiple. To begin with, credit expansion took place against the backdrop of neoliberal restructuring of BiH economy under the auspices of international financial institutions. After the post-war stage of humanitarian aid, financial support from the IMF and the World Bank has been conditional on structural adjustment policies aimed at achieving macroeconomic stability and attracting FDIs

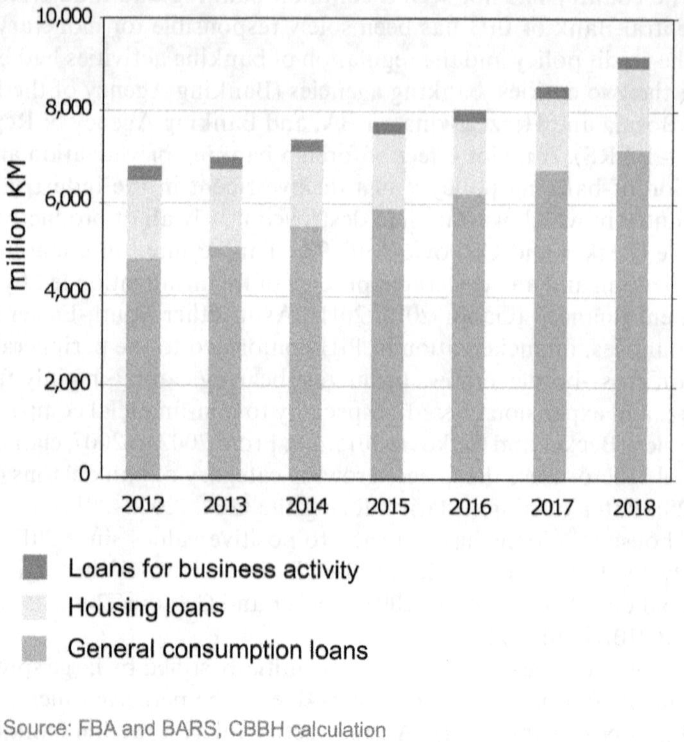

Figure 2.1 Bank loans to households by purpose (KM millions), Bosnia and Herzegovina, 2012–2018.

Source: Reprinted with minor edits from CBBiH (2018: 34).

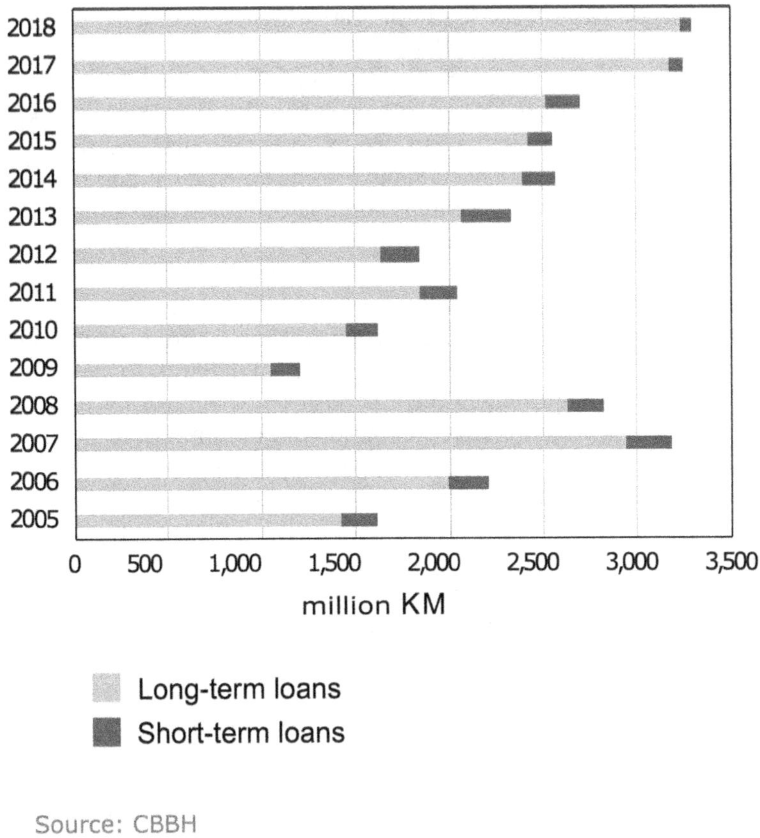

Figure 2.2 Newly approved loans to households by maturity (KM millions), Bosnia and Herzegovina, 2005–2018.
Source: Reprinted with minor edits from CBBiH (2018: 34).

by reducing public spending (including public sector wage bill), privatizing public enterprises and assets, increasing labour market flexibility and so on (Pugh 2002). This resulted in endemic unemployment and job insecurity; persistently low wages; and deregulation and precarization of the labour market, especially in the private sector. In this context, credit has become for many a necessary instrument of periodically supplementing insufficient wages. Indeed, my data suggests that borrowers use general-purpose consumer loans at relatively high interest rates, often repeatedly refinanced, for a wide range of purposes: purchase or improvements to housing, health emergencies, equipment for small-scale business activities, or investments in familial or other social relations. At the same time, the low incomes, the low value of most of the housing stock, uncertain property rights and transaction costs related to mortgages and foreclosures made housing loans less attractive for creditors and less accessible for borrowers. These conditions channelled most of the existing demand for household credit to consumer lending with no cap on the loan amount, which varied depending on the collateral the borrower could offer.

Importantly for the focus of this chapter, consumer lending went hand in hand with the widespread use of guarantorship as a formalized kind of social collateral. This practice had two interrelated purposes: tapping into income streams in debtors' social networks as an efficient and liquid alternative for the general lack of other valuable collateral and suitable repayment insurance, and pushing the frontiers of predatory financial inclusion in a setting of downward socio-economic mobility. Thus, even as interest rates were dropping in the mid-2000s, banks preferred guarantors as a guarantee of creditworthiness over deposits or mortgages. For example, a leaflet of a Western European–owned bank I picked up in Sarajevo in 2007 stated that there was no requirement for a deposit to be eligible for a consumer loan. As long as applicants had co-debtors[11] or guarantors and a continuous income in past six months, they would qualify. Public sector workers were particularly sought after for the role of guarantors; as my research among municipal civil servants has shown, public sector employment is considered a privilege mainly because salary payments are steadier than in the private sector, which, in turn, affords easier access to welfare benefits and above all to bank credit (Lofranco 2016). Especially before the GFC, banks paired their demand for creditworthy guarantors with relaxed lending policies. Guarantors were pitched to customers as a cheaper alternative to mortgage due to lower legal and administrative fees. Even when mortgage was used, combining this with creditworthy guarantors could significantly lower the interest rate and expected monthly instalments, with the latter being the single most important parameter for many borrowers. To further lower instalments, social collateral was frequently combined with long maturities, adjustable interest rates and/or foreign-currency clauses.[12]

Bosnian extended kinship and inter-household co-operation in a historical perspective

As noted in the introduction, the dominant emic explanation of the guarantors' issue pinned it down on the Bosnian extended model of kinship and the resulting (all-too-easy) acceptance of mutual collaboration between nuclear family households. South-East Europeanist scholarship has traced such phenomena to the *zadruga* – a type of extended family household held together by patriarchy, common ancestor worship and collaborative production activities, which has been considered emblematic of South Slav societies inhabiting the Balkan peninsula since the seventh century. Some historians link this family organization to the existence of nomadic and seminomadic populations in the Balkans even before the arrival of South Slavs (Kaser 1994). Although the origin of the *zadruga* has been the subject of a heated scholarly debate whose detailed examination goes beyond the scope of this contribution, it is relevant to highlight that within this debate, anthropologists mostly tended to deconstruct the *zadruga* as an immutable "essence" of premodern South Slav societies.[13] The historical anthropologist Hammel (1972: 370) argued that the *zadruga* should not be approached as an ideal household type. It is rather "an ongoing process of emergence, fission, and reconstitution. Joint families have their origin in nuclear family and can again divide into nuclear families" (Hammel 1972: 30). In other words, shifts of boundaries have been always inherent to the *zadruga* and embedded in its own developmental cycles as well as wider economic, political and cultural transformations.

Pushing further this deconstructive stance, Maria Todorova criticized the image of the *zadruga* as an archaic survival by pointing out that the term itself is a neologism introduced by the Serbian philologist and linguist Vuk Karadžić in 1818 to describe joint families. For Todorova, this implies that their presence in the Balkan region should be limited to specific geographical and political settings (Todorova 2006: 127). More importantly for our analysis of the "guarantors issue", Todorova argued that the *zadruga* has been transformed into a myth invoked in political narratives about the region that oppose Slavic "communal mentality" to German and Anglo-Saxon "individuality and sophistication" (Todorova 2006: 153). She also provided evidence of the ways in which this stereotypical reading of the *zadruga* supported highly diverse ideologies in the region. During socialism, the *zadruga* symbolized the cooperative spirit that would provide the basis for the new social order (Todorova 2006: 157). But the *zadruga* was celebrated also by conservative nationalists as the synonym of traditionalism, indigenism and autochthonism, and the antidote of disruptive Western values (Todorova 2006: 157). In the postsocialist period, the *zadruga* was considered in an evolutionist vein as a marking feature of societies with "retarded" development, and an obstacle to the affirmation of individual private property and market capitalism (Todorova 2006: 153). Beyond deconstructing the essentialist reading of the extended family in the Balkans, Todorova analysed the *zadruga* as a complex and dynamic structure defined by kinship, property relations, residence as well as working arrangements (Todorova 2006: 132). She therefore reiterated the position of other scholars who invoked the *zadruga* to raise a broader point that the relationship between the family as a kinship unit and the household as a productive and reproductive unit marked by space propinquity may vary over time and thus cannot be taken for granted (Todorova 2006; Yanagisako 1979).

The historical development of the *zadruga* has also been an object of enquiry in this critical vein. Several scholars have argued that it was socialist modernization that promoted an irreversible transformation of the *zadruga*, but they did not describe the process as a simplistic transition from extended to nuclear family households (Grandits and Gruber 2012; Todorova 2006). Instead, *zadruga* in rural spaces have been reinvented during socialism as agricultural units and a more progressive alternative to heavy-handed forms of agricultural collectivization (Juriša 1983). In this incarnation, they kept their productive function while including kin as well as neighbours, that is, fellow villagers. These formalized *zadruga* perpetuated collaborative productive practices as well as cultural patterns based on symbolic kinship (godparenthood) and space proximity (neighbourhood),[14] both of which often (but not always) overlap with genealogical proximity (Leutloff-Grandits and Birt 2012). In urban areas, the politically supported household model during socialist modernization were workers' nuclear family households living in flats. Even then, this did not result in an automatic decline of values of collaboration within the extended family. On the contrary, the latter continued to play important roles in facilitating rural-to-urban migration (Halpern 1965: 182). In addition to extended kinship, inter-household co-operation in urban settings was based also on networks of neighbours, *kumovi* (godparents), colleagues and friends.

A serious threat to this form of inter-household collaboration came from the mounting ethno-nationalist ideology during the break-up of the socialist Yugoslavia and especially the 1992–1995 Bosnian War. Substantial literature on the ethnic violence during the war documents its destructive effects on productive structures and social networks in rural and urban settings alike (Christie and Bringa 1993; Henig 2012). However, in a situation of shortages of basic goods, people were in fact forced to rely on ongoing practices of inter-household exchange (and sometimes interethnic barter) as well as on negative reciprocity of looting and illicit appropriation (Broz 2004; Lofranco 2015, 2017; Maček 2009). After the war, despite suspicion and mistrust along ethnic lines, memories of pre-war inter-household co-operation were considered a starting point for reconciliation (Henig 2012; Stefansson 2010). More generally, the role of households as important economic structures of the society (Yanagisako 1979: 199–200) became increasingly evident in post-war BiH. The destruction of the Yugoslav productive system and the ethnicization and retrenchment of the welfare state offloaded to households functions previously satisfied by the socialist state, such as assuring subsistence and providing housing, care and employment opportunities (Kaser 2012: 30). Reliance on inter-household exchanges of resources and favours demonstrated a lack of self-sufficiency of households, especially of urban nuclear family households living off wage labour, many of which belonged to vulnerable categories such as the disabled and female-headed households left behind by warfare (Smajić and Ermacora 2008). In rural-urban fringes, displaced urban nuclear families regrouped into multigenerational households co-residing in self-built family houses and depending mainly on wage labour in urban centres rather than agriculture. All these households faced post-war and postsocialist hardship with a persistent reliance on very extended and, if we include remittances, spatially dispersed (transnational) forms of households, which has been reinforced even more by war-related migration. Furthermore, recent anthropological studies on regimes of exchange of favours and informal lending practices document that Bosnian households engage in informal dynamics of redistribution of public and private resources that are often framed and supported by moral values of trust, honour and reciprocity (Brković 2017; Jasarević 2017; Sorabji 2008).[15]

Thus, in the context of widespread dispossession and retrenchment of formal welfare institutions, the ability of BiH households to expand and draw on their extended familial ties and other social connections became a key "asset" for their reproduction. This interpretation is consistent with Guyer's (1997: 117) argument that the anthropological concept of assets should go beyond "the narrow sense of the term for capitalist economies". The extended family commonly constitutes a powerful set of social ties and the starting point for expanding one's social network in a precarious economy. In the next section, I proceed to examine how the shift to a financialized regime of accumulation has redrawn this set of relations and informal practices.

Extending kinship through the financialization of inter-household solidarity

In the context of social collateral in BiH, inter-household collaboration took, at one level, the shape of a dyadic interpersonal relationship between the borrower and the guarantor. To a significant extent, this was obviously a development introduced by the regulatory framework and financial institutions in a top-down manner. The legal form of the relationship identifies individuals as direct participants. Accordingly, banks do not notify other members of the borrower's and the guarantor's households when their relationship is formally established, although these persons also can be legally obliged to repay in case of a default. In some cases, guarantors themselves reinforced the dyadic nature of the relationship by keeping it secret from their partners. At the same time, the building blocks of guarantorship relations were moral meanings and social relations that structure people's everyday life (Palomera 2014, 2015). This was visible in the ways in which values of extended kinship and inter-household co-operation became entwined with bank requirements and set to work to co-opt creditworthy wage earners into guarantorship relations, thereby introducing the formal legal obligation into existing or newly extended inter-household networks. It was visible also in the way in which many of my interlocutors, when asked about their search for guarantors or their decision to become one, considered indispensable the existence of a relation of "trust". As Sanela,[16] a middle-aged employee of a local post office, explained, "You can be a guarantor for people you trust and who you know will do everything to repay that loan." Mirjana, owner of a fast-food restaurant, told me:

> I preferred to ask good friends, people … whose trust I gained. These are people who know I will do everything to pay the instalments and, thank God, today I can still look them in the eyes without being ashamed.

Clearly, then, this form of co-operation rests on trustworthiness defined as a sense of commitment secured by moral values and social sanctions (Hardin 1996: 29) and here formulated as the primary borrower's absolute commitment and/or capability to repay the debt.

In his work, Webb Keane (2008) explained that moral principles and claims are no strangers to capitalist markets. They become an integral part of capitalism's social reproduction in localized and historically specific contexts through a slippage between regimes of values on the basis of a "semiotic mediation" of a moral metalanguage aimed to socially embed markets' abstract principles. A major example of this process in the financializing BiH is precisely the translation of individuals' trustworthiness into the market principle of creditworthiness, that is, the assessment of trustworthiness by financial institutions. As Lapavitsas remarked, "credit-related trust, which is fundamental to all credit relations, is transformed from a private and subjective into a social and objective relationship as a result of the practices of financial institutions" (Lapavitsas 2007: 418). Trust underpinning capitalist credit is measurable and based on the borrower's ability to repay the principal with interest or to provide a suitable substitute, that is, collateral. Thus, the trustworthiness of guarantors and borrowers that my interlocutors referred to describes often a combination of moral evaluations and objective and measurable creditworthiness criteria. Specifically, "closer" relations, such as familial ones, tend to be marked by a particularly strong moral imperative of collaboration and lower social sanctions in case of the primary borrower's defaulting but also an intimacy that enables the guarantor to evaluate the borrower's ability to repay and thereby potentially trust them. For example, Sanela had been a guarantor for her son and daughter-in-law, and, whenever she needed to borrow money herself, she would ask her cousin who, as she underlined, "knows what I am like". As she further explained, the cousin, employed in municipal administration, agreed to be her "habitual guarantor" because she knew that Sanela would always prioritize repayment and also had the financial capability to do so due to her stable employment. Edina, a jurist at a ministry in her 50s with long-term experience with consumer loans, explained that the prerequisites for the "perfect guarantor" were, in the order of priority, "a stable job, preferably in the public sector (*državni posao*), and that he or she is as close as possible to your family, relatives or acquaintances". As this list reveals, my interlocutors considered the banks' creditworthiness criteria a compelling reason to scan their genealogical tree for the closest relative with a stable public sector wage who could act as a guarantor. When Edina's son needed a loan to refurbish his new flat, she could not act as his guarantor because the repayment of her loans was already taking two-thirds of her wage. As her husband was unemployed, after a few days of thinking, she discovered the perfect combination of desirable moral and economic features in her husband's sister who had a stable job as a nurse in a public hospital.

Within this logic, people who do not have close relatives with stable income are eventually pushed to look for potential guarantors beyond nuclear and extended family ties. In such cases, work colleagues seem to be the most frequent solution, presumably because they are employed and have a daily contact with the borrowers, which gives them a sense of control over the risk of the borrower's insolvency. Like many of my interlocutors, Marina agreed to be a guarantor for a colleague. As she explained, she accepted this request from a non-relative because her colleague had health problems and a wife and two children to support. Besides these moral considerations, she considered the risk low as the borrowed amount was only 2,000 KM (€1,000) and both of them worked for a public publishing house and had high wages. Having succeeded in the search for guarantors outside the family, my interlocutors readily declared those friends or acquaintances to be "like a brother/sister" in the sense that they had been willing to take a risk that only a close relative would have taken. Such cases point to an emergence of new forms of sociability induced by the criteria of financial institutions, as in other settings where social collateral became an important prerequisite for accessing credit (Schuster 2014). Furthermore, they show how familiarity and intimacy as a kind of relation is redefined by the financial market principle of "risk-taking" by households (Martin 2002). Looking for creditworthy guarantors may thus result in symbolically "extending the extended family" and including non-related households in extractive relations. In any case, whether rooted in kin ties or reframed in the semantic field of kinship, the formalization of the borrower-guarantor relationship transformed inter-household exchange into a new relation of intimate interdependence vulnerable to financial risks. The next section shows how the GFC and its aftermath demonstrated this.

Expanding and shrinking inter-household networks in the face of post-crisis debt collection

In 2009 and 2010, the global recession and the EU sovereign debt crisis hit the BiH real economy. The impact was mediated by a reduction in various kinds of monetary inflows that had previously supported local business and consumption, including FDIs, donations, remittances and tourism receipts (CBBiH 2009d: 10). Growing illiquidity in the eurozone resulted in a higher cost of money on EU money markets, a substantial increase in active interest rates and a tightening of procedures for approving loans. The cumulative effect was a decline in overall business activity accompanied by a significant loss of jobs. Unemployment rate reached 24.1% at the end of 2009 (CBBiH 2009a: 26). Arrears on wages in the private sector became more common. Predictably, these developments made debt repayment more difficult for households. In the beginning of 2010, 25.2% of household loans were classified as "non-performing" (CBBiH 2010: 27).

In this context, banks started to collect debts from guarantors and their families in a rushed and secretive manner, often with no prior communication with primary borrowers. The problem was exacerbated by outdated or non-existent legislation, especially the lack of a personal bankruptcy law and inadequate protection of the rights of consumers of financial products. In this sense, the guarantors' issue points also to the extensive liberalization or rather under-regulation of household lending in South-Eastern Europe. The fast-track debt collection instilled mistrust between guarantors and borrowers as the commitment of the latter to debt repayment become doubtful. More importantly, it revealed to both borrowers and guarantors how guarantorship involved them in new financial obligations that went far beyond the boundaries of their own households. Inter-household networks in which people found themselves entangled sometimes extended unexpectedly wide and far, as illustrated by extreme cases presented in the media. For example, a Sarajevo woman was supposedly able to take 52 loans by abusing personal documents of a friend who accepted to be the guarantor for only one of them (Al Jazeera Balkans 2013b; Nezavisne Novine 2011). Such cases revealed the poor and uncoordinated regulation of the post-war banking system. This was also evident from the slow development of a national credit-scoring system, which came to be centralized under the management of the CBBiH only in 2007 and has been updated in real time only since 2019.

Many households had guarantors for their loans while being guarantors for somebody else. As a result, some ended up caught in a chain reaction of insolvency. Mirna, owner of a bakery on the outskirts of Sarajevo, applied several times for a consumer loan with the support of a good friend with a public sector job who was always willing to act as her guarantor. At the same time, Mirna accepted to be a guarantor for her extended family member's 5,000 KM (€2,500) loan. When the relative stopped repaying, she had to assume responsibility for their debt, which, however, undermined her capability of servicing her own debt secured with her friend's guarantee. To solve the problem, Mirna and her husband were forced to sell their car. Another widespread situation was that households found out that guarantorship entangled their domestic budget with other households' transnational strategies to face the post-crisis recession and over-indebtedness. Many debtors in arrears decided to migrate abroad to find a job and repay the debt at home. In some cases, however, they planned to start a new life abroad by throwing onto guarantors the debt burden and compensating them at some point in the future.[17] In such cases, banks would collect the debt from guarantors, sometimes forcing them to turn to their extended family for resource pooling. This was the case of Amra, a retired teacher whom I met in Mirna's bakery. As she heard the story about Mirna's household repaying someone else's debt, she wanted to share the experience of her nephew who accepted to be a guarantor for a good friend for a 20,000 KM (€10,000) loan. The friend moved to Germany, and the nephew was forced to repay the money to the bank. As Amra pointed out, "Not only him, but also his parents who had to take a loan for this. I also contributed with 2,000 KM, despite my poor pension."

The entanglement of guarantors in post-crisis debt collection activated intra- and inter-household co-operation but, in some cases, also led to a disintegration of such relations. Relatives and friends appeared in a new light as a consequence of debt collection that led many to illness and suicide.[18] As debt spread along inter-household ties, marriages broke down and the integrity of nuclear family households was put under serious strain. The marriage of Alma, a hospital nurse, was on the verge of breakdown when her husband found out that she accepted to be a guarantor for several of her colleagues and that she had been called by the bank to repay their debt. When Alma and her husband asked one of the colleagues to repay her loan of 2,500 KM, she refused, arguing that Alma could afford the repayment with her salary. Alma ended up having to pay instalments higher than her salary of 600 KM (€300) while her husband has fallen sick due to the stress of that experience. Their story is representative of the widespread tensions in the post-crisis period among people with stable jobs who had become massively involved in the networks of social collateral despite the low purchasing power of their wages. However, not all cases of repaying guarantors were so conflictual. I frequently encountered cases of "silent repaying" to protect their own reputation and their inter-household network from financial extraction: people were simply ashamed to put their close relatives or friends under pressure over money.

In this context, a "centripetal" tendency (Sabaté, this volume) arose to shrink the relations of inter-household financial solidarity and thereby reverse their pre-crisis expansion, as expressed by the already mentioned statements such as "I would not be a loan guarantor even for my own child." This suggests a rejection of the dangerous interdependence created by guarantorship. For some of my interlocutors, this meant abstaining from the use of credit in practice. As Nina explained:

> Lately, I do not apply for credit because we had had a bad experience in my family … When I could afford it, I bought an oven, when I could afford it, I bought a washing machine, [but] as long as I was not able to afford it, I did not even have a washing machine.

However, for the majority of my interlocutors who did not give up on borrowing, the shrinking of solidarity relations implied a "privatization of risk" (Hacker 2004; Martin 2002) in the specific sense of having persons in their own households act as guarantors or adopting more selective criteria when searching their social networks for guarantors. As Branko, a middle-aged auto mechanic, told me: "I asked my daughter and son-in-law to be my guarantors because these days one does not dare to ask just anyone" (*ne smiješ svakoga pitati*). When this was not possible, the solution was to look for more expensive credit options that dispensed with the need for guarantors altogether. To cope with the problem, my interlocutors started to explore options they had never considered before because of higher interest rates – especially microloans that, starting several years after the war, turned into so-called "flash" consumer loans of small amounts provided by for-profit companies instead of (ostensibly) non-profit microfinance organizations. Flash loan providers secured their share of the market after the GFC by offering credit without guarantors. According to one promotional leaflet for this type of credit, the lender offered "small, quick loans for those who build, those who work in the fields, those who look for credit without guarantors..." (Figure 2.3).

During the period when the guarantors' issue was most hotly debated in the media, lawmakers started to discuss relevant regulations. The 2013 law in the Federation of Bosnia and Herzegovina invalidated guarantorships for outstanding loans issued to borrowers whose solvency was not previously verified by credit institutions. It also obliged credit institutions to exhaust all legal means of collecting from primary borrowers before turning to guarantors. Furthermore, the use of social collateral was declared illegal for loans over 20,000 KM and with maturities longer than three years. Notwithstanding this, banks initially tried to circumvent the law by collecting

Figure 2.3 Microcredit agency advertisement for flash loans "without guarantors", Sarajevo, 2012.

Source: Author.

from co-debtors rather than guarantors and thereby averting their own looming defaults.[19] By doing so, they aimed at tightening the formal obligations for debts as well as restricting the social networks within which debt and risk were shared. The informational website of the Banking Agency of the Federation of Bosnia and Herzegovina thus explains that "in principle, co-debtors should be people from the same household, parents, spouses or business partners" (FBA 2016). The bottom-up resistance to social collateral, together with the new regulations protecting guarantors, pushed credit institutions also to introduce repayment insurance and life insurance as new ways of securing loans. Insurance also enabled banks to continue issuing loans over 20,000 KM that they could not anymore secure with guarantorships. However, insurance made credit more expensive. My interlocutors often accepted insurance as a relief and its higher cost as a price for satisfying the need to limit the reach of extractive relations beyond the debtor's household.

Socializing and privatizing risk in the European financial periphery

This chapter has explored the issue of guarantors repaying other people's debts in the aftermath of the GFC. The origins of the phenomenon were often traced to traditional models of the extended family and household. I sought to deconstruct these oversimplified culturalist explanations and morally disciplining perceptions cropping up in the Bosnian public debate and post-crisis financial education programmes. Reframing this issue in a political economy perspective, the chapter has discussed it as the result of a multiscalar process of financialization of inter-household exchange. It has identified the demand for creditworthy guarantors as a condition for accessing/issuing credit as an important feature of the penetration of foreign finance into BiH household economies. Compared to other settings where social collateral has been employed more selectively to financially include particularly marginalized or impoverished segments of the population, I argued that the financialization of social ties in BiH unfolded as a large-scale strategy targeted at a downwardly mobile population of all strata. Inscribed in these dynamics, Bosnian inter-household collaboration along extended kinship and kinship-like lines appears far removed from a "traditional" cultural attitude. The acceptance of the "collateralization of social ties" by borrowers themselves is rather a direct consequence of the structurally generated need to access credit. Its explanation therefore calls for deeper ethnographic investigation of the relationship between the household's social reproduction and transformations of its internal and external relations under a financialized regime of accumulation.

Anthropological studies of such transformations suggest that they are not purely top-down processes (Narotzky 2015; Palomera 2014). Guarantorship relations expose the ambivalent dynamics of household involvement in contemporary (financial) capitalism whose moral hegemony rests on the blurring of different value regimes and the intertwining of moral and contractual obligations and non-commoditized and commoditized relations of exchange (Narotzky 2015). In BiH, where the last three decades saw a radical privatization of welfare, inter-household exchange became a valuable asset co-opted and transformed by the financial imperative of creditworthiness. The use of social collateral created preconditions for a financialized form of inter-household exchange operating through the extraction of financial value from the income of one household towards the repayment of debts of another household. From the perspective of creditors, this was a wage-based extractive strategy adapted to the conditions of a credit market with a lack of other suitable collateral. Marxian economists grasped the involvement of households in financialization in general as the extraction of financial profits (financial expropriation) from their income streams (Bryan et al. 2009; Lapavitsas 2013). However, it is misleading to assume that each income stream corresponds neatly to an individual, self-standing household. On the contrary, financial expropriation, especially (but not only) in peripheral and semi-peripheral contexts, often involves complex networks of households tied by risky financial interdependence. The extensive use of social collateral in BiH constituted households as hypersocial actors in the credit market, leading them to socialize their risks, multiply guarantorship relations far beyond the usual scope of collaboration in and among households, and thereby expand the social base for financial expropriation.

The economic impact of the GFC revealed the implications of a situation in which various kinds of households (multigenerational, nuclear, transnational, female-headed etc.) were held together by familial and familial-like relations as well as formal financial obligations. These inter-household networks experienced strong material and social tensions as guarantors found themselves forced to prioritize inter-household redistribution of resources for the purposes of repaying borrowers' debts over their own intra-household reproduction, production or consumption. This experience led to a reversal of the unsustainable socialization of risk and a tendency to shrink relationships of financial solidarity, which has been recently supported also by financial institutions.

However, this tendency does not simply reproduce the dynamics of the privatization of risk described for households in Anglo-American cores who had been encouraged to accept risks in their domestic space in a setting of neoliberalization and welfare retrenchment since the 1980s (Martin 2002: 12). The latter process could be more aptly defined as the individualization of risk in the sense that ("fictional") individuals were invited to directly participate in financial markets, invest in financial products and generally internalize the logic of money-making through risk-taking (Martin 2002). In the Bosnian semi-periphery, the privatization of risk also refers to households' resistance to extractive financial practices and their efforts to limit their reach beyond the debtor's household. Furthermore, in a situation of persisting structural conditions of financialization of household economies, my interlocutors' preference for more centripetal relations and more expensive credit solutions should not be read as an outcome of a generalized disillusionment with inter-household relations as such. As de L'Estoile has argued, in situations of political instability and uncertainty about the future, money tends to assume a "transitory value" relative to familial and other social relations that come to play the role of a key welfare asset (de L'Estoile 2013). Credit institutions recently tapped into this shift by starting commodifying the safety of inter-household networks and selling it to borrowers in the form of repayment insurance policies. This latest trend demonstrates the interactive and dynamic character of the relationship between credit institutions and borrowers, which deserves further exploration.

Acknowledgements

I wish to thank all participants in the workshop "Households and Peripheral Financialization in Europe" organized at the Max Planck Institute for Social Anthropology, and in particular Hadas Weiss for her comments on an early draft of this chapter. Thanks also to Don Kalb and Chris Hahn for their support for my research on financialization in Halle and to Marek Mikuš and Petra Rodik for their careful reviews and editing of my contribution.

Notes

1 A guarantor is an individual who accepted a contractual obligation to repay a borrower's debt in the event that the borrower defaults on the obligation. Guarantors pledge their own wages and assets as collateral.

2 The number of NPLs started to increase in September 2008 and has tripled by September 2010 (Ćetković 2011).

3 The exchange rate of the convertible mark to the euro is fixed at 1 EUR = 1.95583 BAM. In other words, 1 KM equals approximately 50 euro cents.

4 The Constitution of BiH, part of the Dayton Agreement signed in 1995, constituted BiH as a federal state consisting of two entities (Republika Srpska and the Federation of Bosnia and Herzegovina) with extensive competencies in multiple sectors, including banking.

5 The "guarantors' issue" was better known under the extended formulation of "guarantors repaying others' loans" (*žiranti koji plaćaju tuđe kredite*).

6 A similar regulatory framework had been previously adopted in Republika Srpska through a 2011 amendment of its Law on Banks. The 2013 federal law was meant to harmonize regulation on the entire national territory.

7 Official data on guarantors repaying the main borrower's debt are available from 2010 to 2016. However, the official data published by the CBBiH are less accurate after 2013. The amount repaid by guarantors each year is not anymore reported, while the emphasis is on a consistent decrease in occurrences: 3,103 in 2014, 2,308 in 2015, and a decrease of 25% in 2016. This is explained by the use of alternative forms of guarantee after the adoption of the 2013 law.

8 This chapter draws on data collected during ten months of ethnographic fieldwork on consumer credit and financialization of household economies in

Sarajevo (Federation of Bosnia and Herzegovina) and East Sarajevo (Republika Srpska), distributed over 2007, 2012, 2013, 2014 and 2019.

9 Funding mainstream banks to provide microloans was just one of the ways through which post-war microcredit sector expanded in BiH in the first half of the 2000s. Microcredit organizations and local and international NGOs were also active in microcredit lending. According to Bateman and Sinković (2017: 129), the Bosnian microfinance sector was at the time the second largest in the world.

10 Some of the increase in loans to households after the GFC consisted in rescheduled claims on the household sector rather than new placements (CBBiH 2013: 27).

11 Unlikely a guarantor, a co-debtor can be required by the creditor to make repayment as soon as repayment by the primary debtor shows any irregularities or delays. A guarantor's obligation should be activated only as a last resort after the creditor has exhausted all other legal means of collecting debt from the debtor.

12 Foreign-currency (FX) loans, sold in BiH by several foreign-owned banks since the latter half of the 2000s, are loans contracted with clauses that set the value of the principal in a foreign currency such as the US dollar, the euro or the Swiss franc while repayment takes place in BiH convertible marks according to the current exchange rate. The appreciation of the Swiss franc in the aftermath of the GFC resulted in a particularly drastic inflation of principals and repayment burden for FX debtors in a number of Eastern European countries (Bohle 2018; Mikuš 2019; Rodik 2015, 2019). In BiH, Swiss franc loans were introduced in February 2006, and by 2009 they amounted to 7.7% of total bank claims on households. At that point, 17.8% of household loans with maturities over ten years were indexed to Swiss franc (CBBiH 2009c: 38). From 2010 on, the percentage of Swiss Franc loans underwent a steep decrease, down to 0.9% in 2018 (CBBiH 2018: 35).

13 For literature reviews, see Kaser (2012) and Todorova (2006).

14 The importance of neighbourhood has been traced to the Ottoman tradition of *komšiluk* that stresses the moral obligation of neighbours to offer prompt mutual help to each other (Bringa 1995; Halpern 1958; Henig 2012).

15 In BiH, drawing on immaterial assets such as social ties (*veze*, *štele*) to exchange favours (*usluge*) can generate material and even monetary assets: for example, future income from a job thus arranged. Alternatively, getting a favour done through familial ties can save money otherwise needed to bribe someone who is not part of the extended familial network (Lofranco 2016).

16 All names of interlocutors are pseudonyms.

17 This problem persists up to now as rampant out-migration from BiH continues. In 2019, the local TV station BN reported that 5,300 indebted people had moved abroad in 2018. As debtors cannot be forced to come back to their home country, the Guarantors' Association is working on establishing bilateral agreements between BiH and the major destinations of BiH migrants (i.e., Austria, Germany, the USA) to enable holding migrants responsible for their debts (BN TV 2019).

18 The Guarantors' Association reported in 2013 that some 40 guarantors had committed suicide by then. For relationships between over-indebtedness and illness (see Rodik 2019: 153–156).

19 In 2016, unpaid loans caused the bankruptcy of two banks in Republika Srpska – Banka Srpska and Bobar Banka. The Guarantor's Association reported that the Banking Agency of Republika Srpska tried unsuccessfully to prevent the defaults by ordering all other banks to block the accounts of guarantors for the non-performing loans given by these two banks.

References

Al Jazeera Balkans (2013b) Ko štiti žirante. Available from: http://balkans.aljazeera.net/vijesti/ko-stiti-zirante [Accessed 21 February 2020].

Bateman, M. & Sinković, D. (2017) Bosnia's microfinance post-conflict experiment: a new Balkan tragedy. In: Bateman, M. & Maclean, K. (eds.) *Seduced and betrayed: exposing the contemporary microfinance phenomenon*. Albuquerque: University of New Mexico Press, pp. 127–146.

Becker, J. & Ćetković, P. (2015) Patterns of financialization in Southeast European and Visegrád countries. In: Radošević, D. and Cvijanović, V. (eds.) *Financialisation and financial crisis in South-Eastern European countries*. Frankfurt am Main: Peter Lang, pp. 71–90.

Becker, J., Jäger, J., Leubolt, B. & Weissenbacher, R. (2010) Peripheral financialization and vulnerability to crisis: a regulationist perspective. *Competition & Change* 14(3–4): 225–247. doi: 10.1179/102452910X12837703615337.

BN TV (2019) Prevareni žiranti – Bijeljina. Available from: https://www.youtube.com/watch?v=TPmlL-VKHLM [Accessed 1 October 2020].

Bohle, D. (2018) Mortgaging Europe's periphery. *Studies in Comparative International Development* 53: 196–217. doi: 10.1007/s12116-018-9260-7.

Bringa, T. (1995) *Being Muslim the Bosnian way: identity and community in a central Bosnian village*. Princeton: Princeton University Press.

Brković, Č. (2017) *Managing ambiguity: how clientelism, citizenship and power shape personhood in Bosnia and Herzegovina*. New York: Berghahn Books.

Broz, S. (2004) *Good people in evil time: portraits of complicity and resistance in the Bosnian war*. New York: Other Press.

Bryan, D., Martin, R. & Rafferty, M. (2009) Financialization and Marx: giving labor and capital a financial makeover. *Review of Radical Political Economics* 41(4): 458–472. doi: 10.1177/0486613409341368.

CBBiH (2007) Financial stability report 2007. Sarajevo: CBBiH.

CBBiH (2009a) Annual report 2009. Sarajevo: CBBiH.

CBBiH (2009b) Fenomenologija i rizici kreditnog rasta u zemljama u tranziciji. Sarajevo: CBBiH.

CBBiH (2009c) Financial stability report 2009. Sarajevo: CBBiH.

CBBiH (2009d) Uticaj globalne finansijske krize na Bosnu i Hercegovinu. Sarajevo: CBBiH.

CBBiH (2010) Financial stability report 2010. Sarajevo: CBBiH.

CBBiH (2012) Financial stability report 2012. Sarajevo: CBBiH.

CBBiH (2013) Financial stability report 2013. Sarajevo: CBBiH.

CBBiH (2015) Financial stability report 2015. Sarajevo: CBBiH.

CBBiH (2018) Financial stability report 2018. Sarajevo: CBBiH.

Christie, D. & Bringa, T. (1993) *We are all neighbours* (film). Granada Television.

Čaušević, F. (2012) Economic perspectives on Bosnia and Herzegovina in the period of global crisis. Available from: www.sant.ox.ac.uk/seesox/opinionpieces/Causevic-Economicperspectives.pdf [Accessed 1 October 2020].

Ćetković, P. (2011) Credit growth and instability in Balkan countries: the role of foreign banks. Research on Money and Finance Discussion Paper no. 27.

De L'Estoile, B. (2014) "Money is good, but a friend is better": uncertainty, orientation to the future, and "the economy". *Current Anthropology* 55(S9): S62–S73. doi: 10.1086/676068.

DeLuca, E. (2017) The household. *Cultural Anthropology* website. Available from: https://culanth.org/fieldsights/1125-the-household [Accessed 4 October 2020].

FBA (2016) Informacije za korisnike finansijskih usluga. Available from: https://www.fba.ba/bs/informacije-za-korisnike-finansijskih-usluga-1 [Accessed 1 September 2020].

FENA (2013) Prevareni žiranti vratili 25 KM tuđih kredita. Available from: https://www.klix.ba/biznis/privreda/prevareni-ziranti-vratili-25-miliona-km-tudjih-kredita/130514068 [Accessed 21 September 2019].

Gabor, D. (2010) (De) financialization and crisis in Eastern Europe. *Competition & Change* 14 (3–4): 248–270. doi: 10.1179/102452910X12837703615373.

Gabor, D. (2011) *Central banking and financialization: a Romanian account of how Eastern Europe became subprime*. New York: Palgrave Macmillan.

Grandits, H. & Guber, S. (2012) The dissolution of the large complex households in the Balkans: was the ultimate reason structural or cultural? In: Kaser, K. (ed.) *Household and family in the Balkans: two decades of historical family research at University of Graz*. Wien: LIT Verlag, pp. 387–486.

Guérin, I. (2014) Juggling with debt, social ties, and values: the everyday use of microcredit in rural South India. *Current Anthropology* 55(S9): S40–S50. doi: 10.1086/675929.

Guyer, J. I. (1997) Endowments and assets: the anthropology of wealth and the economics of intrahousehold allocation. In: Haddad, L., Hoddinott, J. & Alderman, H. (eds.) *Intrahousehold resource allocation in developing countries: models, methods, and policy*. Baltimore: Johns Hopkins University Press, pp. 112–125.

Hacker, S. J. (2004) Privatizing risk without privatizing welfare: the hidden politics of social policy retrenchment in the United States. *American Political Science Review* 98(2): 243–260.

Halpern, J. (1958) *A Serbian village*. New York: Columbia University Press.

Halpern, J. (1965) Peasant culture and urbanization in Yugoslavia. *Human Organization* 24(2): 162–174.

Hammel, E. (1972) The zadruga as a process. In: Laslett, P. (ed.) *Household and family in past time*. Cambridge: Cambridge University Press, pp. 335–373.

Hardin, R. (1996) Trustworthiness. *Ethics* 107: 26–42.

Henig, D. (2012) "Knocking on my neighbours' door": on metamorphoses of sociality in rural Bosnia. *Critique of Anthropology* 32(1): 3–19. doi: 10.1177/0308275X11430871.

Jasarević, L. (2017) *Health and wealth on the Bosnian market: intimate debt*. Bloomington: Indiana University Press.

Juriša, S. (1983) Agrarna politika i problemi kolektivizacije u Jugoslaviji u vrijeme sukoba KPJ s Informbiroom. *Časopis za suvremenu povijest* 15(1): 55–73.

Kar, S. (2017) Relative indemnity: risk, insurance, and kinship in Indian microfinance. *Journal of the Royal Anthropological Institute* 23: 302–319. doi: 10.1111/1467-9655.12608.

Kaser, K. (1994) The Balkan joint family: seeking its origins. *Continuity and Change* 9(1): 45–68. doi: 10.1017/S0268416000004161.

Kaser, K., ed. (2012) *Household and family in the Balkans: two decades of historical family research at University of Graz*. Wien: LIT Verlag.

Keane, W. (2008) Market materiality and moral metalanguage. *Anthropological Theory* 8(1): 27–42. doi: 10.1177/1463499607087493.

Kofti, D. (2020) Financialized kinship and challenges for the Greek oikos. In: Hann, C. & Kalb, D. (eds.) *Financialization: relational approaches.* New York: Berghahn Books, pp. 266–285.

Lapavitsas, C. (2007) Information and trust as social aspects of credit. *Economy and Society* 36(6): 416–436. doi: 10.1080/03085140701428381.

Lapavitsas, C. (2013) *Profiting without producing: how finance exploits us all.* London: Verso.

Leutloff-Grandits, C. & Birt, D. (2012) Seven parish villages in the vicinity of the town of Bijelovar. In: Kaser, K. (ed.) *Household and family in the Balkans: two decades of historical family research at University of Graz.* Wien: LIT Verlag, pp. 603–615.

Lofranco, Z. T. (2015) Refurnishing the home in post-war neoliberalism: consumption strategies in the Sarajevan household economy. *Human Affairs* 25(1): 81–92. doi: 10.1515/humaff-2015-0007.

Lofranco, Z. T. (2016) Party corruption in the Bosnia and Herzegovina public employment system: public discourse, legal and moral legitimation. In: Torsello, D. (ed.) *Corruption in the public administration: an ethnographic approach.* Cheltenham: Edward Elgar, pp. 75–105.

Lofranco, Z. T. (2017) Negotiating neighbourliness in Sarajevo apartment blocks. In: Donnan, H., Hurd, M. & Leutloff, C. (eds.) *Migrating borders and moving times.* Manchester: Manchester University Press, pp. 42–57.

Maček, I. (2009) *Sarajevo under siege. Anthropology in wartime.* Philadelphia: University of Pennsylvania Press.

Martin. R. (2002) *Financialization of daily life.* Philadelphia: Temple University Press.

Mikuš, M. (2019) Contesting household debt in Croatia: the double movement of financialization and the fetishism of money in Eastern European peripheries. *Dialectical Anthropology* 43: 295–315. doi: 10.1007/s10624-019-09551-8.

Narotzky, S. (2015) The payoff of love and the traffic of favours: reciprocity, social capital and the blurring of value realms in flexible capitalism. In: Kjaerluff, J. (ed.) *Flexible capitalism: exchange and ambiguity at work.* New York: Berghahn Books, pp. 268–310.

Nezavisne Novine (2011) Žiranti u BiH još jedna socijalna kategorija. Available from: https://www.nezavisne.com/ekonomija/analize/Ziranti-u-BiH-jos-jedna-socijalna- kategorija/81700 [Accessed 1 October 2020].

Palomera, J. (2014) How did finance infiltrate the world of the urban poor? Homeownership and social fragmentation in a Spanish neighbourhood. *International Journal of Urban and Regional Research* 38(1): 218–235. doi: 10.1111/1468-2427.12055.

Palomera, J. (2015) Investing without wealth: the financialization of social reproduction #crisis. Available at: https://allegralaboratory.net/investing-without-wealth-the-financialization-of-social-reproduction-crisis/ [Accessed 14 September 2019].

Pugh, M. (2002) Postwar political economy in Bosnia and Herzegovina: the spoils of peace. *Global Governance* 8(4): 467–482. doi: 10.1163/19426720-00804006.

Rodik, P. (2015) The impact of the Swiss franc loans crisis on Croatian households. In: Değirmencioğlu, S. M. & Walker, C. (eds.) *Social and psychological dimensions of personal debt and the debt industry.* Basingstoke: Palgrave Macmillan, pp. 61–83. doi: 10.1057/9781137407795_4.

Rodik, P. (2019) *(Pre)zaduženi: društveni aspekti zaduženosti kućanstava u Hrvatskoj.* Zagreb: Jesenski i Turk.

Schuster, C. (2014) The social unit of debt: gender and creditworthiness in Paraguayan microfinance. *American Ethnologist* 41(3): 563–578. doi: 10.1111/amet.12095.

Schuster, C. (2015) *Social collateral: women and microfinance in Paraguay's smuggling economy.* Oakland: University of California Press.

Smajić, S. & Ermacora, S. (2008) Poverty amongst female-headed households in Bosnia and Herzegovina: an empirical analysis. *South East European Journal of Economics and Business* 2(1): 69–88. doi: 10.2478/v10033-007-0017-x.

Sorabji, C. (2008) Bosnian neighbourhoods revisited: tolerance, commitment and *komšiluk* in Sarajevo. In: Pine, F. & de Pina-Cabral, J. (eds.) *On the margins of religion.* New York: Berghahn Books, pp. 97–112.

Stefansson, A. (2010) Coffee after cleansing? Co-existence, co-operation and communication in post-conflict Bosnia and Herzegovina. *Focaal* 57: 62–76. doi: 10.3167/fcl.2010.570105.

Todorova, M. (2006) *Balkan family structure and the European pattern: demographic developments in Ottoman Bulgaria.* Budapest: Central European University Press.

Van der Windt, N., Dauskardt, R., Heimes, M. & Hoessel, J. (2011) Housing finance from post-conflict interventions to market development in the Balkans. In: Köhn, D. & von Pischke, J. D. (eds.) *Housing finance in emerging markets: connecting low-income groups to finance.* Heidelberg: Springer, pp. 211–224.

Yanagisako, S. J. (1979) Family and household: analysis of domestic groups. *Annual Review of Anthropology* 8: 161–205. doi: 10.1146/annurev.an.08.100179.001113.

Zaloom, C. (2017) Finance. *Cultural Anthropology* website. Available from: https://culanth.org/fieldsights/1163-finance [Accessed 1 July 2020].

Section II

Spaces of financialized housing and reproduction

3 Semi-peripheral financialization and informal household solutions

Embedded scales of uneven development in Hungarian urban fringes

Ágnes Gagyi, Csaba Jelinek, Zsuzsanna Pósfai and András Vigvári

Introduction

Based on a collective research project bridging anthropological and political economic perspectives, this chapter contemplates local specificities of financialization of households and housing in postsocialist Hungary in relation to long-term patterns of uneven development. We point to processes embedding macro-scale dependencies within lower geographical scales, specifically to the rolling out of successive waves of financial (over-)inclusion and exclusion through financialized housing structures in Hungary before and after the 2007–2008 Global Financial Crisis (GFC). Our collective work is driven by an interest in the dynamic relationships between capital accumulation and social reproduction in semi-peripheral contexts. This interest implies understanding our case studies in Hungary from the perspective of their embeddedness in the larger dynamics of the capitalist world-system. It also calls for a theorization that can relate our cases to descriptions of global processes, which however are often developed based on cases from global cores. In the latter effort, we build on traditions of research on interpenetrating scales of uneven development in critical geography (Dunford and Liu 2017; Hadjimichalis and Hudson 2014; Harvey 1978; Hudson 2015, 2016; Smith 1984), the critical political economy of uneven development (including *dependentista*, world-systems and neo-Gramscian traditions) and systemic approaches to global anthropology (Friedman and Friedman 2008; Kalb and Tak 2005; Wolf and Silverman 2001).

We understand financialization not as a discrete phenomenon but as a dynamic integrated in broader reconfigurations of capitalist accumulation across productive and financialized phases of long global economic cycles as well as across boom and bust phases of shorter lending cycles. Accordingly, we emphasize that in both kinds of cycles, successive moments of inclusion and exclusion of social reproduction functions into and from the formal circuits of the capitalist economy play an important role in accumulation, including financialized accumulation. Our chapter describes the articulation between this kind of dynamic and mortgage lending before and after 2008 on both the international and sub-national level. We demonstrate how financialized accumulation relies on household resources that meet social reproductive functions. We further show that intermediate spaces through which the "moving frontline" of financial over-inclusion and exclusion passes have a particular significance for the spatial dynamics of financialized accumulation. Our case study of an allotment garden area close to Budapest is an instance of such an intermediate space that also reveals the articulation of financialization and informal reproductive labour. In the allotment area, households that became over-indebted after 2008 resort to informal housing solutions to maintain their reproductive and labour capacity while also fulfilling debt repayment obligations. We further discuss state regulation as an important factor in institutionalizing the moving frontlines of financial inclusion/exclusion and governing the conditions of reproductive adaptation to the pressures of accumulation. Forms of this reproductive adaptation change as the inclusion/exclusion dynamic unfolds: in periods of financial inclusion, the risks of this inclusion are spread across households and their broader social networks (e.g. by using relatives' homes to access mortgage loans), while in periods of financial exclusion, reproductive capacities of households and their networks compensate for losses (e.g. by family and friends helping failed debtors). Ultimately, we demonstrate that the two dynamics of financial inclusion/exclusion and reproductive adaptation in households are inherently intertwined, especially in contexts when formal wage relations are precarious.

Financialization as part of long-term and uneven capitalist development

Literature on the financialization of housing has emphasized a global trend towards a deepening financialization, complemented by differences between local trajectories resulting from specificities of infrastructural and policy environments (Aalbers 2017; Fernandez and Aalbers 2016). Beyond comparing local variations of a global trend, we propose to understand local processes of financialization as part of long-term historical development of local articulations of capital accumulation and social reproduction, themselves embedded in the development of capitalism as a global system. More broadly, we do not conceive of financialization as a new, specific mode of accumulation that "followed" the Fordist regime after its crisis. Rather, we see it as a periodically recurring phase of systemic cycles of accumulation that occurs when profitability in the sphere of production drops and an increasing amount of surplus capital seeks new channels of investment in money markets (Arrighi 1994). While this approach grasps financialization as a stage of global cycles, its foundations in world-systems theory also make it possible to consider relations between local versions of financialization in terms of the interconnected and hierarchical relations of global uneven development. Another main advantage of this approach for our study is that it highlights the continuity between different phases (productive and financialized) of capitalist development across different localities of the global economy.

In our conceptualization of the current local "variety" of financialization in Hungary as a phase embedded in this long-term historical process, we emphasize continuities and overlaps with earlier phases of financialization. For example, in Hungary, the real estate boom of the financialization phase after 1873 played a similar role as today, which is one of the targets for the investment of Western financial capital during a cyclical crisis of accumulation (Gyáni 1992). The connection is illustrated by continuities of the banking infrastructure channelling this investment (Raviv 2008: 304–306) as well as continuities of physical infrastructures built during the nineteenth-century financialization in some inner parts of Budapest that serve as the base for the current wave of gentrification and financialization. Another important connection is the continuity of uneven development relations that bridge financialized and productive phases of integration – from the contradictions of socialist import-substitution industrialization manifesting in the form of the public debt crisis building up from the 1970s onwards, to the sequence of privatization in the 1990s and debt-based development in the 2000s after the inflows of privatization capital stopped. Thus, when looking at the Hungarian housing privatization in the 1990s, the surge of mortgages in the 2000s, the mortgage crisis after 2008 and the present revitalization of the housing market through state-subsidized mortgages, domestic investments and a renewed interest of international capital, we place our case study within this larger frame of continuous and overlapping uneven development. This perspective proves especially useful when investigating the infrastructural, spatial and social hierarchies through which the present phase of financialization is articulated.

Households, social reproduction and inclusion/exclusion dynamics

Cycles of global capitalist development, as well as shorter lending cycles, contain an underlying element of accumulation that consists in successive inclusion and exclusion of social reproductive functions from the formal circuits of capitalist economy. We see this inclusion/exclusion dynamic as an ever-present aspect of the relations of uneven development. In theoretical terms, we think of this dynamic as a moving frontline of what Rosa Luxemburg ([1913] 1951: 366) called capitalism's need for "external" resources and Jason Moore (2015) discussed as capitalism's production of its own "cheaps". Informal labour, and the creative process of managing income portfolios of households, make up crucial components of these "cheap", "external" resources upon which capitalist accumulation hinges. Moreover, the constant pulsation of this frontline – the inclusion/exclusion of certain household practices into/from the formal practices of capitalist accumulation – is especially characteristic for intermediate positions within capital accumulation (Dunaway 2012), that is, positions that are alternately included and then excluded throughout boom and bust periods of accumulation cycles. As we will demonstrate, in the case of mortgage lending in Hungary before and after 2008, we can identify the geographical aspect of this pulsation in what we call intermediate spaces: suburban and urban-fringe areas of the capital, as well as secondary cities (other larger cities beside the capital) and their suburbs, which concentrate households with high-risk mortgages and serve as transitory zones for the hierarchical flows of rural–urban migration.[1]

In critical geography, shifts between financial exclusion and over-inclusion of impoverished areas have been described as a characteristic of the geography of housing financialization, which operates as a dynamic of uneven development (Aalbers 2009). In our case study, we interpret dynamics of financial exclusion and inclusion as relations of uneven development in intermediate positions. We conceive of the national economy and the state as structures that mediate larger world-systemic hierarchies of accumulation. They achieve this by manipulating external connections of the national economy as well as by limiting and managing the local contradictions of uneven development. Policies directly or indirectly affecting households are major means of the latter process. Thinking in terms of uneven geographical development, this dynamic of uneven development corresponds to connections between internal geographical hierarchies and uneven external relations – what *dependentista* and world-systems traditions termed variously metropolis-satellite relations (Frank 1966), structural heterogeneity (Pinto 1973) or externally integrated structures (Amin 2004) within dependent economies.

In line with the world-systems tradition of household research (Smith et al. 1984), we approach households as units of social reproduction of labour that combine resources accessed through formal capitalist circuits with informal reproductive work. As Wilma Dunaway (2012) emphasized, in semi-peripheries as intermediate positions in global relations of uneven development, industrialization and other forms of capitalist penetration never produced a pure form of fully integrated free-wage labour. Social reproduction under consecutive modes of capitalist incorporation has been continuously supported by what Dunaway described as a model of the "semi-proletarian household" – one that complements incomes from the formal economy with various informal activities to secure conditions of its own basic and social reproduction. Structurally, this practice of juggling diverse income sources at the scale of the household provides a constant stream of bottom-up "subsidies" to capital's social reproduction costs, stabilizing accumulation at higher scales in situations when the formal economy does not secure the conditions of labour reproduction. We see forms and variations of this stream as a key arena in which we can grasp empirically the relevance of the social reproduction dynamics to the understanding of capital-society relations. In non-core positions, this is true as much of productive phases of accumulation cycles (as in cases of rural extended kin supporting urban industrial workers with food, and the workers spending weekends doing agricultural or construction work in the rural family hinterland, thereby meeting reproductive costs not covered by industrial wages) as of phases of financialization (as in cases where the costs of mortgages formally taken by individuals are borne by extended families). Geographically, the hierarchical relationship between inclusion into formal relations of the capitalist economy and exclusion from the same (which produces the need to satisfy reproductive needs through informal means) is closely reflected in the functional hierarchy of urban and rural spaces (as in cases of the urbanization of labour in times of conjuncture, and the expulsion of unemployment to the rural hinterland in times of crisis). Intermediate zones of urban-rural migration flows are especially relevant in this regard, as they manifest the effects of accumulation through over-inclusion and exclusion in an intensive way. Our case study shows how these areas also become sites of informal reproductive strategies.

Articulating housing financialization through uneven development in Hungary

In the current wave of financialization in Hungary as well as the lending wave after the 1870s crisis, the embeddedness of internal uneven development in relations of external dependence is reflected in the financialization of the local housing market as an extension of a financialization process of Western capital pushing to penetrate new, "emerging" markets (Hilferding [1910] 1981; Raviv 2008; Tilly 1986). Another important aspect of this embeddedness is the volatile nature of available capital. In boom periods, capital floods housing markets of peripheral economies, while in crisis periods this flow of money is abruptly halted (see Figure 3.1).

During the boom in the 2000s, lending to households[2] surged in Central and Eastern Europe (CEE) at the moment of a saturation of Western and Southern European retail credit markets, and at better conditions for capital than in those markets – in the form of short-term, adjustable-rate loans rather than of long-term, fixed-rate loans, with higher profit margins and with exchange rate risks externalized to borrowers (Pósfai et al. 2018). If this move of inclusion happened as a way of compensating for decreasing profits in Western Europe, the moment of exclusion after the GFC also illustrated the core-periphery relations of the process: lending in CEE came to a halt while continuing in Western Europe. Effects of uneven lending can be also seen from the fact that although the total volume of Western European mortgages is consistently much higher, the rates of non-performing mortgages were higher in Southern and Eastern Europe (EMF 2015, cited in: Pósfai et al. 2018: 175). In Eastern Europe (Hungary being one of the most important examples), structurally dependent forms of lending were pushed to the extreme with mortgages denominated in foreign currencies, most

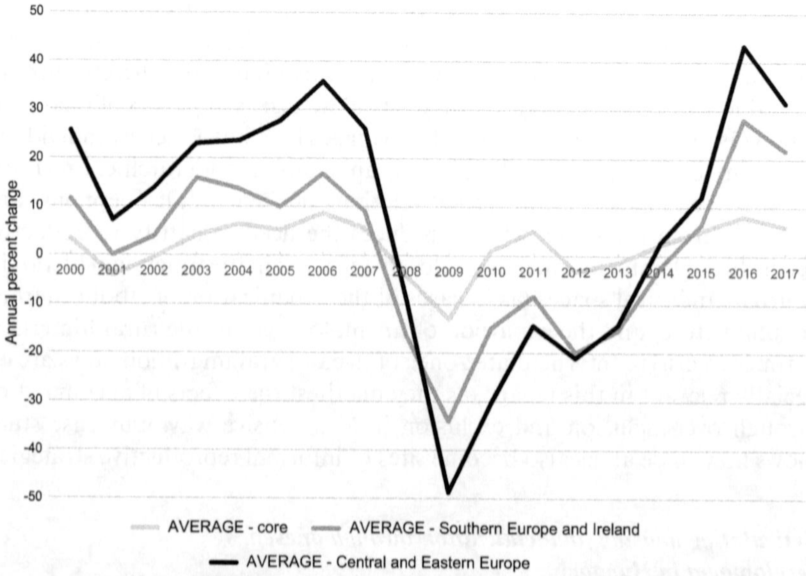

Figure 3.1 Real gross fixed investment in housing (annual percent change), European regions, 2000–2017.

Source: Drawn on the basis of data from EMF (2019). Country groupings as follows: core - AT, BE, DE, DK, FI, FR, GB, IT, LU, NL, SE; Southern Europe and Ireland - CY, ES, GR, IE, MT, PT; Central and Eastern Europe - BG, CZ, EE, HR, HU, LT, LV, PL, RO, SI, SK.

often the Swiss franc. In a loan thus constructed, the principal was determined in the franc, which placed the entire risk of exchange rate fluctuations on debtors earning their wages in the local currency – the Hungarian forint (ISO code: HUF). After the GFC, in combination with active interest rates unilaterally adjusted by lending institutions,[3] the rapid depreciation of the forint left scores of forex debtors unable to pay their instalments while their outstanding debt increased month by month.

The 2000s mortgage boom reproduced a similar pattern of core-periphery relations within the national scale. As Pósfai (2018) demonstrates, the inclusion of poorer Hungarian regions into mortgage finance increased during the CEE lending boom. Similarly to regional differences between Western European and CEE lending, this over-inclusion of poorer areas happened towards the end of the mortgage boom, at a faster pace, and with generally worse lending conditions than in wealthier Hungarian regions like central or north-western Hungary. The areas that had been included during the spatially and socially most expansive phase of mortgage lending immediately before the crisis have become spaces of exclusion from housing finance in the post-GFC period of a relaunch of mortgage lending. Extensive lending in marginal geographical areas has led to an uneven geography of non-performing loans after 2008 – households experiencing the greatest and most persistent difficulties due to over-indebtedness are typically located in smaller settlements in worse-off areas (Dancsik et al. 2015).

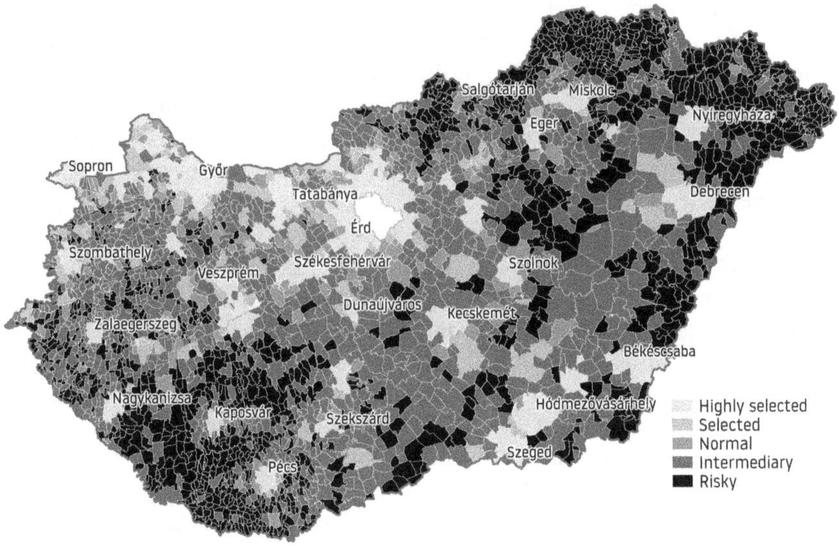

Figure 3.2 Settlement categories used by a Hungarian bank for collateral valuation, 2017.

Source: Reprinted with minor edits from Pósfai (2018: 69).

This geography of non-performing loans has subsequently become the geography of a new financial exclusion through the redlining policies of mortgage-originating banks (see Figure 3.2). This connection is supported also by our interviews with corporate actors in the housing market who underlined that bank policies of collateral valuation rely heavily on current housing market activity and price levels – thus a local market with many defaulting mortgages will necessarily result in worse collateral valuation for new mortgages (Pósfai 2018). (In 2019–2020, this tendency started to change somewhat due to a new policy introduced by the government to support mortgage lending in smaller settlements. However, we have no data on how this affected bank valuation policies.)

Intermediate spaces in the uneven geography of financialization

Intermediate positions (here understood as positions within the national scale) in the uneven relations of financial inclusion and exclusion play a specific role in the process of accumulation. These positions can be grasped both sociologically and geographically. Pósfai (2018) noted a specific geographical positionality of those intermediate spaces that are most sensitive to fluctuations in bank and state policies regulating mortgage loans. During the mortgage lending boom, core areas (urban centres) in Hungary have seen the largest share of direct investments in housing (usually purchases of investor-buyers paying upfront), while mortgages played a comparatively less important role there. It is important to keep in mind that typical candidates for mortgages in Hungary are households that cannot afford upfront payment for a new home but have sufficient income to qualify for a loan. The point where banks' risk assessment meets households' repayment capacities constitutes a moving frontline of credit, which is as important for market actors' accumulation potential as for households' reproduction needs. While in strictly economic terms this frontline is determined by bank lending policies and households' income and spending, in the case of mortgage lending, geographical location also plays an important role through its impact on both real estate prices and accessibility of jobs that guarantee repayment capacity. Together with state mortgage subsidy policies that only make newly built housing eligible for higher-value subsidies, the moving frontline of credit encourages households to buy homes in intermediate areas such as suburbs and urban fringes of large cities that offer available plots and relatively accessible prices. From the perspective of households, these intermediate locations emerge as choices for residence due to a combination of factors including housing affordability, access to employment, access to state housing subsidies and access to a mortgage loan. For financial actors, these areas emerge as a result of their constant balancing of profitability and risk management. Thus, within existing structures of uneven development, this moving structural frontline between financial penetration and households' reproductive work can be grasped not only in terms of income distribution but also geographically.

Pósfai (2018) demonstrated that areas with the highest number of property transactions related to mortgages in 2016–2017 were peripheral districts of the city of Budapest and the inner ring of suburban towns surrounding it. Seen at a larger scale, then, areas on both sides of the administrative boundary of Budapest were where mortgage lending tended to be most intensive within the functional urban area of the capital. Secondary cities and their suburbs are also typical areas for mortgage lending. Housing markets in these places display the highest degree of sensitivity to changes in mortgage markets and relevant bank and state policies. Besides mortgage lending, suburbs and urban-fringe areas are also at the frontline of the domestic migration of households striving towards more central locations from more peripheral ones, and those shifting towards more peripheral locations as they lose ground within urban centres. In these movements, marginal parts of a functional urban area can gain particular importance. Thus, we define them as intermediate locations with heightened manifestations of the inclusion/exclusion process within the national scale. This understanding is similar to the notion of urban fringes in critical urban studies regarding the way unequal development is articulated on the fringes of hierarchical urban-rural flows (Pryor 1968; Vigvári 2016). Our case study is located in one of these areas on the eastern periphery of the functional urban area of Budapest.

The state's role in establishing the frontline of financial inclusion/exclusion

For two decades after the regime change in 1989, Hungary's integration in the global economy was based on a model favouring foreign direct investment (FDI) and loans. This model was a continuation of the marketization and Western-oriented opening of the Hungarian socialist regime that started in 1968 and was reinforced under the pressure of the mounting state debt during the 1970s and 1980s. After the regime change, the elite bloc supporting this model was represented politically by a socialist-liberal coalition whose agenda combined neoliberalism with a symbolic support for democratic values. After the FDI wave based on privatization in the 1990s dwindled, the dependent economic model was perpetuated on the basis of debt-creating inflows from the early 2000s. Besides a growing public debt, this meant a rapidly increasing stock of household debt, much of which was housing loans.

Public spending on housing has been in fact shrinking already since the 1970s as public expenditures became increasingly focussed on foreign debt service. After the regime change, vast majority of public housing stock has been privatized by giving sitting tenants preferential right to buy at heavily discounted prices. Housing policies were characterized by further spending cuts, leading to a dwindling of the remaining public housing stock, the decentralization of welfare obligations to impoverished local governments and the diminished accessibility of utility benefits (crucial for households with low incomes). At the same time, much of the remaining public spending on housing was directed towards market-based housing solutions that integrated the fulfilment of housing needs into capital circuits. The chief forms of such spending were various subsidies supporting access to homeownership through mortgages, with eligibility conditions favouring childbearing middle-class and upper-middle-class households. As these subsidies have been gradually wound up in the early-to-mid 2000s, banks introduced foreign-currency (FX) mortgages to relax their own credit policies and expand the moving frontline of credit. The ensuing wave of mortgage lending has, for the first time since the regime change, allowed lower-middle-class and worker households to gain access to new housing through mortgages (Hegedüs and Somogyi 2016).

The GFC hit Hungary at the time of not only a mounting stock of FX private debt but also deep and escalating public indebtedness and a two-year recession since 2006. The economic and political failure of the development model based on attracting Western capital contributed to the electoral success of Fidesz's nationalist program in 2010. The Fidesz government's response to the financial and social crisis that set in as the forint depreciated, and hundreds of thousands of families with Swiss franc loans found themselves on the brink of default was its wider policy, presented as a national "freedom fight" against a dependence on Western capital, and a centralization of the power field in domestic politics to keep out the latter's "internal agents". Fidesz reacted to the FX mortgage crisis on the housing market with strongly politicized campaigns against foreign banks as well as the Socialist Party as their political representatives. Practical measures to aid debtors included exchange rate and interest-rate caps, a new obligation of banks to accept early one-off repayment and eventually a forced conversion of FX loans to the Hungarian forint. Besides a temporary moratorium on evictions, a National Asset Management Company was set up to help debtors facing foreclosure by acquiring their homes and allowing them to stay as tenants at subsidized prices (Bohle 2014). The FX loans emergency package mitigated the ballooning of debt due to the forint depreciation. Nevertheless, debt service costs of indebted households, now especially those with forint-denominated loans, remained one of the highest in CEE (Dancsik et al. 2015; Misetics 2017: 279). One-off repayment, as well as the conversion of outstanding FX debts to the forint, benefited FX mortgage debtors in better financial positions while leaving those with large arrears in a difficult situation (Dancsik et al. 2015). Moreover, consistently with previous policies' bias towards home acquisition and against subsidizing home maintenance, poor households' arrears on utility bills and rent were not addressed and welfare benefit programmes tackling this issue were scrapped in 2015.

A new phenomenon of the post-crisis housing market has been an increased number of investor-buyers. This form of investment was encouraged by the growing wealth of a new upper-middle class due to the Fidesz government's regressive redistribution policies combined with the general environment of low interest rates. Along with other factors such as the continued inflow of foreign capital into real estate, these forms of investment generated a surge of housing costs in core locations,[4] pushing low-income households towards more peripheral areas.

The most recent wave of housing policies is consistent with Fidesz's class and financial policies driven by its aim to build state-supported national capital. In 2016, the government introduced a housing subsidy scheme that supports construction or purchase of (preferably new) homes by those who are able to make the required down payment. The size of the subsidy depends on the number of children that the applicant's family has or promises to have. This scheme, tagged by the acronym CSOK (meaning "kiss" in Hungarian), was emphatically introduced to support middle-class childbearing families in accessing homeownership with a home purchase subsidy of up to about €30,000, which can be supplemented with a subsidized loan. Single parents on child benefits, those with a gap in their social insurance payments of six months or more, those in workfare programmes and those with a criminal record are excluded from the scheme (Misetics 2017: 279). Pósfai (2018: 79–80) points out that, given these conditions, the CSOK programme intervenes exactly in the area of the market in which banks' lending capacities (boosted by the expansion of savings of the upper-middle class) became constrained by the economic situation and stricter risk assessment regulations after the GFC. The function of CSOK is therefore to widen the channels of investment that contracted following the crisis because of the reduced creditworthiness of potential borrowers. Analysing data from real estate and credit agents operating in secondary cities on the share of their customers combining a CSOK subsidy with a mortgage, Pósfai (2018) demonstrates a co-dependence of these two instruments of housing finance. Potential mortgage clients who struggle to make the required down payment often draw on CSOK for this purpose. This has been made possible by changes in bank policies in the course of 2017 after banks realized that for many of their potential clients this was the only way they could acquire a mortgage (Pósfai 2018: 80). Some banks even have an internal policy of not accepting applications for CSOK subsidies if the person does not apply for a mortgage as well. This points to the controversy of having banks act as front-desk operators of this state subsidy programme: the role is only worthwhile for banks if they can also sell a mortgage on the side. As a result, in 2017, about 80% of households acquiring a CSOK subsidy also took a mortgage (Pósfai 2018: 80).

The impact of state intervention on widening the channels of mortgage lending at the frontline of households' reproductive capacities and banks' risk management can also be grasped in terms of geographical concentration. Pósfai (2018: 75) points out the economic-geographical effects of home purchase subsidies: in the intermediate areas as defined above, the housing market does not move without the push of more forceful mortgage lending and/or state subsidies. However, when those conditions are secured, such areas experience fast localized housing booms. Pósfai mentions the eastern suburban area of Budapest as the most emblematic case of strong housing market response to inclusion into housing finance – and ensuing strong volatility (Pósfai 2018: 75–76). Here, a majority (approximately 60%) of transactions in 2017 were made with a CSOK subsidy, and practically all transactions involved a mortgage. Furthermore, the consequences of pre-crisis mortgage lending were still strongly felt in the area: about 90% of transactions with existing housing units involved property serving as collateral for an earlier mortgage, most often taken in the years before the GFC. New state housing policies such as CSOK served to boost a new wave of mortgage lending that re-integrated these social and geographical positions into the circuits of financial accumulation. To sum up, in such intermediate areas, the effects of the pre-2008 lending boom and the post-2008 debt crisis intersect with the effects of state policies. Lower-middle-class and worker households previously excluded from state-subsidized mortgage have been integrated into the boom of non-subsidized FX lending after 2004. Many of these households were thus able to buy homes in suburban areas or secondary cities. They were particularly hard hit by the post-2008 debt crisis and typically excluded from the benefits of re-stabilization programmes.

Case study: informal housing in the urban fringe of Budapest

Our case study follows the strategies of households who found themselves in intermediate geographical areas as defined above, yet instead of participating in the new wave of inclusion in household lending chose to compensate for their losses through informal housing solutions and inputs of their own informal labour while accepting the risk of an informal dwelling situation. This serves to highlight the organic connection between the consequences of over-indebtedness and the use of informal household-level reproductive strategies within the broader process of accumulation. Our focus is on an allotment garden that has been transformed from a recreational and agricultural place into a residential neighbourhood after the political and economic transformation of the 1990s but that is legally still not considered a residential area. This space has a specific peripheral position in the settlement structure. It is situated on the eastern edge of the Budapest functional urban area while also being a local periphery: it lies just outside the administrative territory of the nearest local town, which is itself one of the more peripheral suburbs of Budapest. Our case shows how people excluded from inner-city neighbourhoods strive to stay within the reach of income opportunities provided by core areas through reliance on informal practices, which has become increasingly significant after the GFC.

In previous sections, we have described how non-core parts of the Budapest functional urban area can be seen as intermediate spaces where the moving frontline of inclusion to and exclusion from housing financialization can be grasped. This pulsation of inclusion and exclusion creates highly diverse spaces where some suburban areas are the most striking examples of rapid mortgage penetration while other, more marginal (fringe) areas concentrate those excluded from the mortgage-based housing regime (Pósfai 2018; Székely 2018). Our case study is an example of the latter while also demonstrating how the movement of households between the two types of zones manifests their exposure and agency in the face of capital's inclusion/exclusion techniques. While the allotment works for some households as a space of (self-) exclusion from direct involvement in circuits of financialization, the residents' turn to informal dwelling is still shaped by the conditions of financialized housing – either through their exclusion from formal channels of housing finance due to previous debt default or through their active avoidance of financialized, debt-based access to housing. Furthermore, their informal work and risk-taking props up their ability to reproduce themselves as labour.

The origins and formation of allotment gardens (zártkert) during state socialism

Although there had been some historical precedents, it was during the state-socialist period that allotment gardens became widespread and very popular in Hungary. Establishing allotments provided small plots for workers that they could use for recreation, leisure activities and small-scale gardening. This development was a widespread phenomenon in the country: according to some estimates, about 7–10% of the population owned a second home in an allotment garden (*zártkert*) by the end of the socialist period, which means approximately 115,000 such estates (Hegedüs and Manchin 1987). A major expansion of allotment gardens between 1965 and 1975 involved authorities dividing agricultural land into small gardening plots with the aim to stimulate private farming activities as a source of informal incomes for households. Owners typically held plots of approximately 300–800 square meters and built a small bungalow to be able to stay in the allotment during the weekend and holidays from spring to autumn. The bungalows were officially registered as small fruit stores or wine cellars, and official urban zoning regulations did not allow their permanent residential use. The expanded provision of the plots created a widespread form of private (real estate) ownership and economic activity within the socialist framework – informal work in the household mixed with a recreational activity. Furthermore, construction on allotments was practically unregulated; almost everybody could build what they wished without any serious need for permits. This facilitated the fast spread of the small plots and bungalows and of the informal economy for which they served as a base.

This multiplication of plots officially allocated for informal reproductive activities formed part of the hidden austerity policy of externalizing the costs of labour reproduction to the "second economy" (Galasi and Sziráczki 1985; Vigvári and Gerőcs 2017), which became legalized after 1982. A part of "the non-monetarized portion of second economy" (Hegedüs 1992: 229) was self-help housing construction, which emerged as a response to the severe shortage of public housing and entailed construction with the help of relatives and friends (Kováts 2020). In this phase, allotment gardens became an important site of private housing and land ownership in functional urban areas. They also supported a state-backed version of the semi-proletarian household model as the informal activities of blue-collar workers on allotments compensated for the widening gap between stagnating wages and inflating prices. Allotments were spatially concentrated either in traditional holiday areas further from the city, where they served as recreational second homes for the wealthier strata, or at new sites on the outskirts of cities and towns, where they provided space for gardening and leisure activities of blue-collar workers, particularly those of rural origin. While the first type of allotments usually survived the transformation of the 1990s, the latter ones began to decline due to the economic crisis of blue-collar households. At the beginning, former "blue-collar allotments" were gradually abandoned; later they have evolved into a housing destination for the losers of housing privatization and the mortgage-based housing regime. By following the housing trajectories through which one such space has become populated after the transformation, we can identify the structural factors at work.

An allotment in the eastern suburban sector of Budapest

Our qualitative empirical data is based on ethnographic research in one allotment garden. The fieldwork was conducted between 2016 and 2019 and resulted in 38 housing trajectory sheets, 22 interviews and 5 household ethnographies. Participant observation was also an important part of the research design. The allotment garden belongs to a small town with about 10,000 inhabitants situated at the eastern edge of the functional urban area of Budapest, about 35 km from the city centre. The town is linked to Budapest by one of the major railway lines, which enables daily commute for households that cannot afford a car. It has traditionally had a high proportion of blue-collar workers commuting to the capital. Despite having a good rail connection with Budapest, the town has never become a site of middle-class suburbanization. Together with the neighbouring villages, it has rather attracted newcomers from rural hinterlands who wished to settle close to the capital and people pushed to the fringes of the city as they could not afford living costs in the capital. In this sense, the town fulfils an intermediary role in demographic flows within urban-rural developmental hierarchies. This function is characteristic for Central and Eastern European suburbanization processes (Stanilov and Sykora 2014) and was even more significant during the state-socialist era due to administrative restrictions that prevented rural migrants from moving to the capital (Tosics 2006). The allotment garden itself was developed in 1970 in the area of vineyards of the local state-owned farm. The former vineyards were divided into small plots that were sold first to local farmers and then, in the 1980s, to blue-collar workers from Budapest. After the transformation of the 1990s, recreational and farming activities gradually declined due to the economic changes of the period. Some of the weekend houses and garden plots have been abandoned while others have been converted to permanent housing.

Push factors: from privatization to the current housing crisis

Our field site can be considered a space in which key housing-related economic and policy changes since the regime change have become personalized and lived through by people mobilizing informal solutions to cope. The first wave of new inhabitants seeking permanent (yet informal) housing in the allotment arrived in the 1990s. These were households that typically lost their formal income due to postsocialist transformation and could not afford growing utility bills (Hegedüs et al. 1996). However, the largest wave of newcomers can be dated to around 2010 when the ranks of over-indebted have been expanding fast. These people had taken mortgages during the boom of the 2000s and encountered difficulties with paying their monthly instalments. Their debt problems ultimately pushed them to cheaper, low-status neighbourhoods, including allotments close to major cities (Hegedüs and Somogyi 2016; Pellandini-Simányi et al. 2015). According to statistics, the number of inhabitants of allotments at the national level doubled between 2001 and 2011.[5] In this context, allotments represent niche areas providing cheap housing not too far from city centres where jobs are more readily available. In our field site, such households often previously lived in nearby suburbs or Budapest's outer districts. Besides the pressure of servicing existing debts, pre-emptive avoidance of indebtedness also played a role. A resident of the allotment in her 60s offered the following comment:

> All I can see is that everyone is fleeing because of the mortgage debt. This young generation especially, because they're not having any luck in Budapest, they don't want to get a mortgage and get indebted. They say, they will give it a go, as in staying here, and if it works out … why wouldn't it? And it is going to work out if one likes to work on their own property.

The mortgage crisis was indeed present in all housing trajectory sheets collected during fieldwork. There were residents who lost their previous housing due to defaulting on their mortgages while several households refused to apply for a mortgage loan due to its bad reputation. At the same time, there were several households that took out consumer loans for refurbishing their facilities at the allotment gardens. However, the conventional residents' narrative frames the allotment as an idyllic natural shelter from the financialized housing market.

The case of a young man (in his mid-30s at the time of fieldwork) and his family is a good example of the second wave of arrivals. He was born in Budapest, but he grew up in a suburban village close to the capital. His parents took out both consumer and FX housing loans during the 2000s, using a half of their house as collateral. After 2008, due to rapidly changing exchange rates, they could not repay the loans, and their house was foreclosed by the bank and auctioned off for a very low price in the middle of the housing market slump. It was bought by an investor from whom the family continued to rent their home. Under the pressure of the economic crisis, the family's former economic status was thus destroyed. The young man decided to escape from this unsustainable situation and get a new private home for himself and his family. He bought a cheap plot on the allotment and gradually decided to build a light-structure house using only his and his friends' labour. He bought all necessary material on the black market, which enabled him to save a big amount of money. The construction took one year, and he worked on it during his free time. As he said:

> I used to go to work by the train at 4:40 am, I got home at 3 pm, and I immediately came over [to the allotment] to build the house. Once when we were working on the bathroom with one of my friends, we realized, oh my God, that's the alarm clock, it is morning, let's finish for today because we have to go work again.

The man was sincerely proud of his house that was built and owned by him, not by a bank. "This is ours," he said, expressing a sense of pride and social safety at the same time. Within the heterogeneous population of the allotment, this household can be seen as part of a second wave of financial exclusion in Hungary's postsocialist world-economic integration. These are households who used to have better work opportunities and housing situations during the period of privatization or were students and lived with their parents in the early 1990s and were included in the 2000s mortgage boom, only to find themselves excluded from labour and housing opportunities of core areas after 2008, forced to give up their homes and earlier investments to satisfy bank repayments and look for substitute housing in more peripheral areas.

Pull factors: the bottom-up emergence of a new residential area

Although local planning and zoning regulations never recognized the allotment as a residential area, since the 1990s there has been a considerable movement into the allotment due to the increasing structural housing issues. Local planning regulations identify the allotment as an agricultural area where residential units are officially not permitted. The former bungalows that were transformed into permanently inhabited houses are therefore still officially listed as fruit stores or wine cellars rather than residential units, resulting in a growing informal housing settlement. The real estate therefore cannot serve as collateral for mortgages; moreover, owners cannot qualify for housing subsidies (such as CSOK) either. However, relevant regulations enable certain contradictions. The most important contradiction ensues from a national regulation that allows one to register as a resident in any kind of building as long as it has an official postal address. Due to this national regulation, inhabitants have official addresses, they can easily access local social and healthcare services (kindergartens, schools, elderly and childcare) and they can participate in local elections.

The first important pull factor of the allotment is that the costs of housing are significantly lower due to the lack of public services. In 1990–1994 alone, the share of utility costs in household expenditures in CEE countries such as Hungary rose from 5.8% to 11.4% (Hegedüs et al. 1996: 116), which became one of the root causes of housing poverty after the transition.

The lack of basic infrastructure such as sewage or asphalt roads can be, on the one hand, considered a major aspect of housing poverty, while on the other hand it can become an advantage and an attractive factor for incoming residents in terms of reducing housing-related costs. In the allotment we studied, only electricity is available. There is no central heating or gas network (dwellers use firewood to heat their bungalows during winter) and no piped water system either (they use private wells or public faucets). Replacing basic infrastructure with self-built solutions and informal practices, dwellers can achieve independence from certain public services.[6] As one resident (woman, 37 years old) commented:

> Then another big advantage of living here is that utility bills are quite alright because we use water from the well. Although, to be fair, we use mineral water to drink and cook, the bills are still quite low. So if you choose to live in a place like this you can save up a lot, for sure. If you live on a housing estate or in an apartment, then you have to pay way bigger utility bills and that can be a lot. Here we don't have this problem.

From the 2000s onwards and especially since the post-2014 house price boom, people moving to allotments have been motivated not only by a reduction of their bills but also by real estate prices. Currently, house prices are up to a half lower in the allotment than in the inner areas of the adjacent suburban town – where, in turn, they are considerably cheaper than in Budapest.[7] Despite the demand, the uncertainty of the legal status and the lack of infrastructure keep real estate prices down. Besides its geographical position, it is this regulatory grey zone that makes it possible for households willing to accept the risks of informal dwelling to fashion one of the cheapest housing solutions in the functional urban area of Budapest.

Conclusions

We proposed to understand financialization as an element of long-term dynamics of uneven development under capitalism as a global system. As part of this process, waves of financialization are built on and operate within relations established by previous (both productive and financialized) phases of cycles of accumulation. We emphasized the importance of multiple temporal layers and geographic scales of the cycles of uneven development for an analysis of the local constitutive process of the global financialization wave that reached Hungary in the 2000s. Among these, we gave special attention to the cumulative effects of inclusion/exclusion dynamics of capitalist accumulation in what we called intermediate positions within core-periphery relations of uneven development. The pulsation of inclusion/exclusion dynamics in these positions can be conceived as a moving frontline between the capitalist potential for accumulation and social reproduction capacities of households. In the case of housing financialization, it is a frontline between interests of financial institutions and household reproductive capacities that moves according to economic and regulatory shifts. Within this relationship, in periods of financial inclusion, households are drawn into a financialized housing regime, which – in the case of lower-middle-class and working-class households – acts as a framework for extracting household resources through disadvantageous loan conditions. Even if the most severe consequences (i.e. foreclosure) are avoided, situations of over-indebtedness often develop, which means that resources and work of the household and its social networks are monetized and directed to satisfying the repayment demands of the lending institution and avoiding bankruptcy. In other, financially exclusive periods of this relationship, households lacking a sufficient income are excluded from formal lending mechanisms and thus rely more extensively on informal solutions to manage their housing situation. In this chapter, we addressed this frontline in terms of geographical dynamics of financial inclusion/exclusion as well as in terms of the articulation of formal and informal modes of reproduction within households. These broader processes are particularly tangible in spaces that we have identified as intermediate, such as suburban and urban-fringe areas around the capital city. In our case study, we showed how households navigate this moving frontline by setting up informal dwellings in a former allotment garden in Budapest.

The chapter pointed to historical continuities that place the current effects of housing financialization in a broader context of uneven development. We demonstrated the contribution of the 2000s housing financialization wave and its inclusion/exclusion dynamics to uneven development through macro- and micro-regional differences between lending conditions and mortgage performance. The differences between Western European and CEE mortgages, implying a late over-inclusion to compensate for the saturation of core markets at the price of higher risks externalized to debtors (through higher and more flexible interest rates and FX loans, all of which led to higher rates of default), are replicated in the differences between core and peripheral locations within the national scale. As a result, households in positions lower in the spatial hierarchy typically accessed loans at worse conditions. Within the national scale, we see a geographical concentration of the effects of financial inclusion and exclusion (through market and state interventions alike) in intermediate areas. To emphasize the significance of these intermediate positions for the optimization of accumulation, we noted the ways in which state mortgage subsidies introduced in 2016 helped widen investment channels narrowed after the crash of 2008 in the precise area of the mortgage market where households' capacities came close to, but without the subsidy still failed to meet, banks' lending criteria. In geographical terms, loans combined with these subsidies (i.e. the loans these subsidies made possible) in the most recent (from 2016 onwards) wave of mortgage lending have been indeed concentrated in intermediate areas: the Budapest functional urban area (excluding its most central zones) and suburban areas of secondary cities, which have traditionally served as transition zones in rural-urban flows of migration related to internal uneven development. These intermediate spaces are highly diversified, and while they are prime areas for new mortgage lending, they also contain places (allotment gardens and other locally peripheral sites) that are excluded from institutionalized forms of housing investment, since they are not legally considered residential areas.

Our case study focusses on one of these allotment gardens at the eastern edge of the Budapest functional urban area. While in the first part of the chapter we characterized intermediate zones with an emphasis on their heightened sensitivity to the macro-dynamics of financial inclusion and its after-effects, we analyse the informal settlement as an example of households' agency in optimizing their reproductive capacities in response to those conditions. We showed that the formation of this informal residential area near Budapest has been driven by a sequence of exclusions that followed previous inclusion waves: first by the privatization of socialist industry and housing, which sent many blue-collar labourers urbanized by socialist industrialization back to rural locations through the effects of unemployment, rising energy costs and growing household utility debts, and second by the mortgage crisis that followed the financial over-inclusion of many CEE households through high-cost and high-risk mortgage lending in the 2000s. Through informal housing solutions fashioned in the allotment garden, the households we studied manage to partially counteract the effects of these expulsions and stay within the reach of income opportunities provided by the capital city despite not being able to afford the typical costs of housing in the area. This strategy can be described as the opposite of the logic of state subsidies widening the channels of financial investment: these households use the "subsidy" of informal dwelling and work to optimize their income portfolio such as to avoid exploitative financial inclusion and thus increase their own chances of reproduction. We see this counter-tendency, resulting in the reproduction of households' resources against the effects of exclusion, as a key element of the inclusion/exclusion dynamics we are looking at. Through this effort, households optimize their chances of reproduction while also stabilizing their contribution as active labour to the process of accumulation. The fact that allotment gardens had been created as part of the socialist state's measures to externalize the costs of rising life standards in the face of economic contraction and growing state debt, by means of providing plots for households' informal reproductive work, illustrates the continuity and temporal layers of this type of interaction. The present regulation of allotments, which rules out formal residence in these areas while in practice tolerating low-cost informal dwelling that enables residents to keep access to jobs in cities, works as a current continuation of the externalizing tendency. Our ethnographic focus on households thus enables us to capture and understand this "hidden" domain of the present moment of financialization as part of the long-term history of articulations between capitalist inclusion/exclusion and the capacities of social reproduction in a semi-peripheral area.

Acknowledgements

The ethnographic case study presented in this chapter was carried out as part of András Vigvári's PhD research, which was partly supported by the Sylff Association. Gagyi's work on this chapter was carried out as part of the project "Housing, social mobilisations and urban governance in Central and Eastern Europe", funded by the Swedish government's research council Formas (contract no. 2016-00258).

Notes

1 The chapter uses three different socio-spatial categories: functional urban area, suburb and urban fringe. These categories refer to different geographical units and different socio-spatial contexts. The concept of functional urban area is usually used in macro-scale approaches and expresses the idea that urban functions stretch beyond administrative city boundaries. The categories of suburb and urban fringe are more often micro-scale concepts used to describe specific housing tendencies in functional urban areas. While the category of suburb refers to recipient locations of a dominantly middle-class housing movement away from central parts of functional urban areas, urban fringe connotes peripheral sites of ongoing socio-spatial housing exclusion.

2 This chapter focusses only on mortgage loans and neglects other types of household loans. In Hungary, a mortgage loan is typically a loan for housing purposes collateralized by real estate. This excludes home equity loans, which also existed before the GFC, as well as non-collateralized loans used for housing purposes.

3 Banks could impose interest rates unilaterally until it was banned in 2014.

4 According to Eurostat, from 2016 onwards Hungary has seen the highest increase in real estate prices in the EU (Pósfai 2019).

5 According to the census of the Hungarian Central Statistical Office, the number of permanent inhabitants of allotments increased from 42,200 to 89,500 in 2001–2011 (Czirfusz et al. 2018).

6 However, some public services have been recently introduced in response to the growing number of inhabitants. At the time of writing, waste removal, post and internet and television services are available for those ready to pay.

7 At the time of writing, the average price for a house in the allotment is around 10m HUF (€27,700), while the average housing price in the inner areas of the nearest suburban town is more than 20m HUF (€55,400). A similar detached house in Budapest costs around 50m HUF (€138,800).

References

Aalbers, M. B. (2009) The sociology and geography of mortgage markets: reflections on the financial crisis. *International Journal of Urban and Regional Research* 32(2): 281–290. doi:10.1111/j.1468-2427.2009.00875.x.

Aalbers, M. B. (2017) The variegated financialization of housing. *International Journal of Urban and Regional Research* 41(4): 542–554. doi: 10.1111/1468-2427.12522.

Amin, S. (2004) Globalism or apartheid on a global scale. In: Wallerstein, I. (ed.) *The modern world-system in the longue durée*. Boulder: Paradigm, pp. 5–30.

Arrighi, G. (1994) *The long twentieth century: money, power, and the origins of our times*. New York: Verso.

Bohle, D. (2014) Post-socialist housing meets transnational finance: foreign banks, mortgage lending, and the privatization of welfare in Hungary and Estonia. *Review of International Political Economy* 21(4): 913–948. doi: 10.1080/09692290.2013.801022.

Czirfusz, M., Pósfai, I. & Pósfai, Z. (2018) A lakhatási szegénység területi folyamatai. In: Pósfai, Z., Jelinek, C. & Czirfusz, M. (eds.) *Éves jelentés a lakhatási szegénységről 2018*. Budapest: Habitat for Humanity Hungary. Available from: https://habitat.hu/mivel-foglalkozunk/lakhatasi-jelentesek/lakhatasi-jelentes-2018/teruleti-folyamatok/ [Accessed 14 August 2020].

Dancsik, B., Fábián, G., Fellner, Z., Horváth, G., Lang, P., Nagy, G., Oláh, Z. & Winkler, S. (2015) *Comprehensive analysis of the nonperforming household mortgage portfolio using micro-level data*. MNB Occasional Papers Special Issue. Budapest: Magyar Nemzeti Bank. Available from: https://www.mnb.hu/letoltes/mnb-occasional-papers-special-issue.pdf [Accessed 14 August 2020].

Dunaway, W. A. (2012) The semiproletarian household over the longue durée of the modern world-system. In: Lee, R. E. (ed.) *The longue durée and world-systems analysis*. Albany: SUNY Press, pp. 97–136.

Dunford, M. & Liu, W. (2017) Uneven and combined development. *Regional Studies* 51(1): 69–85.

EMF (2015) *Hypostat 2015: a review of Europe's mortgage and housing markets*. Brussels: European Mortgage Federation.

EMF (2019) *Statistical tables Hypostat 2019*. Brussels: European Mortgage Federation. [Data obtained on request by the authors].

Fernandez, R. & Aalbers, M. B. (2016) Financialization and housing: between globalization and varieties of capitalism. *Competition & Change* 20(2): 71–88. doi: 10.1177/1024529415623916.

Frank, A. G. (1966) *The development of underdevelopment*. Boston: New England Free Press.

Friedman, K. E. & Friedman, J. (2008) *Modernities, class, and the contradictions of globalization: the anthropology of global systems*. New York: Altamira.

Galasi, P. & Sziráczki, G., eds. (1985) *Labour market and second economy in Hungary*. Frankfurt: Campus Verlag.

Gyáni, G. (1992) *Bérkaszárnya és nyomortelep*. Budapest: Magvető.

Hadjimichalis, C. & Hudson, R. (2014) Contemporary crisis across Europe and the crisis of regional development theories. *Regional Studies* 48(1): 208–218. doi: 10.1080/00343404.2013.834044.

Harvey, D. (1978) The urban process under capitalism: a framework for analysis. *International Journal of Urban and Regional Research* 2(1–4): 101–131.

Hegedüs, J. (1992) Self-help housing in Hungary: the changing role of private housing provision in Eastern Europe. In: Mathéy, K. (ed.) *Beyond self-help housing*. London: Mansell, pp. 217–231.

Hegedüs, J. & Manchin, R. (1987) Az üdülőterületek expanziója (1965–1975) (Egyéni és kollektív stratégiák). *Szociológia* 2: 251–276.

Hegedüs, J., Mayo, S. K. & Tosics, I. (1996) Transition of the housing sector in the East Central European countries. *Review of Urban and Regional Development Studies* 8(2): 101–136. doi: 10.1111/j.1467-940X.1996.tb00113.x.

Hegedüs, J. & Manchin, R. (1987) Az üdülőterületek expanziója (1965–1975) (Egyéni és kollektív stratégiák). *Szociológia* 2: 251–276.

Hegedüs, J. & Somogyi, E. (2016) Moving from an authoritarian state system to an authoritarian market system: housing finance milestones in Hungary between 1979 and 2014. In: Whitehead, C. (ed.) *Milestones in European housing finance.* Oxford: Wiley-Blackwell, pp. 201–217.

Hilferding, R. ([1910] 1981) *Finance capital: a study of the latest phase of capitalist development.* London: Routledge & Kegan Paul.

Hudson, R. (2015) Uneven development, socio-spatial polarization and political responses. In: Lang, T., Henn, S., Ehrlich, K. & Sgibnev, W. (eds.) *Understanding geographies of polarization and peripheralization: perspectives from Central and Eastern Europe and beyond.* Basingstoke: Palgrave Macmillan, pp. 25–39.

Hudson, R. (2016) Rising powers and the drivers of uneven global development. *Area Development and Policy* 1(3): 279–294. doi: 10.1080/23792949.2016.1227271.

Kalb, D. & Tak, H., eds. (2005) *Critical junctions: anthropology and history beyond the cultural turn.* New York: Berghahn.

Kováts, B. (2020) Is there a core-semiperiphery division in housing? Applying world-systems theory in European comparative housing research. *Housing, Theory and Society.* doi: 10.1080/14036096.2020.1813801.

Luxemburg, R. ([1913] 1951) *The accumulation of capital.* London: Routledge & Kegan Paul.

Misetics, B. (2017) Lakáspolitika és hajléktalanság. In: Ferge, Z. (ed.) *Társadalom és szociálpolitika, Magyarország 1990–2015.* Budapest: Osiris, pp. 267–286.

Moore, J. W. (2015) *Capitalism in the web of life: ecology and the accumulation of capital.* New York: Verso.

Pellandini-Simányi, L., Hammer, F. & Vargha, Z. (2015) The financialization of everyday life or the domestication of finance? How mortgages engage with borrowers' temporal horizons, relationships and rationality in Hungary. *Cultural Studies* 29(5–6): 733–759. doi: 10.1080/09502386.2015.1017142.

Pinto, A. (1973) *Heterogeneidad estructural y modelo de desarrollo reciente de la América Latina.* Santiago: CEPAL.

Pósfai, Z. (2018) Reproducing uneven development on the Hungarian housing market. PhD dissertation, Doctoral School of Geosciences, University of Szeged. doi: 10.14232/phd.9753.

Pósfai, Z. (2019) Annual report on housing poverty in Hungary: executive summary. Budapest: Habitat for Humanity Hungary. Available from: https://habitat.hu/sites/lakhatasi-jelentes/wp-content/uploads/sites/5/2020/01/HFH2019EN_V2.pdf [Accessed 14 August 2020].

Pósfai, Z., Gál, Z. & Nagy, E. (2018) Financialization and inequalities: the uneven development of the housing market on the eastern periphery of Europe. In: Fadda, S. & Tridico, P. (eds.) *Inequality and uneven development in the post-crisis world.* Abingdon: Routledge, pp. 167–190.

Pryor, R. J. (1968) Defining the rural-urban fringe. *Social Forces* 47(2): 200–215.

Raviv, O. (2008) Chasing the dragon east: exploring the frontiers of Western European finance. *Contemporary Politics* 14(3): 297–314. doi: 10.1080/13569770802396345.

Smith, N. (1984) *Uneven development: nature, capital, and the production of space.* Athens: University of Georgia Press.

Smith, J., Wallerstein, I. M. & Evers, H. D. (1984) *Households and the world economy.* Beverly Hills: Sage.

Stanilov, K. & Sykora, L., eds. (2014) *Confronting suburbanization: urban decentralization in postsocialist Central and Eastern Europe.* Oxford: Wiley-Blackwell.

Székely, G. (2018) A lakásvásárlás finanszírozása. In: *Miben élünk? A 2015. évi lakásfelmérés részletes eredményei*. Budapest: Központi Statisztikai Hivatal, pp. 67–80. Available from: https://www.ksh.hu/docs/hun/xftp/idoszaki/pdf/miben_elunk15_2.pdf [Accessed 14 August 2020].

Tilly, R. (1986) German banking 1850–1914: development assistance for the strong. *Journal of European Economic History* 15(1): 113–152.

Tosics, I. (2006) Spatial restructuring in post-socialist Budapest. In: Tsenkova, S. & Nedovic, Z. (eds.) *The urban mosaic of post-socialist Europe: space, institutions and policy*. Heidelberg: Physica Verlag, pp. 131–150.

Vigvári, A. (2016) "Rural poverty" in urban spaces of Budapest: research proposal for examining spatial inequality in contemporary Hungary. *Socio.hu* 4: 47–61. doi: 10.18030/socio.hu.2016en.47.

Vigvári, A. & Gerőcs, T. (2017) The concept of "peasant embourgeoisement" in the perspective of different historical conjunctures. *Studia Universitatis Babes-Bolyai Sociologia* 62(1): 85–104. doi: 10.1515/subbs-2017-0006.

Wolf, E. R. & Silverman, S. (2001) *Pathways of power: building an anthropology of the modern world*. Berkeley: University of California Press.

4 The strange non-death of the "normal" household

Ciudad Valdeluz and homeownership across the economic cycle

Natalia Buier

Introduction

The centrality of housing to Spain's contemporary model of accumulation has not been missed by many. As the Spanish financial crisis brought to the fore the limits of the country's highly financialized real estate sector and sunk it into a prolonged crisis, the circulation of images of irresponsible spending, corrupt politicians and the usual range of stereotypes about the sins of the Southerners also accelerated. It did not take long for academic analysis to respond to this. The range of interventions situating the Spanish housing bubble in a broader context goes from explanations that identify the proliferation of new financial instruments and deregulation as its immediate causes to those that trace the overproduction of housing to a longer history of the Spanish state and the political project of constructing a nation of homeowners during the fascist period (Charnock et al. 2014; Di Feliciantonio and Aalbers 2018; Hernández and López 2010; Naredo and Montiel 2011). These discussions were accompanied by reflections about the ways in which the financialization of housing has impacted notions of homeownership and inter- and intra-household relationships (Palomera 2014; Sabaté 2016). Not unlike in other national contexts (Poppe et al. 2016), and in line with broader discussions about the ways in which debt disrupts daily life and draws households into new economic relationships (Montgomerie and Tepe-Belfrage 2017), discussions about housing and financialization situated at the level of the household have been aimed at destabilizing reigning liberal assumptions about homeownership as a source of stability. The focus on the aftermath of the 2007–2008 Global Financial Crisis and the more localized crises it triggered, which laid bare the vulnerabilities of households within a regime of asset-based welfare, has confirmed the entanglement of financialization and crises of social reproduction (Fraser 2014) and resulted in a growing record of fissures in the ideology of homeownership as a route to stability (Weiss 2014).

This chapter seeks to contribute to a processual, activity-oriented conceptualization of the household by focussing on the conduct of Spanish households as agents of investment in housing. In line with other contributions to this volume, I maintain that households should not be treated as discrete units of analysis but as dynamic sites that emerge at the intersection of relations of production, reproduction and investment. Recent discussions about households and financialization have stressed the blurring of the boundaries between "homes as socially valued living environments and homes as investment objects" (Poppe et al. 2016: 59), a reading that implies a softening of the tensions between use value and exchange value of housing. Some of the literature on financialization and housing qualifies this reading. Thus, while implicitly or explicitly conceding that the capitalist logic of financialization tends to blur such boundaries, some authors argue that the experience of indebtedness under conditions of crisis can act as a counter-tendency and result in an unveiling of some of the ideological tenets of economic liberalism (Sabaté 2016; Weiss 2014). Departing from these arguments, my analysis of the experience of crisis in Valdeluz suggests that while the tension between use value and exchange value remains a defining feature of housing as a commodity, we should be wary of the assumption that crisis invariably facilitates a critique of economic liberalism and the capitalist ideology of property.

This chapter presents a cautionary tale in relation to optimistic readings about the role of crisis in redrawing the moral economies of financialization by looking into the case of Ciudad Valdeluz, an urban development project in the proximity of Madrid that was heavily affected by the irruption of the 2008–2014 Spanish financial crisis. The first residents of Valdeluz moved in shortly before the crisis broke out and purchased their property in the boom phase of the economic cycle. Valdeluz is essentially a case of interrupted urbanization, since the crisis hit at a time when only the first phase of construction had been completed and a large number of housing units had not been sold. The conjuncture resulted in a massive devaluation of property, which led to the arrival of what I refer to as a second generation of residents, namely people who took advantage of low property prices in the bust phase of the economic cycle. In order to explore the ways in which the purchase of real estate constitutes households as sites of investment and reproduction, I follow four personal stories about homeownership in Valdeluz. These stories of Valdeluz residents allow me to observe the ways in which the meaning of homeownership is mediated by what I refer to as the "normal" nuclear family household. Scholars have long insisted that nuclear families are inadequate proxies for households (Yanagisako 1979). At the same time, the "second demographic transition" has led to increasingly diverse household forms (Buzar et al. 2005). Whether one subscribes to the thesis of the erstwhile prevalence of the nuclear family household or questions its pervasiveness as an actually existing demographic structure (Harris 1981), contemporary scholarly consensus has been forged around acknowledging the (increasing) diversity of household arrangements. However, the argument of this chapter arising from the analysis of the case of Valdeluz is that the "normalcy of the nuclear family" household (Carter 1995) remains ideologically operative and might even be strengthened as actually existing household forms drift further away from it. In other words, the ideological association of nuclear families and households outlives the real or assumed historical dominance of the nuclear family household.

This ties into the second core argument of this chapter, which is that the instability of housing as a store of value under conditions of financialization and the failures of households as shock-absorbers challenge the division between "mobilities of privilege" and "mobilities of disadvantage" (Wiesel 2014). The distinction between mobilities of privilege and disadvantage emerges from the attempt to build on the concept of "housing pathways" (Clapham 2002) through the lens of residential mobility. Alongside other attempts to overcome the limitations of the concept of "housing career", it breaks with the treatment of housing transitions in terms of a single source or destination, or what has been criticized as the "snake and ladders" metaphor for housing biographies (Beer and Faulkner 2011). Characterized as "valorised, voluntary, comfortable" and offering an "improved housing quality and accumulation of capital" (Wiesel 2014: 320), mobilities of privilege supposedly constitute pathways of high-income households. Low-income households are expected to be characterized by mobilities of disadvantage, which are "stigmatised, forced, painful or costly" and may result in a "deteriorating housing quality and loss of capital" (Wiesel 2014: 320).

While contributions such as these expand the range of possible residential trajectories, reminding us of the variegated movements of individuals through the housing market, they fail to capture the production of the structure of constraints and opportunities for those movements. Moreover, in spite of the broadened view of inter-household relations they afford, they fail to capture the full complexity of intra-household histories of relocation. The inherent instability of "privilege" and "disadvantage" has its origins in the fundamentally relational nature of households' positionality as well as in the volatility of the financialized economy. As I will show, for the privileged households of Valdeluz, what began as a promise of upwards mobility ended up as a costly relocation. Conversely, for the less affluent, the collapse of the housing market opened unexpected pathways to improved housing. The housing pathways literature and its associated variants, such as the literature on residential mobility, operate with the assumption that increased income inequality leads, over time, to increasingly uneven housing outcomes and that these processes are reinforced by the operation of the housing market (Beer and Faulkner 2011). Valdeluz presents a case that does not conform to this pattern; under conditions of economic instability, the spatial polarization of the urban middle class and the working class collapsed, even if it remained inscribed into the promises of the suburban middle-class family home. Even more importantly, if further refinements of the concepts of housing pathways and mobilities of privilege and disadvantage could potentially cover an ever-expanding range of individual trajectories through time, the limits of this classificatory attempt are revealed by the synchronic view it affords. At any given moment in time, as occupants of structural positions, the households of Valdeluz had to juggle constraints and opportunities that escape easy classification. Thus, while first-generation homeowners were going to gain access to higher-quality housing, they also belonged to those unable to access housing in Madrid. By contrast, second-generation homeowners frequently experienced their move to Valdeluz as a forced or painful event in a longer history of household recomposition related to divorce, separation or the onset of illness or disability. The contradictory positions of households that had to navigate a shifting terrain of advantages and disadvantages suggest that their mobility is best understood as simultaneously advantageous and disadvantageous.

Finally, analysis of housing pathways and trajectories treats lifestyles related to housing decisions as a set of values and aspirations that originate from consumers navigating a structure of constraints and opportunities. But as I discuss below, the bundle of values that constitute the suburban family lifestyle is not simply a set of subjective aspirations and expectations that must be realized in a market context. Faced with the instability of the market, the middle-class residents of Valdeluz embarked on a political trajectory that countered the crisis-induced democratization of urban space with a discourse of the normative nuclear family household. Behind this discourse, we find the property-owning investor household recognizing and selecting those "definitions of use values advantageous to accumulation rather than reflective of the real human needs of labor" (Harvey 1976: 277). These use values are produced as part of the functioning of the housing market; suburban lifestyles belong to the extra-economic factors that are part of the financial valorization of housing (Harvey 1976). The "normal" nuclear family household is the ideological backbone of the language in which the first-generation residents of Valdeluz expressed their double dispossession: from the exchange value of suburban housing as well as the use values attached to it. But frustrated expectations about stability and upwards mobility strengthened, rather than weakened, the selection of those use values favourable to capitalist accumulation.

Valdeluz, a symbol of the crisis

I arrived to Valdeluz in the spring of 2017, accompanied by my research assistant Diego, as part of a broader research project about the development of Spanish high-speed rail (HSR). Spain is a European leader in HSR mileage, a development that, as I discuss elsewhere (Buier 2020), is but one pillar of a major infrastructural boom that has also resulted in Spain boasting Europe's largest number of airports and most kilometres of highways. My main research interest in relation to Valdeluz was to understand the way in which the expansion of transport infrastructure had impacted peripheral urban development and existing mobility patterns. Valdeluz is but one of many urban projects that have followed the expansion of HSR. The map of the Spanish HSR, which is locally known as AVE (short for *Alta Velocidad Española*), can be seen as comprised of central nodes and peripheral locations, the latter including those stations and stops that are situated outside established urban nuclei. Valdeluz-Yebes is one of these peripheral locations, yet it is also in many respects unlike any other, given the overlap between its short history and the dynamics of the financial crisis and the particularities of its spatial and administrative structure. The extremeness of manifestations of crisis in Valdeluz makes it both very useful to think with and limited in terms of potential for generalization. As I further discuss, the processes at work in Valdeluz offer us the possibility to observe a set of social and economic relations into which households become embedded in the context of financialization and which are rarely visible to this degree. While the exacerbation of the crisis-induced processes in Valdeluz might not be typical, it allows us to not simply contrast households' differential ways of relating to homeownership but also observe what kind of social tensions and struggles emerge when those varied relationships with homeownership confront each other as actually existing social processes within a shared urban space.

Arrested development

The history of Valdeluz begins with the story of the Madrid-Barcelona HSR line. A decision was made to locate the Guadalajara HSR station (positioned approximately 60 km from Madrid on the Madrid-Barcelona route) approximately 10 km outside the municipality of Guadalajara. The official explanation for the choice of the location was that it was the best solution from a technical point of view. The location for the new station fell within the boundaries of the small municipality of Yebes, a Castilian village with a population of 214 in 2005. The plots that the station would be eventually built on, administratively an exclave of Yebes, belonged to Teresa Valdés, related to the husband of Esperanza Aguirre, at the time a high-ranking member of the People's Party (PP), the leading right-wing party of post-Francoist Spain. It was not long after the decision was announced that a massive construction project was born: Ciudad Valdeluz was an urban development project (*Proyecto de Actuación Urbanística*, PAU) born around the location of the new HSR station.

Planned as a town for approximately 34,000 people inhabiting 9,500 housing units, Valdeluz was supposed to be built in four phases (see Figure 4.1). The main developer of the project was Reyal Urbis. The first residents moved in in 2006 when construction was still advancing at a fast pace. When crisis hit in 2008, however, construction was brought to a halt with only the first phase of the project completed. Reyal Urbis is nowadays primarily remembered as one of the spectacular bankruptcies in the Spanish construction sector. After long negotiations about the company's debt, Reyal Urbis was finally liquidated in 2017. At the time of my fieldwork, the housing stock

Figure 4.1 Details of a scale model of Valdeluz, Valdeluz, 2017.
Source: Author.

of Valdeluz was still basically that of 2008 (see Figure 4.2). The centrepiece of the planned town was the HSR station, which, it was claimed, would leave the residents of Valdeluz 20 minutes away from the centre of Madrid. The expectation that accompanied the project was that the station would be serviced by Avant, Spain's regional HSR service, rather than the long-distance Madrid-Barcelona service. This was supposed to ensure a frequent and subsidized (or otherwise put relatively cheap) connection to Madrid. This service was never implemented, and any informed observer is likely to draw the conclusion that it will not be implemented in the foreseeable future. At the time of the fieldwork, none of the seven daily trains to Madrid that stopped in Valdeluz ran early in the morning or late in the afternoon. But more importantly, at approximately €20 for a one-way trip to Madrid, this was a form of luxury travel inaccessible to most. The €11m Valdeluz-Yebes station, with an estimated annual maintenance cost of €122,000, is one of Spain's most underutilized HSR stations. Only 108 people a day on average were estimated to use it in 2015, and my own research suggests that most were not residents of Valdeluz.

The years that followed the collapse of the real estate market were characterized by a spectacular fall in the value of property, as house prices

Figure 4.2 Closed office of Reyal Urbis and pre-installed infrastructure in Valdeluz, 2017.
Source: Author.

dropped as low as 30% of pre-crisis levels. With only the first phase of the project completed, most of the promised amenities were lacking. These were the years during which, as Spain's real estate crash made the news, Valdeluz became a symbol of the aberrations of the crisis. During the following three years, national and international media flocked to Valdeluz for the best shots of abandoned property and still cranes. After all, as some of the residents of Valdeluz I talked to ironically pointed out, Valdeluz was only 20 minutes away from Madrid by HSR. These were the years during which Valdeluz became tied to the label of "ghost town". That the label stuck is not exactly surprising. In 2010, only 726 people were officially registered as living in Valdeluz, while housing capacity was estimated at close to 10,000. The presentation of Valdeluz as a symbol of the crisis has not been confined to mainstream media. Academic analysis has also turned Valdeluz into a widely used example of the destructive effects of financialized real estate development, although most of the times its role is that of a simple, if impressive, illustration (see, for example, Naredo and Montiel 2011). And while critical analysis is radically distinguished from popular media through its concern with the origins and development of the housing boom, these two genres coincide in their description of the contemporary state of Valdeluz: what this place is primarily characterized by is absence. Residents who never arrived, trains that never made it, facilities that were never built, supermarkets that never opened: Valdeluz, the ghost town.

From a ghost town to a town of hope

Shortly after moving in, the first homeowners found themselves contemplating the breach of a promise: the promise of life in a comfortable suburban environment fit for the start of family life. Two aspects had been central to the marketing of real estate in Valdeluz: connectivity and houses fit for becoming homes. It is the latter that is primarily of interest to me in this chapter. As my interviews with first-generation homeowners confirmed, and as evidenced by the trail of ads and promotional campaigns left behind by Reyal Urbis, the commercial image of Valdeluz was built around the three- or four-member nuclear family household. The nuclear family represented by generic white, upper-middle-class parents accompanied by one or two children was essentially the only actor, in addition to the occasional business traveller or golf player, who populated the commercial imaginary surrounding the project. Slogans such as "Valdeluz, we create homes, we make cities" or "Valdeluz, start living" echoed the idea that homeownership is the early necessary milestone in the process of establishing a family.

Such images were not entirely disconnected from the reality on the ground. While assessing the precise composition of the first generation of homeowners remains very difficult (a lack of data and absentee owners being among the main problems), some insight could be gained from interviews with members of that generation. At minimum, it is safe to say that most first-generation homeowners who came to stay in Valdeluz and were still there at the time of my research did fit the profile of young married couples looking for housing that could accommodate family life. These were typically households that relocated from Madrid or its surroundings, financially stable enough to access homeownership at the height of market prices, but not wealthy enough to afford similar homes in Madrid. Comfort and affordability versus centrality was a trade-off that featured prominently in their decisions to move to Valdeluz. Initially marketed as luxury homes for middle-class and upper-middle-class families, the properties of Valdeluz – apartments, semi-detached and detached houses – featured amenities such as pools, paddle tennis courts, private gyms as well as the promise of security associated with a semi-gated environment. Following the collapse of the real estate market, these households were confronted with the devaluation of their property. This had as much to do with the financial crisis and the burst of the housing bubble in general as with the interruption of construction in Valdeluz in particular. The latter not only affected these households' status as investors but resulted in immediate, everyday strains upon their possibilities of reproduction. The collapse of the project meant that essential facilities and services such as a medical centre, a school, and waste collection were missing. Some of this public urban infrastructure was supposed to be completed by the developer, while public services depended on reaching a minimum number of residents, a criterion Valdeluz did not meet. Additionally, the large number of unoccupied houses contributed to the reputation of Valdeluz as a ghost town, which drove down property prices even more.

The homeowners of Valdeluz seeking to restore the value of their property and re-establish a dynamic of growth became dependent on two partially antagonistic strategies. On the one hand, any hopes of quieting the corrosive effects of the ghost town reputation and securing basic amenities depended on simple demographic growth. On the other, the homeowners saw recovering the value of their property as dependent on reinstating the image of Valdeluz as an urban environment suited for middle-class family lifestyles. The latter, however, was threatened by the type of demographic growth Valdeluz registered, as the accidentally democratizing effects of the collapse of real estate prices had resulted in a diversification of the social composition of homeowners. This contradiction marked the trajectory of the neighbours' association[1] (*asociación de vecinos*) composed of first-generation homeowners[2] that came to dominate political life in Valdeluz. Formed in 2010 on the basis of a neighbours' association in existence already since 2007, 40 Compromisos (40 Commitments) was a local political structure through which homeowners sought to address the double economic and reproductive crisis they faced. However, the restorative politics of 40 Compromisos found itself in an uneasy relationship with the kind of growth Valdeluz would eventually see.

Around 2011, with property prices still well below pre-crisis levels, a new generation of homeowners started making its presence felt. These people, who unlike those who had purchased their homes before 2008 did not conform to the image of the middle-class homeowner, were taking advantage of the general collapse of the real estate market as well as the fact that the situation of arrested development in Valdeluz and its persistently negative reputation kept prices here even lower than the average. While the demographic growth based on the arrival of these new residents brought with it the possibility of quieting the ghost town reputation of Valdeluz, it also threatened the lingering hopes that it would become a safe haven of middle-class family life. The more the actual social composition of Valdeluz diversified, the more the nuclear middle-class family seemed to occupy the heart of 40 Compromisos's politics. As the stories that follow show, the nuclear family household became the leading character of the local political imaginary. In the process, residents who were contributing most to actually restoring growth in Valdeluz were those whose households had the biggest chances of being airbrushed from the image of the town considered conducive to growth. This is a dynamic condensed in a series of events in the relentless PR war waged by 40 Compromisos. As Joaquín, former mayor of Valdeluz, and other members of the local administration told me, their priority upon taking office was to change the reputation of Valdeluz as a ghost town. In order to achieve this, they had to not only control the type of information that would make the media rounds but also promote those aspects of life in Valdeluz that were directly opposed to this reputation. *Valdeluz, de ciudad fantasma a ciudad esperanza* ("Valdeluz, from a ghost town to a town of hope"), a slogan used in several newspaper articles, metonymically embodied the type of image 40 Compromisos sought to build.

Underneath the normative nuclear family household

The broken windows of Valdeluz

Gonzalo moved to Valdeluz in May 2007, shortly before the mirage of perpetual growth disappeared. According to his recollections, no more than 100 people lived in Valdeluz at the time. The first residents had arrived in the summer of 2006. According to Gonzalo, these were people from Madrid with high purchasing power who purchased detached houses costing more than €300,000 at the time and more than €400,000 at the peak. Originally from Colombia, he moved to Madrid to do a PhD in civil engineering, facilitated by the fact that his brothers had emigrated to Spain and settled down in Madrid in the 1980s. Both he and his wife were connected to the development of Valdeluz through their jobs. Gonzalo's wife was working for ADIF, the public company in charge of HSR infrastructure development. As for Gonzalo, he learned about the project first-hand through his work in a private company specializing in cadastral updating before even the first brick was laid. Before moving to Valdeluz, Gonzalo and his wife had been living in a studio in the centre of Madrid. Since they were thinking of having children, they decided Valdeluz would be a good place to settle down.

Gonzalo was a founding member of the neighbours' association that eventually took the shape of a political association and ran for local elections under the name of 40 Compromisos. The neighbours' association was formed early on, even before some of its members moved to Valdeluz. He recalled their first meeting in a franchise restaurant in Madrid where they all worked and about their gradual realization that if they wanted to effect change in Valdeluz they had to take over the local administration. Participating in the neighbours' association was not the only change brought about by his decision to move to Valdeluz. Following the dissolution of the dreams of connectivity, he started looking for work closer to home and eventually found a job in a small company in Guadalajara. After the victory of 40 Compromisos in the 2011 local elections, he gave up his job and took up a full-time position as a local council member. At the time of our meeting, Gonzalo was in his second term in office.

As a member of 40 Compromisos from its beginning, Gonzalo had contributed significantly to defining its orientation. He was preoccupied with the image of Valdeluz and, in his self-description, was interested in establishing a dynamic of slow and steady growth (as opposed to the unsustainable forms of pre-crisis growth). He repeatedly emphasized that Valdeluz is a place for young families and expressed his belief that local politics must be responsive to this. According to him, the crisis has significantly altered the profile of those moving to Valdeluz. The main change he saw was a shift from mostly young couples from Madrid as the initial arrivals to couples from Guadalajara and the region of Guadalajara after the crisis. If this was initially supposed to be a dormitory town for people working in Madrid looked upon with hostility by the residents of Guadalajara, with prices dropping below those in Guadalajara it became an attractive option for intraregional relocation. The crisis indeed seems to have altered Valdeluz's integration into regional core-periphery dynamics, as its position transformed from one of a suburb-in-the-making on the expanding urban frontier of a sprawling capital to one of a poorly connected but not too distant suburb of a neighbouring regional centre. Gonzalo was actively involved in the efforts to promote a positive image of Valdeluz and to correct its corrosive reputation as a ghost town. His stress on Valdeluz as a young family town appeared seamlessly integrated with his discourse about stability. His preoccupation with image-building was pervasive:

GONZALO: [talking about public gardens in Valdeluz] Everything has to be clean, perfect, spotless (*impoluto*).

DIEGO: Yes, a basic concept (*premisa*) of the [local] government…

GONZALO: Yes, mine personally.

[laughter]

GONZALO: My philosophy is the one of… Well, I didn't invent anything, it has all been done before. This is basically what Giuliani was doing in New York, the broken windows theory – the building has a broken window and unless you fix it the next day, you will have two, three [broken windows], and then it is going to get vandalized. You have to have everything already in order (*todo lo tienes que tener bien ya*) and regarding this I am very tiresome.

At the time of his relocation to Valdeluz, Gonzalo appeared to be on his way to becoming a member of a model nuclear family. However, his actual life course diverged from this trajectory, and while he was still married at the time of the interview, he ended up not having children. Like many others, Gonzalo bought a home on the frontier of the urban expansion of the Madrid metropolitan region to secure use values deemed essential for raising children. At the same time, according to his own description, he made the purchase in a context in which no one anticipated the dramatic drop in prices that would follow. Unanticipated personal circumstances and times of economic instability combined to send him down a path in which he became, as a local councillor, an architect and spokesperson for an urban environment whose basic social unit was represented as the nuclear family household – an ideal that he did not quite meet himself. But even if that pursuit was not fully aligned with his own family status, it allowed him to project the type of urban space that would restore Valdeluz to its former commercial promise: "Designed for living, planned for growth".

How does somebody from San Sebastián end up living in Valdeluz?

Joaquín shared with Gonzalo more than residence in the same apartment complex. Like Gonzalo, he was one of the founding members of 40 Compromisos and went on to become the first independent mayor of "Spain's first town built from scratch"[3] in 2011–2015. He declared an admiration for what he described as Gonzalo's extreme intelligence and resourcefulness. For more than four years, the pair worked on promoting a positive image of their unfinished town. Originally from San Sebastián, a wealthy coastal town in the Basque Country and a tourist hub with cosmopolitan reputation, Joaquín was a law graduate with a career of a high-level officer in a series of banks. When he took up the office of the mayor as a representative of 40 Compromisos, he was the manager of a Guadalajara branch of one of the biggest Spanish banks. For half a year after being elected, he tried to harmonize his job and his new duties as a mayor, but in the end decided it was impossible and gave up his job at the bank in order to devote himself full-time to his duties at the town hall. He retired from politics and returned to working in a bank in 2015 after a local coalition government formed by 40 Compromisos and the Spanish Socialist Workers' Party (PSOE) resulted in the election of a socialist mayor.[4] He could have stayed in the governing administration as a councillor but decided not to.

During what ended up being a more than five-hour meeting, Joaquín walked me through his adventures as the mayor. He described his politics as centre-left, and it seemed that centre-left was some sort of arithmetical average of values he assigned to the range of his own political views. He was, he told me, very much to the left on some issues (he was, for example, a staunch defender of public schooling, which he believed was the greatest social leveller), and more to the right on what he repeatedly identified as issues of national unity and public order. Joaquín further presented himself as a former believer in the type of residential dream that Valdeluz was supposed to deliver. He justified his former naiveté and attraction to the project by conjuring the image of experiments with greenfield urban projects in the proximity of London where he had studied in the past. After studying the history of 40 Compromisos and talking to him and other people who knew him, I came to believe that Joaquín was fully committed to recreating the Valdeluz brand and its promise of tranquil, suburban civility. I am however sceptical he ever fully believed in it. He finished our long conversation by saying, "So you wonder how somebody from San Sebastián ends up living in a place like Valdeluz? Well, as always: love and work."

Brought to the region of Guadalajara by contingencies of love and work, Joaquín's relocation to Valdeluz was one of his multiple house moves in the area. Looking back at his otherwise fortunate housing pathway, he used it as an illustration of the aberrations of the uncontrolled, speculative Spanish real estate market. He sold his first house in the middle of the frenzy of real estate development in the mid-1990s only three years after he bought it and at a profit of €60,000. He subsequently bought a new house in a village in the Guadalajara region for €200,000, and, after a divorce a few years later, he sold it for €365,000. All of this is madness, it's not normal to extract such surplus value (his wording) from simply reselling your house in a few years, he told me. Yet those were very mad times when everybody was speculating, he added, from individuals to municipal administrations. Joaquín is also an LGBT activist and has been much more active as one since leaving the town hall. A gay man from the Basque country, he was a prime target for both Spanish nationalist and homophobic attacks, which more than once took the form of death threats. He has navigated his difficult circumstances with contradictory impulses. As a mayor, Joaquín actively pursued progressive identity politics. From renaming one of the squares after Federico García Lorca, "assassinated homosexual poet", to insisting on having a feminist section in the local library, Joaquín pursued his dream of a transformative cultural politics and yet, as he himself admitted, has been often afraid of pursuing more radical ideas. The world that surrounded him remained resolutely conservative, as even his well-meaning socialist colleagues often rejected harmless, tame actions. Even then, among his happiest recollections are those of officiating gay marriages in a place that he had insisted on including on the list of "Spanish municipalities free from homophobia".

The longer I talked to Joaquín, the more it became obvious that he was not the ideal candidate for the suburban family dream. As his final confession suggests, to present his housing trajectory as an instance of mobility of privilege is hardly a straightforward choice; rather, it is a delicate balancing act adjusted to the audience. Yet it is also true that he was one of the main architects of a local politics that sought to define Valdeluz as an ideal town for young nuclear family households and that he stayed loyal to the class politics he was elected to carry out throughout his mandate. It was from him that I learned about many details of 40 Compromisos's relentless, even obsessive pursuit of changing the reputation of Valdeluz as a ghost town. Upon assuming his office, Joaquín immediately formed a media team, a decision later criticized by locals. He explained his choice in terms of an effort required to alter the notoriously negative image of Valdeluz, which, in his account and that of other local councillors, was one of the main hindrances to putting the locality on a pathway of growth. The vision of Valdeluz that Joaquín and his team tried to fortify was one of a privileged space for young couples looking to establish a family and take advantage of amenities that they would be excluded from in other places. The young couple seeking to establish a family features so prominently in the imaginary of 40 Compromisos members that it overshadows most other categories of Valdeluz residents.

More than stories about the image-building efforts of the municipality, it was Joaquín's recollections about threats to the image of Valdeluz as an ideal suburban family setting that revealed the way in which the normative nuclear family household operated as a principle of exclusion. Thus, when he remembered some cases of squatting that occurred in Valdeluz, he simultaneously conjured his anxiety at the time about news of these cases circulating widely: "Just imagine this would have made it to the media, the last thing we needed." But the *okupa* (squatters) surfaced as only one in a range of actors that posed a threat to the tranquillizing social homogeneity of the suburban promise. I listened to Joaquín as he talked to me about his fears: one of his greatest fears while he was a mayor, he told me, was that a machoistic murder (*asesinato machista*) would take place. At first, it was unclear whether he meant personally afraid or afraid because it would damage the reputation of the town. As the conversation went on, the line between the two became increasingly blurred. Hardly a racist, as he defended himself while invoking his marriage with a Dominican man as a proof, he nonetheless admitted to being afraid of the pervasive sexism and homophobia of Poles, Latin Americans and other minority ethnic groups that have begun to take up residence in Valdeluz.

Valdeluz is not a place where you work

Carmen was one of those who moved to Valdeluz after property prices fell. She obtained a mortgage for a €162,000 semi-detached house, the starting price for which had been almost €500,000. Unlike in Madrid, it was easy for her to obtain a mortgage even though she did not quite meet the conditions. She attributed her luck to the bank's desire to get rid of unsold property in Valdeluz. But it took Carmen three years to be able to move into her new house. In the meantime, she, her partner José and their first child, aged 3 at the time of the interview, stayed in her grandmother's flat in Carabanchel, a traditional working-class district of Madrid. Carmen and José were both working as shop assistants in two of Spain's largest supermarket chains, and one of their biggest challenges was finding work closer to home. She recalled in detail the complicated scheduling resulting from having to juggle raising children, working in shifts and commuting. The difficulties and costs of both of them commuting to Madrid by car were unaffordable, so the only solution they had was to postpone their relocation until at least one of them found work in Guadalajara: "The bad thing about Valdeluz is that this is not a place where you work."

Carmen was the first to obtain work closer to home after transferring to the Guadalajara branch of the same supermarket chain she had been working for in the capital. For some months after they started living in Valdeluz, and before he found work doing technical support for a telecommunications company in Guadalajara, José kept working afternoon shifts in Madrid. He would look after the baby in the morning, but in order to make the 80 km journey to his workplace, he had to drop off the child with Carmen at the supermarket in Guadalajara, usually one hour before the end of her shift. Their hardships did not end with both of them finding work in Guadalajara. "I tell him: son, you are breaking my heart, I must go to work, I have to eat every day, it is a custom we like to follow," Carmen said to express the difficulties that arose from the little time she could spend with her son between his mornings at the kindergarten and her evening shifts (5–10 pm, Monday to Saturday). "This here is life with a car," she added. While she never believed they could become daily users of the AVE, they did have hopes that the subsidized short-distance HSR service that failed to materialize would at least facilitate the occasional visits of their extended families and friends, something a €8–9 ticket would have allowed for.

Carmen described the residents of Valdeluz as divided between those with high purchasing power who arrived early and those like herself who bought their flats and houses after the collapse of the real estate market – those making ends meet with odd-jobs and the young ("*curritos y jovenes*"). "Ours will predominate," she said, referring to those sharing her socio-economic background. However, she added that in spite of the numerical minority of the first-generation homeowners, they were a pain in the neck ("*tampoco es que haya muchos pero dan mucha guerra*"). She knew some of them but they were not friends; it was only the children of first- and second-generation residents who socialized since they were indifferent to class markers. "I think neither them nor us feel comfortable," she said, "they like other things, they do different things." She could not afford eating out at a very good restaurant in Guadalajara every Saturday, she said by way of example: "If I am lucky, I order delivery pizza once a month, you know?"

While Carmen's household seemed to conform to the normative nuclear family household, she has not bought into the image of Valdeluz as an ideal place for family life. Critical of 40 Compromisos and the PSOE, she held Joaquín personally responsible for many of the problems in Valdeluz. "A lot of propaganda, a lot of publicity, but then there is nothing," she concluded as she talked about the lack of a medical centre and the inadequate bus service. Like Joaquín, Carmen feared the *efecto llamada* (pull effect). Unlike Joaquín, however, her fears were unambiguously concerned with insecurities of urban life rather than property prices in their own right. Originally from a poor, working-class and historically migrant area of Madrid, she recalled the settlements of "South Americans, Romanians and Gypsies" and the fights and drug trafficking that accompanied them. Her parents' current neighbourhood in the same district was better, she thought, but there as well "they have lost the park during weekends." In Valdeluz too, there was a time, when rents were at their lowest, "when you could see the riffraff", but not anymore. However, Carmen feared this might be temporary. She was particularly afraid of an appearance of social housing in Valdeluz and with it the arrival of "Gypsies" and drugs. Unlike first-generation homeowners, her household was a beneficiary of the accidental democratizing effects of the collapse of the market. But Carmen's contradictory position meant that what allowed her to access improved housing and security as coveted use values of suburban living simultaneously threatened to erode the suburban dream. Tranquilizing social homogeneity is a use value favourable to accumulation but one, it turned out, that the market is willing to discard.

Valdeluz, paradise of divorcees

Elena's trajectory illustrates the need to treat households as a set of dynamic relations rather than pre-given units (Mikuš and Rodik, this collection). It also confirms the importance of understanding the multiplicity of inter-household relations instead of assuming households as coherent actors following a unitary logic. There is no point in Elena's story in which she appears unquestionably aligned with her household's trajectory of social mobility. She was among the first arrivals in 2006. At the time, she was married with two children: a seven-year-old daughter and a four-year-old son. Moving to Valdeluz was her husband's idea. She did not want to leave her peripheral but well-connected working-class neighbourhood in Madrid, and, as she put it, she found nothing attractive about Valdeluz. She finally gave in to her husband's insisting that the quieter environment would be better-suited for raising children, even though leaving Madrid took her further from her parents and cut her off from the busy city life she enjoyed. "This cost me the world," she said as she remembered the move. Together with her husband, they ended up taking out a mortgage of almost €250,000. Yes, unfortunately they bought the flat just before the collapse of the real estate market, she said. However, she also underscored that while they bought the flat for €240,000, a similar property in Madrid would have cost more than €400,000. For an entire year, they lived alone in a 58-apartment complex. She recalled the eerie silence and how it spooked her children.

For Elena, the financial crisis and the collapse of the real estate market is the background story to a deeper personal crisis that included a painful divorce and onset of health problems. Elena retained custody of the children and retired early due to her poor health. Her only income at the time of the interview was a modest disability pension. Her former husband, with whom she was not in contact anymore, had stopped paying his share of the mortgage. Following problems with the mortgage, Elena joined the PAH (Plataforma de Afectados por la Hipoteca – Platform for People Affected by Mortgages) assembly in Guadalajara. Two other families from Valdeluz were active in PAH Guadalajara, she said, but there were more people at risk of being evicted. She stopped repaying her mortgage when she realized that the fact that her ex-husband stopped repaying together with a change of the mortgage servicer made it uncertain that her own payments would be deducted from the debt.

Elena talked at length about the uneven intra-household effects of what might outwardly appear as a privileged form of mobility of a middle-class household. Most women among first-generation residents were housewives or stay-at-home moms, she said, while the husband would typically be the one to take the family car to drive to his workplace in Madrid. She laughed at the possibility of roles being reversed and described it as "a bit utopian". One of the earliest residents' initiatives she remembered was a short-lived neighbours' association whose main objective was to find solutions to problems arising from the inadequate public transport in Valdeluz. Elena's life trajectory brings to the fore what the ideology of the normative nuclear family household tends to silence: gendered unevenness of intra-household relations; a process of household recomposition after a divorce that put her and her children at risk of losing their home. Elena's early retirement also made her sensitive to the needs of people who were far removed from the image of the nuclear family household and marginalized by the PR exercise of 40 Compromisos. At the time of the interview, she was a member of the Valdeluz and Yebes Volunteers' Association, a small collective comprising mostly women. The association organized a give-away shop that they referred to as a "social wardrobe" (*ropero social*) and tried to reach out to the invisible in Valdeluz: the retired, the elderly, the disabled. Activities of the association included helping out locals with everyday chores or simply trying to create opportunities for bringing together those most afflicted by solitude through activities such as tending to a community garden.

Like Elena, all members of the association that we talked to spoke at length about those left in the shadow of the image of Valdeluz as a place for young families. Unlike her, most members were second-generation homeowners, some of whom had started out as renters and whose diverse life circumstances had put them on a trajectory of residential mobility. "We joke about this being a paradise of divorcees," Elena said, perhaps taking a cue from a 2015 newspaper article titled "Valdeluz, paradise of divorcees and *mileuristas*"[5] (Villarino 2015). Joaquín had mentioned the article as an uncomfortable episode for the local administration. Of course, Elena did not think of Valdeluz as a paradise. However, she did believe that many found there an opportunity to rebuild their lives in a tranquil environment, even as she talked about how Valdeluz was too small for her and dreamt of retiring in a coastal town. The rest of the women from the association we talked to echoed Elena's sentiments. According to these women, most of whom were freed from the ties of devalorizing property, interrupted urbanization was just what had made Valdeluz a quieter place than expected. None of them seemed to entertain hopes of financial gain from an increase in property prices, as most had experienced non-voluntary relocations and failures of households as shock-absorbers. "If they start building again, we'll leave," Isabel, another retired member of the association told us. Some of the councillors we talked to made small public gestures of support for the association, but in our conversations most of them dismissed its activities as *asistencialista* (welfarist) and of limited interest since they were not directed at the typical Valdeluz household.

The strange non-death of the nuclear family household

Both first- and second-generation residents of Valdeluz have had to make choices under conditions not of their choosing. "The strange non-death"[6] of the normative nuclear family household is a symptom of an attempt to respond to market forces with non-market means. The idiom of the nuclear family at the heart of institutional local politics in Valdeluz emerged as an instrument of the revalorization of property whose financial value was tied to extra-economic considerations and constructed use values. Suburban family lifestyles are both an outcome and a consequence of the "market order of worth" (Davies 2013: 37). The lifestyles attached to the suburban home enter the considerations that determine the financial value of property. They also constitute a bundle of use values that can be accessed through market exchange. Order, predictability and security become scarce goods that are both accessed through and shielded by the exclusionary effects of residential markets. Suburban lifestyles are not a simple set of values that express themselves through consumer choice, but a bundled ideological construct that emerges from the interplay of use value and exchange value. They are produced as part of the everyday functioning of housing markets.

However, as the case of Valdeluz shows, the relationship between the market and these use values is opportunistic and amoral. Under conditions of crisis, market processes are indifferent to the use values that depend upon the exclusionary effects of the pricing mechanism, favouring the incorporation of those whose entrance to suburbanity was previously denied. The political trajectory of first-generation homeowners expressed in the history of 40 Compromisos reveals, however, that the ideological inscriptions favoured by the market remain operative at the household level beyond the boom phase. When the market ceased to act as an exclusionary mechanism, first-generation homeowners became the carriers of a political project that promised to restore both the use value and the exchange value of suburban housing through defining Valdeluz as a town of, and for, the "normal" family household. If first-generation residents are likely to emerge as aligned with an exclusionary politics of growth, the differences between Carmen and Elena serve to remind us that anticapitalist struggle must also seek freedom from the power of capital to define use values in the built environment. The dissolution of expectations of stability tied to homeownership is only the first step in the challenge to define an urban environment that can accommodate an existence beyond what money can buy.

Acknowledgments

Diego Ruedas Torres generously accompanied me as a research assistant in Valdeluz. His help, guidance and insight were indispensable resources for completing the project. I would also like to thank my colleagues in the "Financialisation" research group at the Max Planck Institute for Social Anthropology for their insights and supportive criticism throughout the years, from which this chapter has also benefited. Finally, I would like to thank Marek Mikuš and Petra Rodik for their hard work and generous support as editors.

Notes

1 A neighbours' association is a non-governmental community association composed of residents of a delineated geographic area, potentially legally constituted. Neighbours' associations have been an important actor in Spanish social movements, markedly so during late Francoism and the Transition years.

2 While no exhaustive data is available, the first-generation residents appear to have been exclusively homeowners. The neighbours' association was composed entirely of homeowners. After the collapse of the housing market, renters did begin to appear in Valdeluz, but seem to have remained a minority, mostly on account of the available housing stock being overwhelmingly owned by banks. Conditions imposed by banks favoured the sale of flats and a lease-to-buy rental model, which, according to interviewees, resulted in renters frequently buying the flats they initially rented. Interviews with members of 40 Compromisos indicate a negative valorization of renters who, alongside more dangerous figures such as the squatter, appear as more likely to be disruptive social elements. Recalling a meeting with a dissatisfied renter-resident, Joaquín, former mayor of Valdeluz, remembered asking: "Are you an owner?" (*¿Es usted proprietaria?*).

3 A recurrent advertising slogan for Valdeluz.

4 The mayor of Valdeluz is appointed by the elected councillors.

5 Literally "one who earns a thousand euros" – a term used to designate the precariously employed in the aftermath of the financial crisis.

6 I borrow the wording from Crouch (2011).

References

Beer, A. & Faulkner, D. (2011) *Housing transitions through the life course: aspirations, needs and policy*. Bristol: Policy.

Buier, N. (2020) The second coming of rail: the Spanish high-speed rail-finance complex. *Antipode*. doi: 10.1111/anti.12672.

Buzar, S., Ogden, P. E. & Hall, R. (2005) Households matter: the quiet demography of urban transformation. *Progress in Human Geography* 29(4): 413–436. doi: 10.1191/0309132505ph558oa.

Carter, C. (1995) Nuclear family fall-out: postmodern family culture and the media. In: Adam, B. & Allan, S. (eds.) *Theorizing culture: an interdisciplinary critique after postmodernism*. New York: New York University Press, pp. 186–200.

Charnock, G., Purcell, T. & Ribera-Fumaz, R. (2014) *The limits to capital in Spain: crisis and revolt in the European south*. Basingstoke: Palgrave Macmillan.

Clapham, D. (2002) Housing pathways: a post modern analytical framework. *Housing, Theory and Society* 19(2): 57–68. doi: 10.1080/140360902760385565.

Crouch, C. (2011) *The strange non-death of neo-liberalism*. Cambridge: Polity.

Davies, W. (2013) When is a market not a market? "Exemption", "externality" and "exception" in the case of European state aid rules. *Theory, Culture & Society* 30(2): 32–59. doi: 10.1177/0263276412456567.

Di Feliciantonio, C. & Aalbers, M. B. (2018) The prehistories of neoliberal housing policies in Italy and Spain and their reification in times of crisis. *Housing Policy Debate* 28(1): 135–151. doi: 10.1080/10511482.2016.1276468.

Fraser, N. (2014) Can society be commodities all the way down? Post-Polanyian reflections on capitalist crisis. *Economy and Society* 43(4): 541–558. doi:10.1080/03085147.2014.898822.

Harris, O. (1981) Households as natural units. In: Young, K., Wolkowitz, C. & McCullag, R. (eds.) *Of marriage and the market: women's subordination in international perspective.* London: CSE Books, pp. 48–67.

Harvey, D. (1976) Labor, capital, and class struggle around the built environment in advanced capitalist societies. *Politics & Society* 6(3): 265–295.

Hernández, I. L. & López, E. R. (2010) *Fin de ciclo: financiarización, territorio y sociedad de propietarios en la onda larga del capitalismo hispano (1959–2010).* Madrid: Traficantes de Sueños.

Montgomerie, J. & Tepe-Belfrage, D. (2017) Caring for debts: how the household economy exposes the limits of financialisation. *Critical Sociology* 43(4–5): 653–668. doi: 10.1177/0896920516664962.

Naredo, J. M. & Montiel, A. (2011) *El modelo inmobiliario español y su culminación en el caso valenciano.* Barcelona: Icaria.

Palomera, J. (2014) How did finance infiltrate the world of the urban poor? Homeownership and social fragmentation in a Spanish neighbourhood. *International Journal of Urban and Regional Research* 38(1): 218–235. doi: 10.1111/1468-2427.12055.

Poppe, C., Collard, S. & Jakobsen, T. B. (2016) What has debt got to do with it? The valuation of homeownership in the era of financialization. *Housing, Theory & Society* 33(1): 59–76. doi: 10.1080/14036096.2015.1089934.

Sabaté, I. (2016) Mortgage indebtedness and home repossessions as symptoms of the financialisation of housing provisioning in Spain. *Critique of Anthropology* 36(2): 197–211. doi: 10.1177/0308275X15614636.

Villarino, Ángel (2015) Valdeluz, de ciudad fantasma a paraíso de mileuristas y divorciados. *El Confidencial*, 26 September. Available at: https://www.elconfidencial.com/espana/2015-09-26/valdeluz-de-ciudad-fantasma-a-paraiso-de-mileuristas-y-divorciados_1037338/ [Accessed 15 November 2020].

Weiss, H. (2014) Homeownership in Israel: the social costs of middle-class debt. *Cultural Anthropology* 29(1): 128–149. doi: 10.14506/ca29.1.08.

Wiesel, I. (2014) Mobilities of disadvantage: the housing pathways of low-income Australians. *Urban Studies* 51(2): 319–334. doi: 10.1177/0042098013489739.

Yanagisako, S. J. (1979) Family and household: analysis of domestic groups. *Annual Review of Anthropology* 8: 161–205. doi: 10.1146/annurev.an.08.100179.001113.

Section III

Financialized households in public discourse and culture

5 Household credit in the making and breaking of Greek households

Two decades of financialization

Aimee Placas

Introduction

In recent decades, the Greek economy and society have undergone a tremendous transformation through a process of financialization intimately connected to the economic boom in the late 1990s and the 2000s, followed by what has come to be called generically "the crisis": the government debt crisis and deep recession after 2009 that precipitated social and political crises as well. Household credit was part of this transformation, charting a trajectory from the creation and expansion of the market for consumer credit and mortgage products in the 1990s and early 2000s through its abrupt contraction in the aftermath of the Global Financial Crisis (GFC). The reversal of capital flows (in common with much of the European periphery) and the harsh austerity regime that followed dramatically affected everyday economic life in Greece, with increased labour precarity and high unemployment suddenly making household debt levels unmanageable. The restructuring of Greece's economy under the Troika – the consortium of the International Monetary Fund (IMF), the European Commission (EC) and the European Central Bank (ECB) that decided on the terms of the Greek bailout – underscores Greece's subordinate position in the core-periphery relationships of European capitalism. In response to the growing number of over-indebted households, the Troika consistently opposed pro-debtor interventions of the state and favoured interests of Greek banks (e.g. IMF 2013: 56), many of which are owned by foreign banks from core countries (Kolliopoulos 2020).

My ethnographic research on the usage of household credit during its expansion in the early 2000s and experiences of over-indebted consumers after 2009 revealed the ways in which responsibilities for accrued debts were often distributed among nuclear and extended family members.[1] The Greek state uses the "household" as the main statistical unit for the measurement of levels of indebtedness, defining it as a co-resident group of people whose members pool their resources and consume collectively. Against the background of such technocratic and administrative notions of the household (DeLuca 2017a, 2017b; Guyer 2017: 324; Zaloom 2017; Mikuš and Rodik, this volume), this chapter shows how ideologies and practises of kinship create networks of economic obligation that are not bound by co-residence. Considering the family as something that people "do" rather than what they "are" (Nethercote 2019: 135) and following anthropologists who have recommended that the household not be considered an a priori unit (Harris 1981, Netting et al. 1984), I outline a local normative concept of the household (the *noikokyrió*) that is distinct from the technocratic notion and consider how it shapes the use of credit products and comes into tension with liability for debts. Although household credit products have an individualizing tendency in their form (their use is formally restricted to individuals, and the resulting debt is likewise assigned to individuals), and emerge in a context of neoliberal market deregulation that has itself individualizing effects (Bourdieu 1998), in practice they are caught up in networks of economic interdependence and shared responsibility.

I begin this chapter with a brief background section on the creation of the household credit market in Greece as an outcome of the "market-creating and market-conforming EU regulation in the financial sphere" that transformed the peripheral countries of the European Union (EU) (Rodrigues et al. 2016: 482, see also Bohle 2018; Bródy and Pósfai 2020). The section also introduces the technocratic definition of the household used by the Bank of Greece. I then examine a local conceptualization of the household, the *noikokyrió*, and the tensions between its autonomy and the larger family network in which it is embedded, which exist even as the make-up of the *noikokyrió* changes from its normative co-residential nuclear family form. Ethnographic examples demonstrate how these tensions, and the ideals of the *noikokyrió*, shape credit use and debt obligations. Last, I look at the introduction of Greece's first personal insolvency law for the protection of over-indebted consumers and consider the law's pedagogical nature in shaping understandings of debt repayment. At the same time, I again show how familial ideology encourages responsibility for debts beyond the individual, a fact capitalized upon by both banks and the courts. Following others who have demonstrated how lenders and public institutions mobilize social and familial relationships in Europe's periphery to reduce the risk of their lending practices and secure repayment (Bródy and Pósfai 2020; Kofti 2020; Palomera 2014; Lofranco and Sabaté, this volume), this chapter examines how finance-led capitalism succeeds in tapping into the ambiguous tensions between the individual and the family, autonomy and unity, and the technocratic household and the *noikokyrió* to expand value extraction and the socialization of risks.

A brief background

From the years following World War II and the subsequent Greek Civil War up until 1987, the Greek state heavily regulated the banking system and directed its capacities to economic development in specific sectors. The system included several specialized state-controlled credit institutions, relatively few private banks, and low levels of competition. The state determined interest rates and access to credit, first through the Currency Committee and then the Bank of Greece. The banking system underwent two stages of deregulation in the 1980s. The first stage, after Greece's accession to the EU in 1981, included the abolition of the Currency Committee in 1982, while the second stage, after 1987, saw further liberalization guided by the EU's regulatory framework and the process of the completion of the European Single Market. Importantly, the late 1980s was also the time when the effects of banking deregulation began to be felt at the level of everyday life (Gortsos 1998; Pagoulatos 2003).

It is in the context of this deregulation that the market for household credit as a standard and widely available "bank product" was developed. Households did have access to credit and loans for individual consumption prior to this development – through loans intended for business and industry, credit and instalment sales offered by shops (Arvanitaki and Stratigaki 1994), instalment notes (*grammátia*), mortgages offered as part of a social assistance programme, moneylenders, and employers. However, the new credit products offered by banks greatly increased the availability of credit and its ease of use, moving it into the realm of everyday economic practices. This development is not unique to Greece: a similar shift from a state-controlled financial system to a liberalized one occurred as a requirement of EU integration across Southern and Eastern European peripheries. EU accession and euro adoption enabled substantial inflows of cheap capital that fuelled the expansion of both government and private debt in eurozone peripheries in the 2000s (Bohle 2018; Brissimis et al. 2014; Rodrigues et al. 2016). Households in the periphery thus absorbed both exports and surplus capital from European core countries by utilizing credit products more expensive than equivalents in Western Europe (Bródy and Pósfai 2020). In Greece, household spending was a significant driver of economic growth in the 1990s and 2000s, and the expansion of household credit was central to that spending (Athanassiou 2006, 2012). With the annual increase in loans to resident households peaking at 40.4% in 2001, household credit growth remained steady during those two decades until 2010 when its contraction (still ongoing as of 2019) began (see Figure 5.1).

Many people living in Greece during that time can tell stories of phone calls from banks offering open credit lines ("we have a million drachma in an account under your name, come sign up") or of the ubiquity of the offers of "interest-free instalments" (*átokes dóseis*) through a credit card in retail stores and chains that were themselves multiplying rapidly. Outdoor, print and television advertisements marketing new credit cards, credit lines, "holiday loans", home mortgages and more were inescapable. The retail market was being deregulated at the same time, opening up a new landscape of consumer goods as well as a new geography of spaces where plastic money and credit could be used (see Placas 2018 for the concurrent development of consumer culture in Greece).

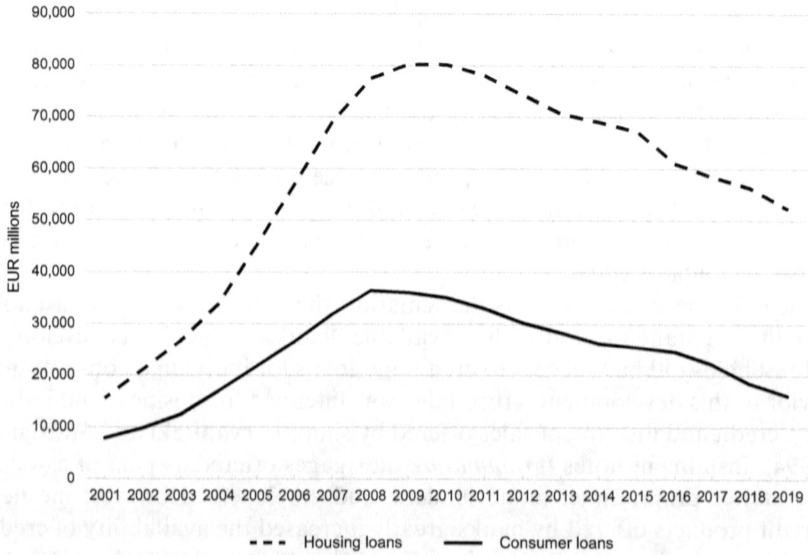

Figure 5.1 Credit to households (end of year, EUR millions), Greece, 2001–2019. Source: Drawn on the basis of data from BoG (2020).

The household credit boom driven by the combination of banking deregulation and later eurozone accession made credit money a significant method for enabling Greek consumer participation in the common market, thus tying EU belonging inextricably to financialization and a speculative imagining of the future. Aitken (2007) has argued that "the economy" is a construction through which we imagine the nation and that popular finance (and the methods by which it is performed) is one of the ways in which this construction is imagined and experienced. Participation in the common market and the eurozone provided a medium for imagining and directly experiencing not just the nation and its economy but also the national economy in relation to other EU national economies, thus exposing inequalities within the supposed union. At the level of everyday life in Greece, the introduction of euro banknotes and coins in January 2002 was certainly a crucial performative point of EU belonging (Malaby 2002). Refrains like "Athens wages, Brussels prices" expressed perceived economic disparities between the periphery and the core of the eurozone and the experience of rising costs of living after the euro adoption. The same is true of the ubiquitous price comparison charts in the Greek press: graphs comparing the price of a cup of coffee in major EU cities and Athens, or the price of a Greek brand of yogurt in multiple countries, with the Greek price being invariably the highest (and the irony of it being cheaper in Germany always highlighted). Wages were stagnant during this period, and the gap between wages and increasing consumption was filled by credit (Pagoulatos 2014).

In order to track the expansion of the household credit market and speak to emerging concerns about over-indebtedness, the Bank of Greece (BoG) began to conduct more detailed survey studies of household borrowing beginning in 2002–2003 (BoG 2003). The surveys measure personal debt and (over-) indebtedness at the level of the household, employing indicators such as outstanding debts per household, ratio of the household's monthly income and loan instalments, and so on. The BoG follows the European System of Accounts in defining households as "small groups of persons who share the same living accommodation, who pool their income and wealth and who consume certain types of goods and services collectively, mainly housing and food" (Eurostat 2013: 45).[2] Accordingly, the household here is a collective economic and social endeavour, with the assumption that the walls that create the residence also create that collectivity and bound it (and bind it) in a meaningful way. Meanwhile, the household as an analytical concept has been thoroughly critiqued for decades, with a focus on its naturalization through its association with the "family" (and their common treatment as synonyms; Harris 1981). Moreover, it has been pointed out that the normative nuclear family household tends to influence the methodology of studying households (VanEvery 1999), even as it declines as an actually existing household form (Buzar et al. 2005). Two insights of these critiques are particularly relevant to this chapter. The first is Jane Guyer's (1981: 98) observation that "individuals can exercise rights and be subject to obligations which are normally thought of as economic beyond the household in which they live." The second is the argument that boundaries of the collective endeavour that supports those who reside together in a "household" cannot be assumed a priori (Nethercote 2019; Netting et al. 1984; Lofranco, and Sabaté, this volume). The ethnographic exploration of household indebtedness I offer in this chapter allows us to see the ways in which economic obligations may be shared on a basis other than co-residence, resulting in a misalignment between the technocratic definition of the household and the household-in-practice.

At the same time, however, the household – as a co-residential nuclear family unit – does function as an ideal form in Greece, and the ideals associated with that form continue to influence practices even as actual household formations become increasingly diverse. In discussing the household as a normative ideal, with a specific history and cultural connotations, I will use the Greek term *noikokyrió*. However, the reader will likely notice commonalities of familial ideologies between the *noikokyrió* in Greece and other cultural contexts in the European periphery (Allen et al. 2004; Bohle 2018; Kováts 2020), which will also resonate with other chapters of this volume.

The noikokyrió

The Greek normative concept of the household (*noikokyrió*) intersects significantly with local moral discourses about the family and finance. The word *noikokyrió* differs from the everyday term *spíti* (house/home), and *spíti*'s more formal synonym *oíkos*, which also implies both residence and family (for a consideration of *oíkos* in relation to family and debt, see Kofti 2020). *Noikokyrió* carries an explicit idea of a shared residence that encompasses dimensions of individual membership of the co-resident group and the members' activity oriented to the group. Additional related words inform its cultural connotations: *noikokýris* and *noikokyrá* are the master and mistress of the house, respectively, gendered terms that relate to an understanding of the household as a heterosexual project with biological reproductive goals, and *noikokyrévo* (verb) and *noikokyreméno* (adjective) both relate to putting things in order, whether they be physical objects, tasks or economic resources.

While the household is and was used as a technocratic unit of measurement in Greece by other social science discourses and the state, as described above, there is extensive anthropological literature on its functioning as a hegemonic form of domestic social organization underpinned by ideologies of gender, sexuality and social reproduction, and as a significant site in the construction of selfhood (Παπαταξιάρχης 2005).[3] Thus, anthropology in Greece has rarely treated the *noikokyrió* simply as a stable metric for counting co-residential, resource-pooling units. Instead, post-war[4] anthropologists have examined the concept as a nexus of normative and moral values about the gendered roles of married men and women, seen as cooperating in the heteronormative reproductive project of running a home and producing children who must then be equipped with tools for their own success. This necessarily includes the fraught transition from the *noikokyrió* of one's childhood to establishing one's own household and thereby attaining adulthood. Changes in the Greek society in recent decades, including challenges to established gender roles and the ideology of marriage, as well as the social and legal recognition of same-sex relationships, have created conditions for the rise in number of other forms of households, such as single, single-parent, unmarried and same-sex households, as well as households that break from kinship completely in their construction (see Yannakopoulos 2009 on the latter). Nevertheless, certain elements of the ideology of the *noikokyrió* persist and continue to be significant factors in the organization of social life.

At the same time, Papataxiarchis (2013) reminds us that the normative model of the *noikokyrió* is far from being an organic expression of timeless cultural ideals. Just as the nuclear family emerged as a relatively recent, nineteenth-century norm elsewhere in Europe (Carter 1995), the *noikokyrió* has been strongly shaped by an "external discipline 'from above'" from the late-nineteenth and early-twentieth century as both the state and the Greek Orthodox Church worked to assert a model of reproduction based on marriage and neolocality (Papataxiarchis 2013: 221). The contemporary model of the *noikokyrió*, the heterosexual nuclear family household formed towards reproductive goals, had become fully established as a "criterion of 'being modern'" (Papataxiarchis 2013: 218) as recently as the post-Junta period of the late 1970s through the 1990s. Adulthood was linked inextricably to marriage, having children and the establishment of a new autonomous household, and this model spread from urban elites to rural areas and all social classes (Loizos and Papataxiarchis 1991; see also Paxson 2004 and Halkias 2004 on the strong linkage between adulthood, marriage and parenthood).[5]

The *noikokyrió* is thereby a familial collective enterprise where every member contributes to its well-being and where success and failure are results of corporate endeavour. Anthropologists have repeatedly demonstrated that the collective self-interest (*symféron*) of the *noikokyrió* is meant to supersede individual concerns, as a result of which concepts of the self that are tied to exclusively individual goals, failures and accomplishments are inadequate for understanding selfhood in this cultural context (Hirschon 1989: 141; Kirtsoglou 2004: 107; Salamone and Stanton 1986: 99). The collective self-interest in the *noikokyrió* is the main driver of decisions regarding labour, consumption, marriage, the sharing of information and so on (Du Boulay 1974; Theodossopoulos 2003). There is an echo here of the technocratic definition of the household, which however reifies this project into a temporally static concept rather than one grounded in social reproduction and potential success or failure.

The technocratic household is also spatially bounded in a way that the *noikokyrió* is not. The collective economic endeavour of the *noikokyrió* is embedded in a broader collective endeavour of the family that is not limited to co-residence. Most significant here is the tension between the ideal autonomy of the *noikokyrió* and its economic rights and obligations that extend beyond the *noikokyrió* along kinship lines.[6] These concerns are common themes in the anthropology of Greece, but Vlahoutsikou and Baharopoulou-Kouli offer a particularly detailed discussion of these conflicts in their ethnographic account of the transition from a patrilocal to neolocal residence pattern in a village on the rural mainland (Βλαχούτσικου and Μπαχαροπούλου-Κούλη 1991). They discuss "intergenerational unity" as a system of expectations and ideals where new nuclear family households have an economy intertwined with the economy of the paternal household (Βλαχούτσικου and Μπαχαροπούλου-Κούλη 1991: 97). Many ethnographies of Greece from the 1980s and the 1990s describe how the building and furnishing of a new *noikokyrió* relied on direct assistance from parents of the newlyweds, but the authors of this ethnographic work show that this assistance is rejected tactically. The goal of the new bride to attain autonomy is pitted against the goals of her mother-in-law for unity (and with it economic control), and the bride asserts her own control over the household by making consumption choices for the household space autonomously instead of seeking intergenerational consensus. Consumption is the means through which the desire for autonomy shapes the reproduction of the *noikokyrió*.

Building on these observations, one could expect the processes of household financialization to be caught up in similar negotiations between ideals of autonomy and extended family unity. Consumer credit provides individuals expanded access to financial resources for the establishment and maintenance of their *noikokyrió*, whether it be founded through a new marriage or otherwise (as is increasingly the case). Household credit products allow for the expression of the ideal of household autonomy, particularly in situations where economic circumstances forestall this autonomy. At the same time, these credit and loan products, ostensibly belonging to specific individuals and attributed to specific households in state statistics, are caught up in networks of familial obligation that extend beyond the individual as well as beyond the *noikokyrió*. The autonomy of the household is in tension with another ideology of kinship: that of economic and material support between generations and along bilateral kinship lines in times of need. This was a consistent theme in my research into household finances and debt in the early 2000s, and again after 2009 as my interlocutors frequently noted either receiving or giving support from/to extended family members they did not live with, which was just as likely to be accompanied by complaints and criticism as by positive evaluation. What follows are several ethnographic vignettes that flesh out the contradiction between credit (which belongs to the borrower) and the resulting debt (where responsibility extends beyond that borrower).

Collective responsibility for debt

The story of Kimon's debt begins with a divorce. The home he lived in with his wife belonged to her (as part of her dowry, as he himself put it, although dowry as a legal category of property transmission had been eradicated almost 20 years earlier), and their separation meant that he moved out and rented an apartment. The financial difficulties of his new situation soon led him into credit card debt: €25,000 spent in one year on furnishing his apartment, a car, cash withdrawals to pay his rent when his pay cheque was not enough, restaurants when he was not in the mood for the cooked food his mother (a widow) sent over and filled his freezer with, and so on. I met and interviewed Kimon for the first time in 2004, just when he was beginning to shop around for a consolidation loan[7] because he could not afford to make the minimum monthly payments on all the cards that he owned. He was a professional in his early 30s whose former steady employment had become more sporadic. When I interviewed him, I noted that his mother made him meals and sent over her cleaner to clean his home as well; I asked him what she thought about his debt. He told me that he had largely managed to keep it from her. "She found a bill once when she was here and insisted on paying it" (with a sarcastic emphasis on the word "found", implying some sort of snooping on her part). Why not tell her the whole amount of his debt, since he was having trouble keeping up with his payments? Because she would insist on repaying it, because it would cause a huge fight between them, because she already thinks he is bad with money, because she gives him money regularly to help him out and he does not want that to stop, and because she thinks owing money is really, really bad. A consolidation loan would be better; he could continue repaying it in smaller instalments every month, and the money she was already giving him to help him out could go towards repayment. She would not need to know.

I ran into Kimon a month or two later, and he told me he had a story for me. His mom found out about the consolidation loan he had eventually taken. There was some sort of address mix-up (he was unclear on this point), his bank mail went to her house, and she opened it. She was furious. Beyond furious: she threatened to cut him off financially, told him that he would "ruin her name" with his actions, and that the only reason that the bank gave him a loan was because she was herself a good customer there and thus he used her without telling her.[8] He should have told her about it; he should have told her before it got out of control; he should have sought her advice and help. "She has to be the one that saves me. I took away her right to yell at me and then fix everything for me."

Another interlocutor in his 40s who worked in the media, Nikos, had received a call from a bank for a Nikolaos Konstantinidis to query him about problems with the repayment of his loan. However, Nikos had no loan at that bank. "Is this Nikolaos Konstantinidis, son of Dimitris?" "No, this is Nikolaos Konstantinidis, son of Thanassis." "Oh, we're sorry, our mistake." When Nikos told me this story, he looked at me expectantly, as if he had delivered a punchline in the end. I made it clear that I did not get it. He laughed: "You see, they did it on purpose. I am his cousin." Family naming traditions in much of Greece give first-born sons the given name of their paternal grandfather, meaning that if that grandfather had multiple sons who then had their own sons, there would be a crop of male cousins with the same name, distinguishable from each other only because formal paperwork also states one's father's name. His wife laughed even harder: "It was my bank, too!" She happened to be an employee of the bank, which lends some weight to their interpretation of this "mistake" as purposeful. What they implied was social shaming within the extended family network as a debt collection technique. In the case of another interlocutor, a man in his late 20s who lived with his parents, family pressure was more direct: the bank called the house and when his mother answered the phone, they informed her that he was behind in his credit card payments. Which, of course, she paid immediately.

These examples typify the ways in which the individualizing aspects of consumer credit are subject to a larger framework of financial responsibility both within and beyond the *noikokyrió*. By mobilizing these norms and practices, actors insert household credit into pre-existing social relations. Even privacy built into the billing and servicing of household credit is subject to circumvention by family members and creditors seeking to collect debts. We see here a disjunction between a technocratic definition of privacy (personal bank information belongs to the individual alone) and an ethic of shared concern; this disjunction is being mobilized towards the collection of debts.

Maintaining autonomy through credit

In my fieldwork, I accidentally stumbled upon another subset of heavy borrowers: divorced or widowed women with children. Within the pool of individuals I spoke with during the years of credit expansion, those least able to keep up with their debts on their own fell into this group. These women had stable, solidly middle-class jobs as civil servants, office workers and so on. They were able to service their debts as far as their banks were concerned, but none of them made these payments solely from their own earnings or from support payments from their ex-partners; each of them had significant financial assistance from a sibling or a parent.

At the same time, all of these women ran their own *noikokyrió*. They lived alone with their children, in some cases near to the rest of their family, in other cases not. Each used a credit card for everyday purchases, and several had taken out consumer loans to repay their card debts when they maxed out their cards. And each of them consistently received financial assistance from other family members specifically to pay back their card debts and loans. This assistance was quite substantial in some cases – 25–50% of the woman's salary – and in all cases it was ongoing. Thus, the everyday running of the household is managed here by its female head who uses credit products to facilitate the daily practices of provisioning and care. Part of the logic derives from the ideology of the autonomous *noikokyrió* adapted to the more recent reality of women's wage labour. The female head of the single-parent household bears the responsibilities of both *noikokýris* and *noikokyrá* (master and mistress of the house), while structural changes in the labour market have expanded the gendered role of *noikokyrá* (Lazaridis 2000).

In my interviews with these women, most of our talk about their debt led them directly to discussing their children:

> When they [her college-age sons] are out with me, they know how I am. "Come on, mom, it's six interest-free instalments!" It doesn't seem like that much then, you have half a year to pay it off, but of course we do it over and over. Clothes, clothes, shoes. They have to have them, so what can I do?

The frequency of this practice – using interest-free instalments – can be only partially explained by the rationale of saving money; as the quote above implies and discussions with my research participants made clear, the resulting debt is usually not paid off before the interest-free period ends. The use of credit allows the female household head to defer external financial assistance from her family to the exceptional (the moment when bills get too high and unmanageable) instead of the everyday (say, assistance with paying monthly bills or money given ahead of necessary purchases). The credit is under her control, and consumption decisions under her authority;

the debt is separate, shared as a fait accompli that needs resolution. This method of running the household is more expensive, with the added cost of high interest accumulated through credit cards and consumer loans (see also the discussion on "defensive consumption" in Mikuš and Rodik, this volume). The performance of autonomy is an important component, and the space of contradiction between autonomy and economic circumstance is filled by techniques of managing credit and debt.

Credit expansion in Greece allowed for the establishment of new households and consumption practices that would have exceeded the resources available through intergenerational assistance, and the cultural significance of autonomy suggests that credit has been used also to disentangle the ties of intergenerational unity. At the same time, the tensions between autonomy and intergenerational support are renegotiated around the issue of debt; credit affects the balance between autonomy and intergenerational unity but not in a unidirectional or constant manner. The financialization of these new households, established with the same expectations of economic growth that had been prevalent throughout the entire post-war era, would make them particularly vulnerable when that growth ended after 2009.

Protecting the household in crisis

The *noikokyrió* in its material instantiation as the physical home also features importantly in the development of the household credit market. This section looks at the development of Greece's first personal insolvency law – Law 3869/2010, commonly known as the Katseli law (after the MP who proposed it). We again find that family obligation is mobilized to maximize repayment from defaulted debtors, but here in the setting of neoliberal reforms and austerity that have decimated the state's protections for its citizens. While the state has seized on the law's implementation to position itself as the protector of the Greek family, the law is also a tool for training citizens to develop a "payment culture" (IMF 2013: 56) where state intervention in consumer over-indebtedness is limited.

By the time that the GFC was underway in 2008, total credit to households in Greece had reached 55.7% of the GDP, nearly the eurozone average of 60.7% (BIS 2020). Household debt burden, as expressed by the share of debt in net disposable income, has continued to increase for some years after the GFC and has still not returned to pre-crisis levels (see Figure 5.2). What to do about over-indebted households had thus emerged as a burning policy concern, with no insolvency protections in place for such consumers despite the significant growth in the household credit market. Other countries in Europe that had developed household credit markets earlier than Greece have found it necessary to put in place personal (consumer) insolvency and debtor protection laws from the 1980s onward. The European perception of over-indebtedness as a serious social and economic problem emerged in the context of a proliferation of credit products on offer and, in some cases, a

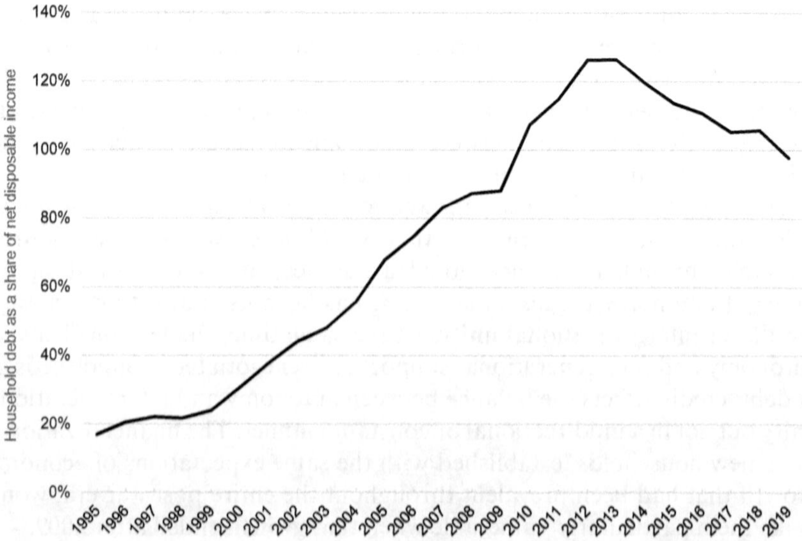

Figure 5.2 Household debt as a share of net disposable income, Greece, 1995–2019.
Source: Drawn on the basis of data from OECD (2020).

weakening of the welfare state (Kilborn 2008). These laws (typified by Germany's consumer insolvency law, which has served as the model for others) most often allow the court to determine a monthly repayment plan based on the debtor's financial capacity that the debtor must follow for a set number of years; if they do, the remaining debt is discharged. This required waiting period of "good behaviour", usually coupled with the requirement to search for employment, highlights the stress on personal responsibility typical for a neoliberal approach to conceptualizing the consumer (Ramsay 2015: 403; see also a similar discussion on the self-responsible subject encouraged through consumer protection law in the Czech Republic in Hoření Samec, this volume).

George Papandreou, then head of the Panhellenic Socialist Party (PASOK, an opposition party at the time), promised to adopt such a law in the campaign for the 2009 elections, which PASOK won. By the time the PASOK government passed the law in 2010, Greece fell under the austerity regime of the Troika (the EC, ECB and IMF). Household indebtedness at that point had increased by 348% from its 2002 levels (Manou et al. 2019: 12). The Katseli law was thus adopted in a moment of emergency and exception. This period after the GFC saw a number of new protections for over-indebted consumers and relief programmes for individuals facing insolvency in European countries (Ramsay 2015). The Greek law shares the basic form of most personal insolvency laws in the EU as described above, but with the addition of a provision that was less common among equivalent EU laws at the time: while the defaulted debtor's real estate must be generally sold off towards repaying their debts, their primary residence (real estate serving as their main home) can be saved through a restructuring of the repayment plan.[9]A repayment plan that allows the debtor to keep their home is a testament to the deep significance of the *noikokyrió* for the construction of both the Greek family and personhood, as discussed above, as well as to the very high rates of homeownership in the country; the mortgage boom that enabled younger generations to participate in homeownership, despite increasing prices (with the latter two features typical to the European periphery at large; see Bohle 2018); and, finally, the massive economic impact that large numbers of foreclosures would cause. It was estimated that there were 100,000 applications for protection under the Katseli law pending in the courts as of March 2014 (Mentis and Pantazatou 2015: 39); in the fall of 2018, there were over 135,000 pending cases (Θεοδωρόπουλος 2018).

The protection of the primary home reflects the deeply symbolic place where real estate, family wealth and security intertwine. While the over-indebted Greek citizen can be locally coded as a victim of the crisis as well as its perpetrator ("conspicuous consumption" is an easy target of criticism, and the "profligate" Greek state gets written small on the person; see also Kofti 2020), the spectre of bank foreclosures on family homes resonates in potentially dangerous ways. The household debt crisis unfolded against the backdrop of the liquidation of state assets and the sale of "public patrimony" as heavily contested requirements of Troika-mandated austerity measures. A strong connection, which equates local banks with the IMF and the ECB, has emerged between the idea of "the banks" requiring the sale of the individual property of Greeks and "the banks" requiring the sale of collective property of the Greek people. Speculations about an imminent sale of archaeological sites, islands and other particularly symbolically "Greek" spaces cropped up everywhere from legitimate news sources to rampant memes. The emic conceptual and moral linkages between the family, the residence and the *noikokyrió* would make widespread foreclosures read as one further indignity gone too far: the dissolution of the family and the destruction of the house and the *noikokyrió* it enables as symbols of basic dignity and selfhood.

The Katseli law as a lesson in neoliberalism

The passage of the Katseli law, for all of its protective potential, can also be seen as a pedagogical moment in the financialization of the household. When Papandreou proposed a law protecting the over-indebted in the 2009 election campaign, the governing party criticized this promise as an irresponsible act of "populism". This critique gained some weight by evoking the Greek history of politicized debt forgiveness, reframing what Papandreou put forward as a necessary response to increased household over-indebtedness into an old politicians' trick aimed at winning votes. This form of debt forgiveness was practiced in the latter half of the twentieth century when banks were state-controlled and their lending was often a process based on clientelistic exchange of favours instead of profit logic and credit risk assessment. The government carried out several sweeping rounds of debt forgiveness through the Agricultural Bank of Greece in the run-up to elections; these were formally development rather than consumer loans, which however had been used for purposes that extended to households (Papataxiarchis 1999). Condemning the Katseli law as populist and an attempt to buy votes placed it firmly within this history.[10]

Some lawyers representing applicants for personal insolvency and debtor protection under the Katseli law – specialists in consumer protection issues for whom this became the chief agenda after 2010 – expressed to me impatience and frustration over clients who expected to get their debts written-off easily and without a process. Lawyers who had given talks for the general public about the Katseli law and how it worked relayed the same experience. The law has seen numerous revisions since it was put into effect, some seeking to increase its effectiveness and scope (such as making the process faster or allowing for the incorporation of commercial loans together with personal ones; EC 2020; Mouzouraki 2012), others toughening rules intended to prevent strategic defaults, a particular concern of the IMF, the ECB and Greek banks (Ramsay 2015: 218) as well as credit rating agencies (Moody's 2020). The development of personal insolvency laws in Europe has been accompanied by recurrent concerns about "moral hazard" created by debt forgiveness and a reticence towards write-offs of outstanding debt. These laws uphold the hegemonic norm that debts must be paid, promoting a "payment culture" without "undermining borrower repayment behavior" (IMF 2013: 55) while placing a limit on suffering and deprivation that this ideal can command. Through the restructured repayment plan, they create a process of a strict financial discipline by which forgiveness can be earned, placing responsibility for debts firmly on the debtor.[11] In practice, however, this neoliberal model of individual responsibility triggers corporate familial responsibility, turning family obligation into a conduit of financial extraction.

In conversations I had with individuals facing this process, and with lawyers discussing their experiences with clients, it was often the case that the financial resources of the extended family had been exhausted by the time the individual sought insolvency and protection under the Katseli law. The loss of income and the increased taxation in the conditions of recession and austerity depleted everyone's ability to assist others. In her recent ethnographic study of the implementation of the Katseli law in courts in Thessaloniki, Kofti (2020: 372) notes that the judges she observed evoked familial support in two contradictory ways: asking applicants about relatives of the members of their household to see if they were available to offer financial assistance, but criticizing applicants as irresponsible if they mentioned supporting such family members. In the proceedings I have followed in Athens, while the debt belonged to the individual applicant, the court might look at all members of their household (as resources or drains on resources) to calculate how much they could afford to repay monthly; the debt may have been individual, but the repayment restructuring considered the household. The court thus becomes another point at which creditors and state apparatuses enforcing legally binding credit/debt relations capitalize on the ambiguity of familial obligation and its tension with autonomy, utilizing it towards extraction when possible but rejecting it when it threatens those ends.

The significance of the household as a concept deeply connected to the construction that is "the Greek family" plays a role in the development of this law and its instantiation in courts. With it, the state can posit itself as the protector of the Greek family and home, but only to a degree; debtor protection, with its positive and negative outcomes, is added on as one more technique through which the financialized household manages its finances and engages with the future. Public discussions of the Katseli law become a medium through which the population understands a new reality: forgiveness of debts to banks is no longer a gift that can be granted by the state. Furthermore, the law lays bare the fact that financial institutions are not subject to the democratic process (i.e. elections), as reforms to the law often came through IMF/Troika requirements (Ramsay 2015: 395); this is particularly relevant in an era when the sovereignty of the national economy had been surrendered to the Troika's management. Adkins (2018: 73) argues that under finance-led capitalism, public policies in relation to (over-) indebted households do not seek to reduce their exposure to debt and risk but rather ensure that they are able to "withstand and tolerate" the former. What we find in Greece – and as this volume shows, in other countries of the European periphery as well – is the mobilization of familial obligation as an additional instrument for increasing households' "tolerance" of their debts and risks.

Conclusions

Nethercote (2019: 134) notes that there is frequently an assumption that capitalism is "inherently destructive" to the bonds of the family. It is certainly the case that financialized capitalism and neoliberal policies in Greece have wrought changes in the ways in which the family and co-residence intersect, with ever-increasing numbers of adult children living with parents, the rejection of inherited properties burdened with debt (Knight 2018), a tendency of popular culture to depict the home as a space of violence and conflict (Aleksić 2016) and much more. Indeed, if we consider the family as something people *do* rather than what they are, inability to economically assist one's family according to the ideologies of familial support may challenge one's selfhood as a good parent, sibling, child and so on. What an analysis of the sharing of debt in Greece shows us, however, is that neoliberal capitalism harnesses the bonds of the family to maximize value extraction whenever possible. After using credit to fill the gap between wages and consumption, debtors often end up turning to familial ties to avoid financial ruin from the resulting debt. The family is not "used" in this way only by debtors; it is used by banks, by courts, by the state. The economic crisis in Greece has exposed rather than caused the contemporary tensions of the family as a biopolitical entity, as Papanikolaou argues in his text on the changes surrounding this "sacred" institution (Παπανικολάου 2018). Its ideologies of obligation and responsibility have been intensified in the credit bust period, but as I have shown above, they had been contributing to and shaping household financialization already during the boom.

As we can see from some of the other chapters in this volume, the housing and welfare regime in Greece is similar to other economies in Europe's periphery in significant ways, one of them being familial tendencies and their role in household financialization. Familialism has been framed as a factor that inhibits economic development (Katrougalos and Lazaridis 2003; Liagouras 2019). However, a close analysis of the actual workings of households and their dynamic boundaries shows that kinship networks can function as significant sites of profit extraction in an expanding (and collapsing) household credit market, as seen in this chapter, as well as this volume's chapters by Sabaté and Lofranco. Although developments in these markets, such as the adoption of the Katseli law on personal insolvency, indicate state investment in a formulation of neoliberal subjects who successfully internalize responsibility for their economic welfare, in practice familialism continues to be put to work to reduce creditors' exposure to non-repayment.

Acknowledgements

My fieldwork on the development of consumer credit market in 2001–2004 was supported by a grant from the National Science Foundation. During my fieldwork on consumer over-indebtedness in 2011–2012, I received significant help from one of the more active consumer protection associations in making contacts; I will keep this organization anonymous but owe them a great deal for their expertise and assistance. I would also like to thank Marek Mikuš, Petra Rodik and Tracey Rosen for their significant feedback on this chapter.

Notes

1 I conducted fieldwork on the development of the market for consumer credit in Athens intensively in 2001–2002 and more sporadically in 2003–2004. I did further systematic fieldwork focussing on over-indebtedness related to household credit in 2011–2012. All names for interlocutors used in the chapter are pseudonyms.

2 More recent BoG surveys (after 2009) follow the methodological framework of the Eurosystem's Household Finance and Consumption Survey (EHFCN 2013) in order to produce data comparable at the EU level. They seem to differ from

the earlier surveys in only requiring a household representative (rather than each household member) to respond to the survey but not in the definition of the household.

3 Anthropologist Evthymios Papataxiarchis (2013) points out that anthropological discussions of the household in Greece have benefitted from the fact that the increased attention to the economic realm of everyday life in Greek ethnography occurred concurrently with the "cultural turn" in anthropology, and thus this economic term was considered in its emic capacity (and complemented by a strong feminist deconstruction that predated the cultural turn).

4 In the Greek context, "post-war" refers to the period after the end of the Greek Civil War in 1949.

5 Much has also been written about the gendered ideals of the heads of the *noikokyrió*, the *noikokýris* and *noikokyrá* (e.g. Salamone and Stanton 1986, among many others), but limitations of space keep me from a longer discussion on gender here.

6 My chapter neglects other significant networks of obligation and assistance, like those of friendship or politics. See Kofti (2020) for an analysis of financial assistance in the face of debt that includes friendship.

7 A consolidation loan allows the debtor to repay their existing debts towards multiple creditors and replace them with a single new loan. Some ads for these loans appeal to an emotional association with the orderly household by using the adjective *noikokyreména* (in order, orderly, organized) with ad copy such as "All in one, in order."

8 Kimon would have qualified for the loan on his own, but his mother was more familiar with the Greek banking of the pre-deregulation era where personal relationships played a greater role in arranging loans.

9 See Ramsay (2015) for a comparison of protections for the primary residence and restructuring mortgage debt among European countries. Mouzouraki (2012) gives a detailed explanation of how the exemption for the primary home functions in the Katseli law. Mentis and Pantazatou (2015) offer a detailed history and evaluation of the law's early development and structure.

10 Ramsay addresses the potential "populism" of such laws as a worry of the IMF:

> An early IMF paper by Luc Laeven and Thomas Laryea in 2009 noted that governments might develop household debt restructuring based on 'social considerations' but 'the design of … debt restructuring programs should be based on sound economic principles'. This seems to reflect a fear of populism distorting political decision-making in a crisis.
>
> (Ramsay 2015: 404)

11 On several occasions during the peak of the economic crisis and again in 2020 in response to the COVID-19 pandemic, limited emergency measures for protecting homes from foreclosure – both general moratoria and payment subsidies – have also gone into effect as temporary measures that supplement the Katseli law. However, one of the purposes of consumer insolvency laws is to limit such direct interventions from the state as acts that undermine "credit discipline" (Liu and Rosenberg 2013: 17).

References

Adkins, L. (2018) *The time of money*. Stanford: Stanford University Press.

Aitken, R. (2007) *Performing capital: toward a cultural economy of popular and global finance*. New York: Palgrave Macmillan.

Aleksić, T. (2016) Sex, violence, dogs and the impossibility of escape: why contemporary Greek film is so focused on family. *Journal of Greek Media & Culture* 2(2): 155–171. doi: 10.1386/jgmc.2.2.155_1.

Allen, J., Barlow, J., Leal, J., Maloutas, T. & Padovani, L., eds. (2004) *Housing and welfare in Southern Europe*. Oxford: Blackwell.

Arvanitaki, K. & Stratigaki, M. (1994) Computerization in Greek banking: the gendering of payment and practices. In: Cockburn, C. & First-Dilic, R. (eds.) *Bringing technology home: gender and technology in a changing Europe*. Buckingham: Open University Press, pp. 59–77.

Athanassiou, E. (2006) Prospects of household borrowing in Greece and their importance for growth. Centre of Planning and Economic Research (KEPE) Discussion Paper 84. Available from: https://www.kepe.gr/pdf/D.P/dp_84A.pdf [Accessed 15 October 2020].

Athanassiou, E. (2012) Household debt and domestic demand: Greece versus other euro zone economies. *International Journal of Business & Social Science* 3(10): 157–166. Available from: http://www.ijbssnet.com/journals/Vol_3_No_10_Special_Issue_May_2012/16.pdf [Accessed 15 October 2020].

BIS (2020) Total credit to households. BIS Statistics Explorer (database). Available from: https://stats.bis.org/statx/srs/table/f3.1 [Accessed 11 November 2020].

BoG (2003) *Report on monetary policy 2002–2003*. Athens: Bank of Greece.

BoG (2020) Credit to domestic non-MFI residents by domestic MFIs excluding the Bank of Greece (table). Available from https://www.bankofgreece.gr/en/statistics/monetary-and-banking-statistics/credit-aggregates [Accessed 11 November 2020].

Bohle, D. (2018) Mortgaging Europe's periphery. *Studies in Comparative International Development* 53(2): 196–217. doi: 10.1007/s12116-018-9260-7.

Bourdieu, P. (1998) The essence of neoliberalism: what is neoliberalism? A programme for destroying collective structures which may impede pure market logic. *Le Monde diplomatique*, December. Available from: https://mondediplo.com/1998/12/08bourdieu [Accessed 11 September 2020].

Brissimis, S. N., Garganas, E. N. & Hall, S. G. (2014) Consumer credit in an era of financial liberalization: an overreaction to repressed demand? *Applied Economics* 46(2): 139–152. doi: 10.1080/00036846.2013.835482.

Bródy, L. S. & Pósfai, Z. (2020) *Household debt on the peripheries of Europe: new constellations since 2008*. Periféria Policy and Research Center Working Paper 3. Available from: https://www.periferiacenter.com/periferia-working-papers [Accessed 15 October 2020].

Buzar, S., Ogden, P. E. & Hall, R. (2005) Households matter: the quiet demography of urban transformation. *Progress in Human Geography* 29(4): 413–436. doi: 10.1191/0309132505ph558oa.

Carter, C. (1995) Nuclear family fall-out: postmodern family culture and the media. In: Adam, B. & Allan, S. (eds.) *Theorizing culture: an interdisciplinary critique after postmodernism*. London: UCL Press, pp. 186–200.

DeLuca, E. (2017a) The household. *Cultural Anthropology* website, August 4. Available from: https://culanth.org/fieldsights/1125-the-household [Accessed 8 September 2020].

DeLuca, E. (2017b) Transition. *Cultural Anthropology* website, August 14. Available from: https://culanth.org/fieldsights/1164-transition [Accessed 8 September 2020].

Du Boulay, J. (1974) *Portrait of a Greek mountain village*. Oxford: Clarendon Press.

EC (2020) Enhanced surveillance report – Greece, May 2020. European Commission Institutional Paper 127. doi: 10.2765/329491.

EHFCN (2013) The Eurosystem household finance and consumption survey: methodological report for the first wave. European Central Bank Statistics Paper Series 1. Available from: https://www.ecb.europa.eu/pub/pdf/scpsps/ecbsp1en.pdf [Accessed 15 October 2020].

Eurostat (2013) *European system of accounts: ESA 2010*. Brussels: European Commission. doi: 10.2785/16644.

Gortsos, C. (1998) *The Greek banking system*. Athens: Ant. N. Sakkoulas.

Guyer, J. I. (1981) Household and community in African studies. *African Studies Review* 24(2/3): 87–137. doi: 10.2307/523903.

Guyer, J. I. (2017) Survivals as infrastructure: twenty-first-century struggles with household and family in formal computations. In: Harvey, P., Jensen, C. B. & Morita, A. (eds.) *Infrastructures and social complexity: a companion*. Abingdon: Routledge, pp. 323–334.

Halkias, A. (2004) *The empty cradle of democracy: sex, abortion, and nationalism in modern Greece*. Durham: Duke University Press.

Harris, O. (1981) Households as natural units. In: Young, K., Wolkowitz, C. & McCullagh, R. (eds.) *Of marriage and the market: women's subordination in international perspective*. London: CSE Books, pp. 49–68.

Hirschon, R. (1989) *Heirs of the Greek catastrophe: the social life of Asia Minor refugees in Piraeus*. Oxford: Clarendon.

IMF (2013) Greece: third review under the extended arrangement under the extended fund facility. International Monetary Fund Country Report 13/153. Available from: https://www.imf.org/en/Publications/CR/Issues/2016/12/31/Greece-Third-Review-Under-the-Extended-Arrangement-Under-the-Extended-Fund-Facility-Staff-40636 [Accessed 15 October 2020].

Katrougalos, G. & Lazaridis, G. (2003) *Southern European welfare states: problems, challenges, and prospects*. New York: Palgrave Macmillan.

Kilborn, J. J. (2008) Comparative cause and effect: consumer insolvency and the eroding social safety net. *Columbia Journal of European Law* 14 (3): 563–596. Available from: https://www.iiiglobal.org/node/2022 [Accessed 15 October 2020].

Kirtsoglou, E. (2004) *For the love of women: gender, identity and same-sex relations in a Greek provincial town*. London: Routledge.

Knight, D. (2018) The desire for disinheritance in austerity Greece. *Focaal* 80: 30–42. doi: 10.3167/fcl.2018.800103.

Kofti, D. (2020) Financialized kinship and challenges for the Greek oikos. In: Hann, C. M. & Kalb, D. (eds.) *Financialization: relational approaches*. New York: Berghahn, pp. 360–384.

Kolliopoulos, A. (2020) Bank recapitalizations in Greece: from state-led bailouts to the ownership transfer of banks to foreign hands. Hellenic Foundation for European & Foreign Policy (ELIAMEP) Working Paper 112/2020. Available from: https://www.eliamep.gr/en/publication/bank-recapitalizations-in-greece-from-state-led-bailouts-to-the-ownership-transfer-of-banks-to-foreign-hands/ [Accessed 15 October 2020].

Kováts, B. (2020) Is there a core-semiperiphery division in housing? Applying world-systems theory in European comparative housing research. *Housing, Theory and Society*. doi: 10.1080/14036096.2020.1813801.

Lazaridis, G. (2000) Filipino and Albanian women migrant workers in Greece: multiple layers of oppression. In: Anthias, F. & Lazaridis, G. (eds.) *Gender and migration in Southern Europe: women on the move*. Oxford: Berg, pp. 49–80.

Liagouras, G. (2019) On the social origins of economic divergence: familism, business and state in Greece. *Western European Politics* 42(5): 1115–1139. doi: 10.1080/01402382.2018.1564870.

Liu, Y. & Rosenberg, C. (2013) Dealing with private debt distress in the wake of the European financial crisis: a review of the economics and legal toolbox. International Monetary Fund Working Paper 13/44. Available from: https://www.imf.org/en/Publications/WP/Issues/2016/12/31/Dealing-with-Private-Debt-Distress-in-the-Wake-of-the-European-Financial-Crisis-A-Review-of-40326 [Accessed 15 October 2020].

Loizos, P. & Papataxiarchis, E. (1991) Gender and kinship in marriage and alternative contexts. In: Loizos, P. & Papataxiarchis, E. (eds.) *Contested identities: gender and kinship in modern Greece*. Princeton: Princeton University Press, pp. 3–25.

Malaby, T. M. (2002) Making change in the new Europe: euro competence in Greece. *Anthropological Quarterly* 75(3): 591–597.

Manou, K., Palaios, P. & Papapetrou, E. (2019) Housing wealth, household debt and financial assets: are there implications for consumption? Bank of Greece Working Paper 263. Available from: https://www.bankofgreece.gr/Publications/Paper2019263.pdf [Accessed 11 November 2020].

Mentis, G. & Pantazatou, K. (2015) Country report Greece. In: Micklitz, H. & Domurath, I. (eds.) *Consumer debt and social exclusion in Europe*. Farnham: Ashgate, pp. 29–45.

Moody's (2020) Ratings action: Moody's upgrades Greece's rating to Ba3, outlook remains stable [Press release]. 6 November. Available from: https://www.moodys.com/research/Moodys-upgrades-Greeces-rating-to-Ba3-outlook-remains-stable--PR_435205 [Accessed 11 November 2020].

Mouzouraki, M. (2012) Adopting and implementing the law on debt adjustment and debt relief in Greece at the time of the economic crisis. Paper presented at the conference on "Legislating for personal insolvency in Ireland", 12 April, Dublin. Available from: https://flacdebtconference2012.wordpress.com/papers-presentations [Accessed 1 June 2020].

Nethercote, M. (2019) Revisiting the household for housing research. *Housing, Theory and Society* 36(2): 129–148. doi: 10.1080/14036096.2018.1453865.

Netting, R. M., Wilk, R. R. & Arnould, E. J., eds. (1984) *Households: comparative and historical studies of the domestic group*. Berkeley: University of California Press.

OECD (2020) National accounts at a glance. OECD National Accounts Statistics (database). doi: 10.1787/data-00369-en.

Pagoulatos, G. (2003) *Greece's new political economy: state, finance, and growth from postwar to E.M.U.* New York: Palgrave Macmillan.

Pagoulatos, G. (2014) State-driven in boom and in bust: structural limitations of financial power in Greece. *Government & Opposition* 49(3): 452–482. doi: 10.1017/gov.2014.6.

Palomera, J. (2014) How did finance infiltrate the world of the urban poor? Homeownership and social fragmentation in a Spanish neighbourhood. *International Journal of Urban and Regional Research* 38(1): 218–235. doi: 10.1111/1468-2427.12055.

Παπανικολάου, Δ. (2018) *Κάτι τρέχει με την οικογένια: έθνος, πόθος και συγγένεια την εποχή της κρίσης*. Αθήνα: Εκδόσεις Πατάκη.

Papataxiarchis, E. (1999) A contest with money: gambling and the politics of disinterested sociality in Aegean Greece. In: Day, S., Stewart, M. & Papataxiarchis, E. (eds.) *Lilies of the field: marginal people who live for the moment.* Boulder: Westview, pp. 158–175.

Παπαταξιάρχης, Ε. (2005) Το «νοικοκυριό», ναι, σε εισαγωγικά: για την «οικονομική ανθρωπολογία», την «ελληνική εθνογραφία» και την πολιτισμικήσυγκρότηση της οικιακής εργασίας. In: Φύλο, Χρήμα *και* Ανταλλαγή, 9–11 Δεκεμβρίου, Μυτιλήνη, Λέσβος. Πανεπιστήμιο Αιγαίου. Available from: http://www1.aegean.gr/gender-postgraduate/Documents/Fylo_Chrima_Antallagi/Fylo%20kai%20oikiaki%20ergasia-10-edraft.pdf [Accessed 1 June 2020].

Papataxiarchis, E. (2013) Shaping modern times in the Greek family: a comparative view of gender and kinship transformations after 1974. In: Dialla, A. & Maroniti, N. (eds.) *State, economy, society (19th-20th centuries): essays in honor of emeritus professor George B. Dertilis.* Athens: Metaixmio, pp. 217–224.

Paxson, H. (2004) *Making modern mothers: ethics and family planning in urban Greece.* Berkeley: University of California Press.

Placas, A. (2018) Disrupted and disrupting consumption: transformations in buying and borrowing in Greece. In: Doxiadis, E. & Placas, A. (eds.) *Living under austerity: Greek society in crisis.* New York: Berghahn, pp. 321–346.

Ramsay, I. (2015) Two cheers for Europe: austerity, mortgage foreclosures and personal insolvency policy in the EU. In: Micklitz, H. & Domurath, I. (eds.) *Consumer debt and social exclusion in Europe.* Farnham: Ashgate, pp. 189–227.

Rodrigues, J., Santos, A. C. & Teles, N. (2016) Semi-peripheral financialisation: the case of Portugal. *Review of International Political Economy* 23(3): 480–510. doi: 10.1080/09692290.2016.1143381.

Salamone, S. D. & Stanton, J. B. (1986) Introducing the nikokyra: identity and reality in social process. In: Dubisch, J. (ed.) *Gender and power in rural Greece.* Princeton: Princeton University Press, pp. 97–120.

Θεοδωρόπουλος, Νίκος (2018) Οι δανειολήπτες σπεύδουν να καλυφθούν κάτω από την ομπρέλα προστασίας του νόμου Κατσέλη. Bankingnews.gr, 12 December. Available from: https://bankingnews.gr/index.php?id=399278 [Accessed 11 November 2020].

Theodossopoulos, D. (2003) *Troubles with turtles: cultural understandings of the environment in a Greek island.* London: Berghahn.

VanEvery, J. (1999) From modern nuclear family households to postmodern diversity? The sociological construction of "families". In: Jagger, G. & Wright, C. (eds.) *Changing family values.* London: Routledge, pp. 165–184.

Βλαχούτσικου, Χ. & Μπαχαροπούλου-Κούλη, Ά. (1991) "Να χαρώ κι εγώ το σπίτι μου και το κλειδί απ' τα μέσα": γυναίκες και κατανάλωση σ' ένα χωριό της Βοιωτίας. *Σύγχρονα Θέματα* 45: 94–100.

Yannakopoulos, K. (2009) Cultural meanings of loneliness: kinship, sexuality and (homo) sexual identity in contemporary Greece. *Journal of Mediterranean Studies* 18(2): 265–282. Available from: https://muse.jhu.edu/article/676513/pdf [Accessed 15 October 2020].

Zaloom, C. (2017) Finance. *Cultural Anthropology* website, August 7. Available from: https://culanth.org/fieldsights/1163-finance [Accessed 8 September 2020].

6 "For the sake of consumer protection"

Blending paternalism and neoliberalism in the discursive financialization of households in the Czech Republic

Tomáš Hoření Samec

Introduction

The relationship between financialization of the economy and the increasing role of finance in everyday life has been subject to substantial scrutiny (Beggs et al. 2014; French and Kneale 2009; Langley 2007, 2008, 2009; Langley and Leyshon 2012; Martin 2002; Reid 2017). Some authors have argued that various discourses, technologies and practices transform people into rather coherent (in terms of their attributes, skills and actions) financialized subjects who embrace a calculative investor logic and reliance on financial products (Hillig 2019; Joseph 2014; Martin 2002). Other authors have gone on to problematize this idea, uncovering an inconsistent and uneven nature of the financialization of subjects (Fligstein and Goldstein 2015; Lai and Tan 2015; Lazarus 2017; Montgomerie and Tepe-Belfrage 2019; Pellandini-Simányi and Banai 2020; Pellandini-Simányi et al. 2015; Reid 2017; Samec 2018; Watson 2010). While not necessarily agreeing on the success of the financialization of subjects, most studies share the argument that it is an important technique of governance and identify the state and public institutions as important actors in this endeavour, encouraging the use of financial products and markets to secure one's well-being as part of a broader process of state retreat from welfare provision (Crouch 2009; Doling and Roland 2010; Lai 2017; Lai and Tan 2015; Palomera 2014; Soederberg 2014).

In this chapter, I aim to contribute to this body of literature by demonstrating how public institutions in the Czech Republic blend paternalistic and neoliberal arguments and appeals, thereby engendering a specific mode of discursive household financialization. Focussing on discursive artefacts (websites and parliament speeches) on household finance produced by public institutions (the Czech National Bank, the Ministry of Finance) and representatives of political parties, the chapter develops two arguments. The first argument explores modes of construction of various subject categories that figure in this discourse: households, families, individuals, consumers and citizens. These categories are employed in a manner that acknowledges to some degree the social character of finance and debt but eventually obscures their structural conditions and causes, resulting in an individualization of responsibility for managing risks related to loans and other financial products. Households in particular are constructed as simultaneously unitary and compound actors: consisting of individuals who are understood as forming a compact unit while also having their specific and possibly diverging individual characteristics, interests and preferences, thereby forming a compound actor. This argument brings new insights to the literature on the financialization of subjects that tends to use the terms households, individuals, families, consumers and citizens interchangeably.

The second argument delves deeper into the normative content of this discursive production and relates it to the semi-peripheral character of the Czech economy and financial system and its structural and legal characteristics. More specifically, I show how the country's punitive debt enforcement system may serve as a potential source of legitimacy for a paternalistic rhetoric towards subjects and how the patterns of use of various types of loans (mortgages, consumer loans) by people of different socio-economic backgrounds is to certain extent reflected in discourse. Public institutions and politicians embrace both a seemingly empowering accent on consumer rights and a paternalistic emphasis on protection and surveillance for those deemed irresponsible in their financial practices. This discourse admonishes and educates its subjects to be cautious and careful in their budgeting, loan-taking and investing, rather than emancipated or empowered in relation to lenders and financial markets. It takes for granted using financial products and relying on financial markets and presents it as a morally correct code of conduct for those who proceed reasonably, responsibly and cautiously. Eventually, such discursive practices not only normalize the financialization of subjects but moralize it as a sign of good citizenship (Bryan and Rafferty 2014; Clarke 2015; Hanna et al. 2015; Kear 2013). Thus, paradoxically, even ideologies and moral codes linked to rather non-investor (risk-averse, credit-aware, savings-oriented) behaviour may be employed to promote a vision of a financialized national economy consisting of households that rely on financial markets.

The chapter is structured as follows. The next section discusses the conceptualization of the financialization of subjects in relation to the concepts of household financialization and the financialization of daily life. The third section describes the semi-peripheral characteristics of the Czech Republic with a focus on the emergence of its credit markets. The fourth section recounts the character of the Czech Republic's debt enforcement system, which enables a maximization of profit extraction from vulnerable debtors and constitutes an important context for the discursive financialization of households. The fifth section briefly introduces the concept of discursive financialization and analyses acts of household moralization in the discourse surrounding the adoption of the 2016 Consumer Credit Act, which was essential for regulation of loan-taking. Conclusions discuss the chapter's findings and present an argument that even a discourse warning households against excessive loan-taking may contribute to their financialization and the moralization and individualization of finance by creating two categories of households: those (in)capable of taking on loans and thus (un)worthy of protection and participation in the financial system.

Conceptualizing the financialization of subjects and the financialization of households

Financialization is characterized by the retreat of the state and public institutions from the provision of welfare, housing, education and healthcare, their replacement with financial markets and products, and the related shift of responsibility for welfare provision to households (Finlayson 2009; Forrest and Hirayama 2015; French and Kneale 2009; Lazarus 2017; Montgomerie and Büdenbender 2015; Trumbull 2012; Watson 2010). Various theoretical frameworks and analytical approaches have been employed to understand how financialization transforms the economy and daily life (for literature reviews, see Pellandini-Simányi 2020; van der Zwan 2014). Among these, the Foucauldian approach enables a focus on institutionalized hierarchies of power that discursively construct desired, ideal human actors – financial subjects. These subjects (should) possess specific moral, rational and emotional characteristics that naturalize use of finance and investor-like attitudes. In this chapter, I approach the financialization of subjects with the main focus on discursive modes, such as those that Foucault described as "normation" and normalization of certain characteristics and practices of human actors (Hillig 2019: 1462). These modes also comprise construction of docile subjects who discipline and govern themselves by embracing certain (calculative, investor-like, individualistic) rationalities and moralities (García-Lamarca and Kaika 2016; Joseph 2014; Kear 2013; Lai 2017; Langley 2007; Reid 2017; Türken et al. 2015). While Foucauldian scholars have so far mainly focussed on individuals as financial subjects, in this chapter I extend this analytical framework to collective actors such as households.

The Foucauldian approach is intrinsically related to the study of the financialization of daily life since both strands of literature overlap in their focus on specific actors of financialization, conceptualized variously as individuals, households, citizens or just subjects. While Hillig (2019: 1463–1464), for instance, includes a concern with subjectivity and its governance in the framework of the financialization of daily life, the latter, in my understanding, implies a focus on an actual performance of prescribed practices, such as taking out a mortgage to finance a buy-to-let investment, creating a portfolio of financial products and so on. The literatures on the financialization of subjects and daily life overlap also with work that explicitly employs the concept of household financialization (e.g. Beggs et al. 2014; Hillig 2019;

Montgomerie and Büdenbender 2015). The studies from these three strands of literature share the understanding that the discursive formation of financial subjects as enabling a smooth intrusion of finance into everyday life and life-cycle events, such as the transition to homeownership, university enrolment or retirement. For example, they draw attention to how political and financial elites expect households to embrace the responsibility for collectively self-managing financial risks while securing one's welfare through financial products and financial markets (Beggs et al. 2014). Notably, in all three strands of literature – on the financialization of daily life, subjects and households, respectively – we often encounter the concepts of individual, household, citizen and consumer being used interchangeably, which obscures the potential differences between them as categories of financial subjects. In contrast, this chapter unpacks the specificities of discursive construction of Czech households as ideal financial subjects. As we will see, the key distinguishing characteristic of households is that they are constructed as hybrid actors: at the same time compound – consisting of individuals with specific and possibly diverging characteristics, interests and preferences – and unitary, since these individuals need to, at least to a certain degree, coexist and co-operate.

A specific field of research that has emerged within the literature on the financialization of subjects and that is relevant to my focus in this chapter concerns financial education and financial literacy. It has been argued that the aforementioned shift of responsibilities for risk-taking and financial management onto individuals and households has been achieved also through financial education and financial literacy discourses (Beggs et al. 2014; Clarke 2015; Kear 2013; Maman and Rosenhek 2020), which also contribute to the individualization of the causes and effects of (financial) success or failure (Hanna et al. 2015; Türken et al. 2015). Financial education discourse also promotes certain moral codes, such as reliability or entrepreneurial spirit, which should guide economic action such that individuals are enrolled in financial relations in "proper" ways (Lai 2017). In the case of financial education, we see how various actors, including public institutions, non-governmental organizations and private businesses such as banks and other financial providers, act together to promote a certain vision of reality where individual knowledge, capacities and actions play a decisive role in life fortunes, an argument which also resonates in the case of Czech public institutions, as will be shown later in the chapter. However, outcomes of such subject construction and responsibility ascription are not always as expected. The logic may fail to be fully adopted due to the more or less subversive resistance of its prospective subjects (Hájek et al. 2020) or even due to a lack of will or capacity of the governmental apparatus to actively promote it (Čada 2018). In sum, then, the financialization of subjects is far from uniform, definite and unchallenged (Lazarus 2017; Pellandini-Simányi and Banai 2020), although pressures to normalize a particular version of the self and, more broadly, economic practices reliant on finance are immense.

Varieties of financialization: the Czech Republic as a double semi-periphery

Anglo-Saxon countries such as the United States, the United Kingdom or Australia tend to be generally described as the "most advanced" in terms of the role of finance in the daily lives of individuals and the financialization of households (e.g. Fligstein and Goldstein 2015: 576; Langley 2007; van der Zwan 2014: 114–115). However, continental European countries have also been exposed to financialization at various scales and to different extents; hence this collection's focus on household financialization in Europe's peripheries. Housing is one of the domains in which the effects of financialization on households in these spaces have been most obvious. Households in countries such as Spain (García-Lamarca and Kaika 2016; Palomera 2014; Buier and Sabaté, this volume) or Hungary (Pellandini-Simányi et al. 2015; Pósfai 2018; Gagyi et al., this volume) have been enrolled in particularly risky and exploitative relations of housing financialization due to a lack of legal protection and other factors.

The concepts of periphery and semi-periphery have multifaceted meanings and usages in the literature, as discussed by Mikuš and Rodik in their introduction to this volume. I build on their distinction between real and financial accumulation relations as two dimensions of core-periphery relations, and the notion of the semi-periphery as an intermediate position in these relations, in order to characterize the Czech Republic as a double semi-periphery. Thus, the Czech Republic occupies a semi-peripheral position within the core-periphery relations of real accumulation inasmuch as it has developed complex industries that, nevertheless, still rank lower than their counterpart industries in the core (including their parent companies) in the hierarchies of autonomy, sophistication and added value (Bohle and Greskovits 2012: 44–48).[1] This implies a significant share of low-wage jobs and sets the stage for widening social inequalities. The Czech Republic's position within the core-periphery relations of financial accumulation is also characterized by a certain in-betweenness. On the one hand, as in other settings of peripheral financialization, the financialization of the Czech economy has been extraverted in the sense of reliance on cross-border capital inflows (Becker et al. 2010: 229–230; Gabor 2011: 126, 176). Similarly to the Czech industry, the financial and banking system is dominated by subsidiaries that export significant revenues out of the country to their parent companies, based typically in the core (Gabor 2011: 149). On the other hand, some key characteristics of peripheral financialization in Central and Eastern Europe were relatively moderate in the Czech Republic or absent altogether: net capital inflows tended to be smaller than in other countries and did not rely on debt instruments, while low interest rates on the domestic currency mitigated speculative inflows and carry-trade activity, including foreign-currency lending (Gabor 2011: 176, 178–179).

Transformation from the former Czechoslovak socialist political and economic system to liberal democracy and capitalism has decisively shaped the Czech Republic's trajectory towards semi-peripherality. The so-called bank socialism era of the 1990s saw a high level of state intervention in the banking sector in the form of bailouts for banks facing bankruptcy. After completing the privatization of major banks, the first half of the 2000s was marked by a steady growth in mortgage lending, which accelerated just before the US mortgage crisis. Mortgage lending has remained under the relatively strict regulation of the Czech National Bank, and banks did not offer foreign-currency mortgages as in Hungary, Poland or Croatia (Halawa 2015; Mikuš 2019; Pellandini-Simányi et al. 2015; Rodik 2015). The volume of mortgage loans to households currently accounts for almost one-quarter of the Czech GDP, which is still under the EU average and on a level similar to Ireland or Poland (Bertalot et al. 2019: 124). Nevertheless, the Czech trajectory of housing financialization is distinctive in that the largest expansion of mortgage lending did not occur during the 2000s boom as in most European countries, but in 2014–2018 when the total volume of mortgage loans grew by a half and their average size almost doubled from €41,000 to €72,000 (Bertalot et al. 2019: 122). The expansion of the mortgage market was accompanied by a sharp increase in house prices and rents in major cities, such as Prague and Brno, as well as a drop in housing affordability for those first entering the market and vulnerable social groups.

In the Czech Republic, mortgage loans and consumer loans operate as relatively distinct debt circuits that target different social groups. While mortgages are mostly used by middle- and high-income groups, consumer loans have predominated among those without savings and assets and with precarious incomes, such as single-income households.[2] These loan categories also carry different cultural meanings, as we will also see in the following empirical sections. Major mainstream media have constructed mortgages as a normal and inevitable tool for achieving homeownership (Samec 2020). Mortgages have been supported by state policies such as tax deductions and may be invoked as a proof of their holders' success and responsibility, despite also generating fear and anxieties (Samec 2018). The expanding mortgage market with its low level of defaulted loans – approximately 1% in 2020 and 3% during most of the economic recession and stagnation in 2009–2014 (CNB 2020) – contrasts with a high level of arrears and defaults on consumer loans. In terms of its structure, the consumer credit market is more complex than the mortgage market. Three segments may be distinguished: (1) bank lenders with relatively strict lending criteria and transparent terms ("bank consumer loans"); (2) non-bank lenders targeting low-income social groups with loans for hire purchase of consumer goods ("subprime consumer loans"); and (3) non-bank lenders actively seeking out potential borrowers (often those already indebted) and offering legal but highly exploitative "fast" loans ("predatory consumer loans"). The Czech subprime credit market is therefore mostly comprised by the second and third segments of the consumer credit market, whereas experiences with subprime mortgages or FX mortgages have absented. In addition, consumer loans are intrinsically linked to the Czech system of debt enforcement, which is the subject of the next section.

The debt enforcement system in the Czech Republic

The combination of a, until 2016, poorly regulated consumer credit market and a comparatively punitive debt enforcement system (Ošťádlová 2017) constitutes an important material context for the discursive financialization of Czech households. Before 2016, providers of loans below CZK 5,000 (approximately €200) only needed to register as self-employed entrepreneurs in order to run a business and were not subject to any regulatory requirements whatsoever. Unregulated subprime and predatory lending contributed to a situation whereby approximately 821,000 people (almost one-tenth of the Czech adult population and almost one-fifth of Czech households) faced legal debt enforcement (*exekuční* řízení or *exekuce*) at the end of 2018 (Otevřená společnost and Ekumenická akademie 2019). In practice, this means wage and property seizures and life on the brink of poverty unless one is able to secure sufficient income in the informal labour market. Private bailiffs (*exekutoři*) have the right to seize money from bank accounts such that only a monthly "unimpoundable minimum" remains. At the time of writing, this minimum, depending on the debtor's monthly income and presence of dependents, may be as low as CZK 7,771.50 (about €310), which corresponds to three-quarters of the living wage.

Bailiffs also have the right to seize non-financial property, such as most consumer goods (with some exceptions, such as a refrigerator) and when the amount of debt exceeds CZK 100,000 (about €4,000) also the real estate. The origins of the current debt enforcement system may be traced back to 2001 when the system was privatized. No longer employees of the state, private bailiffs (*exekutoři*) became freelance professionals (required to have a legal education) who could enforce debt collection on the basis of court authorization. The privatization of the debt enforcement system together with other legal conditions, such as disproportionately high bailiff and lawyer fees as well as large fees for overdue repayments, resulted in the creation of so-called "debt business" (*obchod s dluhy*). This term refers to extremely profitable practices of debt enforcement that may result in a debtor with an originally minor debt, such as an unpaid fine of CZK 200 (about €8), eventually having to repay up to 100 times more in fees and sanctions related to the enforcement proceeding itself.

Although there is no central debt enforcement registry that could be mined for evidence on reasons for these proceedings, a survey (Prokop 2018) of individuals facing them indicated three main causes: 57% of respondents had been unable to repay a consumer loan, 24% had not paid rent or utility bills and 17% had not paid bills for phone or financial services. This points to a widespread issue with the inability to repay consumer loans, which may be attributed either to the insolvency of debtors or the intentional lenders' strategy of making the loans practically unpayable in order to expand value extraction from debtors via debt enforcement proceedings. Another study based on interviews with people facing debt enforcement identified a complex set of reasons for their inability to repay, which often coincided with and reinforced each other: serious health problems, family and relationship issues, job loss or parental leave (Szénássy et al. 2017: 48–49). Available statistics further suggest that over-indebtedness is more concentrated among low-income households and that the debt enforcement system pushes them out of formal labour and housing markets into (semi-) illegal jobs and substandard housing (Trlifajová and Hurrle 2019).

Consumer Credit Act (CCA) no. 257/2016 was expected to change this situation while also harmonizing the Czech legal system with EU requirements. The thorough discussion of the law among politicians, bank representatives and social workers from NGOs helping over-indebted people started in 2014. The law did bring more regulation. It banned "arbitration clauses" (*rozhodčí doložky*) in loan agreements through which the debtor waived the right to a trial and left disputes to be resolved by a private arbitrator, often clientelistically linked with the loan provider. It also capped the debt enforcement fees of lawyers and bailiffs, and limited sanctions for debt repayment arrears. It charged the Czech National Bank with supervision of special new licences for loan providers, now required under rather strict conditions. Finally, it also allowed for early repayment of loans (including mortgages) without sanctions from the lender (such as additional fees). As the next section shows, the discourse surrounding the adoption and implementation of the CCA serves as an example of the moralizing discourse on the patterns of household financialization shaped by the Czech consumer credit market and debt enforcement system.

For the sake of consumer protection? Czech public discourse on household finance

This chapter adopts an approach inspired by the Foucauldian framework that emphasizes the role of discourse and the interplay of power relations between formal institutions (such as the government) and members of social institutions (such as households). Inspecting discursive artefacts produced by Czech public institutions and political actors, the chapter focusses on how they construct an ideal of financial behaviour and financial subjectivity based on moralization, evoking emotions and confirming certain structural conditions or attributes of individuals and households as taken-for-granted. The concept of discursive financialization is employed here to underscore that many transformations of subjectivities and, subsequently, everyday life would hardly be possible without a way of naming and talking about finance and without circulating instructions for people or institutions on how to act in relation to it. Thus, only through a set of discursive practices does the "purple haze" of finance become filled with meanings, emotional attachments and moral evaluations, thereby constituting finance as a discoverable, communicable and knowable reality that subjects may relate to and interact with (de Goede 2005: 5–8). In this sense, discursive financialization refers to two aspects of discourse: *language in action*, conceptualized here as discursive artefacts (e.g. laws, websites, parliamentary speeches), and the *rules* of making these texts, especially the rules of what and how may be said to be accepted as a relevant actor in public debate (Hájek 2014: 115). The following two sub-sections analyse the ways in which the discourse of public institutions, through an accent on certain moral codes and attempts to invoke emotions, constructed households as subjects acting in a financial context and promoted the ideal vision of the household as a financial subject.

Households educated to self-protect: public institutions promoting financial responsibility

The adoption of the 2016 Consumer Credit Act was an important milestone in the regulation of consumer loans, particularly subprime and predatory loans. In addition to significantly changing the legal setting and thereby the overall character of the consumer credit market, the CCA was also accompanied by communicative efforts by public institutions related to the law specifically (speeches surrounding its approval in the Czech parliament) or household finance more broadly (websites published on behalf of the Czech National Bank [CNB] and the Ministry of Finance [MoF]). As such, the resulting discursive artefacts are particularly relevant for the analysis of discursive household financialization in the Czech Republic.[3]

Addressing the general public and, in the case of the CNB, also explicitly targeting young adults (as a social group perceived as less responsible in financial management), both the CNB and the MoF referred to their audience explicitly as "households". At the same time, they often explicitly or implicitly linked this concept with the one of the nuclear family. For example, the CNB's educational website *Money on the Run*, in a section titled "Family", discusses the issues of a joint family/household budget where the household is depicted as a joint project, something to be "built up". Financial products, such as a joint bank account, are there to facilitate proper household functioning – proper from the point of view of the national economy and financial markets – and provide welfare through a better overview and control of the household economy:

> How will you manage your household [finances]? The joint bank account is a useful helper in family finance planning. … Remember that only one person is the owner at a time. That person can cancel the account at any time, disable access, or take out a loan.[4]
>
> (CNB 2016a)

This excerpt indicates a theme that is emblematic throughout the various discursive accounts: the hybrid character of households as financial subjects. While the text speaks about a "joint" account, it also states that only one person is its legal owner. This is the case despite underscoring the need for coordination between household members; for example, the website also advises prospective joint bank account holders to agree on how much each will contribute before deciding to open a joint account. Households thus appear as simultaneously unitary and compound subjects: unitary since they are discursively constructed as economic *units* (sharing the budget, for instance), and compound since they, of course, consist of individuals who may have different interests and preferences – though they usually (must) co-operate. This is further illustrated by a discussion of the issue of debt of married couples in the same website section:

> Be honest with each other. For obligations and debts taken on before the marriage, the obliged one [by contract] is usually the only one responsible; however, potential debt arrears and enforcement may affect common matrimonial property.
>
> (CNB 2016a)

The CNB's website seeks to moralize readers through a call for honesty, which is reinforced by a bogeyman in the form of debt enforcement. The moralization is justified by the fact that while an individual can take out a loan on their own, stop repaying it and be subjected to debt enforcement, their spouse is also legally liable for repayment, making it a problematic issue in cases of divorce or the original borrower's death. Here, we can also see how the notions of the family and the household overlap; the website speaks about household finance while assuming a familial (marital) relationship as a framework for the management of debt. Moreover, there is a hint at complex relationships between actions and responsibilities of individual family (or household) members and possible power asymmetries between them inasmuch as the mentioned legal setting reproduces gender power asymmetries in the domain of finance. A qualitative study of Czech over-indebted households revealed a pattern of (former) wives/female partners having to repay the debts of their (former) husbands/male partners (Szénássy et al. 2017). With debt enforcement hanging in the air as a phantom that may ruin one's life, financial education is presented as a universal solution. Although the CNB website (in a section titled "Debts") provides detailed instructions on how to cope with debt arrears and debt enforcement, neither the CNB nor the MoF ever closely describe (not to mention criticize) the actual social and legal circumstances of over-indebtedness, taking them for granted as background conditions. This contrasts with the discourse of politicians, as we will see in the next section.

The dangers of excessive indebtedness are often moralized through the use of affective language that should evoke fear of irresponsible borrowing, as in the section of the CNB website titled "Loans and Credit". The CNB warns against even small debts ("remember that even small loans can cause big debts"), categorizes particular debts as bad ("loans for Christmas gifts or holidays") and questions the rationality of household decisions ("an object of desire quickly recedes"; "do you really need a loan?"). Paradoxically, it achieves these objectives by itself employing affective language intended to evoke fear of consequences ("nobody wants a crowd of bailiffs at their door") and the moral code of self-responsibility ("the burden of repayment can weigh down on you for 20 years"). This would seem to suggest that authors of the

CNB and MoF websites argue against the use of financial products (loans) and becoming an entrepreneurial, investor-like subject. In reality, however, they only discourage taking out what they understand as non-productive loans (for gifts and optional consumption in general) and borrowing by those who do not have enough resources to repay. The following is the introduction to another section of the CNB website titled "Housing":

> It is tempting to fulfil your dream of homeownership. However, everyone must realistically consider whether his own housing [i.e. owner-occupied] is appropriate for his life situation and whether his budget will withstand such a big commitment in the future.
>
> (CNB 2016b)

The introduction again invokes the principle of self-responsibility ("big commitment in the future"). It states that mortgage loans and, by implication, the good life that can be achieved through homeownership, are here only for those who can "realistically consider" their situation (i.e. be careful and rational), "withstand [the] big commitment" (i.e. be responsible) and plan their household budget (i.e. be calculative). Thus, entering the world of finance and loans is morally right only for careful and responsible subjects:

> Although the activity of providing consumer credit is legally regulated … this legal regulation cannot replace rational judgment that each consumer must make on their own before concluding a credit agreement.
>
> (CNB 2016b)

Practically the same rhetoric may be found in the article *Christmas on Credit?* published on the MoF website in 2019. While referring to the 2016 Consumer Credit Act, it moralizes loan-taking by introducing the category of "reasonable debt", which includes "homeownership and investment in one's own education". After an overview of relevant consumer rights, the piece concludes:

> Thus, the law does remember consumer rights. However, it cannot save us from our own irresponsibility. Irresponsibility for spending on something we do not really need. … Please do not forget, even during Christmas time, that when debts grow over our heads, we face the risk that the next time (when we might need it all the more) nobody will lend to us and that we can cause many problems for our family and sleepless nights.
>
> (MoF 2019)

Again, the moralistic distinction between good and bad borrowing and spending practices and the evocation of fear of the consequences of indebtedness that may affect the family are used to influence readers. The overarching motivation seems to be instilling caution, reason and prudence in dealings with finance. However, the article also states that "consumer credit is part of the market economy, whether we like it or not" (MoF 2019), thus normalizing it as an inevitable feature of the capitalist economy. The discourse of protection articulated by the emphasis on consumer rights thus merges with calls to self-monitor household finances and limit one's emotional decision-making – being a reasonable and therefore reliable financial subject is the ultimate value (Beggs et al. 2014: 987). Implicitly, only subjects (individuals and households) that act responsibly are worthy of (legal) protection, while others are depicted as irresponsible and debt enforcement against them as their individual fault. While everybody is admonished to be reasonable and cautious in their loan-taking, the use of financial products is presented as an unavoidable and normal part of life. At the same time, the article again points to the hybrid (unitary/compound) character of households by marking the subjects of household finance as "consumers" while discussing their conduct during Christmas, which is generally perceived as an emblematic family event. The article therefore suggests that our subjectivity is, first, one of a consumer (i.e. subject of market choices) who only secondarily acts within a social and cultural context (having a family, experiencing Christmas, etc.), which, nevertheless, should not influence their reasonability and prudence.

Households must be responsible: consumer credit act in parliamentary debates

In April 2016, Andrej Babiš, then the minister of finance, introduced a draft of the Consumer Credit Act in the Chamber of Deputies (the lower house of the Czech parliament) during its second hearing. He emphasized consumer protection as its rationale and invoked the argument of consumer rights to back his claim that the law should be swiftly adopted (Parlament ČR 2016b). This led to a general discussion about causes of the proliferation of debt arrears, debt enforcement and the appropriate (effective and morally correct) extent of regulation. Two distinct kinds of arguments emerged in the discussion: one about debtors' (lack of) rationality, intelligence and responsibility, invoked to call into question their deservingness of protection and regulation, and the other about social aspects of indebtedness, such as constructing certain vulnerable categories of people and revealing the social (specifically familial) dimension of debt.

The first theme was illustrated by Marek Benda from the liberal-conservative Civic Democratic Party (ODS), who questioned borrowers' moral right to legal protection, arguing that taking out a loan is always a *voluntary* choice and a question of one's intelligence: "The idea that we must always protect everyone from their own stupidity – I just want to point out that no one has ever forced anyone to take out a consumer loan." (Parlament ČR 2016b). However, this idea of a complete and unlimited freedom of choice, regardless of relevant structural and individual conditions, was discarded by most other politicians who made the second type of arguments. This included MPs representing a coalition of leftist and centrist parties as well as those from the right-wing nationalist populist party Dawn (Úsvit). Martin Lank (Dawn) thus argued that predatory lending techniques affect mostly "seniors" who need protection:

> I don't think this is really about intelligence. … They [predatory lenders] are abusing people who are currently in a difficult, desperate situation or simply do not understand the economy and cannot do the maths. They are simply not all geniuses when it comes to economics and finance. And they are often seniors. I believe these people need to be protected.
>
> (Parlament ČR 2016b)

Karel Fiedler (Dawn) also disagreed with the argument that people *always* take out a loan voluntarily and went further in emphasizing the social and economic conditions that may lead people into the hands of predatory lenders:

> People get into various life situations; I could come up with a lot of examples. For example, a single woman with children: the ex-husband does not pay the mandatory alimony, she gets into trouble. When her washing machine stops working, she can wash her laundry by hand; when her refrigerator or stove stops working, it is a bigger problem. She lives simply from pay check to pay check – and here comes a forced loan (*nucený úvěr*).
>
> (Parlament ČR 2016b)

Interestingly, when referring to the subjects of the CCA, the politicians used the terms "families" and "households" only rarely; instead, they talked about "consumers", "citizens" and specific categories such as "single mothers" or "seniors". This stands in contrast to the categorization of financial subjects by the CNB and the MoF. While these institutions were unable or unwilling to explicitly nuance their advice for different social groups that face significantly varied economic conditions, the politicians attempted to reflect the situation of specific social groups. Furthermore, the idea of the absolute voluntariness of loan-taking shared by liberal and conservative right-wing politicians was questioned by left-wing and populist right-wing politicians on the grounds that people cannot always influence their own life circumstances and the social and economic conditions in which they find themselves.

However, ultimately, politicians of all parties proved willing to individualize the issue of "consumer" protection from excessive debts through an accent on financial education and literacy. Such an argument was made by, for example, Miroslav Kalousek, leader of the liberal-conservative party TOP09:

> Without higher financial literacy, the problem will simply not be solved – and the level of financial literacy is desperate. … And we will not protect anyone from their own irresponsibility and stupidity by [adopting] any norm.
>
> (Parlament ČR 2016c)

The call for financial literacy enabled a consensus between politicians who supported stronger regulation of (predatory) lending and those who doubted its practical effectiveness. In their speeches, politicians of all allegiances repeatedly referenced individual financial literacy as something necessary for the financial system to work well. The objective of achieving financial literacy on the part of "ordinary people" (seen as currently lacking it) was thus defined as essential and beyond dispute, even by those who saw predatory lending techniques as the main cause for the proliferation of debt arrears and defaults. Such discursive production paints a picture where the fundamentals of the financial system are principally right and beyond questioning, and it is only its specific flaws that need fixing. Only one voice, again Karel Fiedler's (Dawn), offered a hint of a counter-narrative introducing the idea of possible structural causes behind over-indebtedness, such as poverty:

> Increasing the financial literacy of citizens – that has been here before. I think that it would be a good idea to also increase the financial self-sufficiency of those citizens so that they do not have to borrow for a washing machine. I can understand that they will borrow for housing … but many are in a financial situation that they must borrow three or four thousand crowns [ca. €120–160].
>
> (Parlament ČR 2016b)

However, even this supposed counterargument did not question the hegemonic view of finance as an instrument for delivering welfare ("I can understand that they will borrow for housing"). Even the word choice "financial self-sufficiency" (*finanční soběstačnost*) speaks in favour of individualized solutions and obscures the social dimension of debt, that is, that indebtedness (and debt enforcement) has implications not only for individuals but also, possibly, their household members. Therefore, although some politicians acknowledged the social implications of credit and debt and criticized the predatory lending techniques as immoral, eventually, they resorted to the individualized solutions (financial education) and causes of the problem (lack of financial literacy and proper financial rationality).

Conclusions

This chapter has examined the role of public institutions and political representatives in the discursive financialization of households in the Czech Republic through a focus on their discursive production dealing with consumer credit and its legal regulation. This focus brings another important element to the literature on household financialization in the semi-peripheral countries of Central and Eastern Europe (Halawa 2015; Halawa and Olcoń-Kubicka 2018; Mikuš 2019, 2020; Olcoń-Kubicka 2020; Pellandini-Simányi et al. 2015; Pósfai 2018; Rodik 2015; Rodik and Žitko 2015; Stenning et al. 2010) and enables comparison with other countries, especially those comprising the Anglo-Saxon and Western European cores. The chapter has advanced two arguments. The first concerns the discursive construction of various kinds of financial subjects – households, families, citizens, consumers – and especially the hybrid (unitary/compound) character of the household (overlapping with the family) when evoked in the discourse of public institutions. The discursive artefacts produced by the Czech National Bank and the Ministry of Finance thus constructed the financial subject as an individual actor embedded within certain social relations – those of the household/family. At the same time, they failed to acknowledge the broader social and economic context of (over-) indebtedness – they did mention the threat of (over) indebtedness spreading to those social relations but avoided discussing the characteristics of the consumer credit market, the debt enforcement system and so on. They used the terms household and family interchangeably and connected the concepts of the household as an economic unit and the (nuclear) family as a social unit to certain traditional roles. In other words, households were constructed as coextensive with nuclear families, and the possibility of different household forms and money management arrangements went unrecognized (e.g. when partners share funds only partially, when an adult individual cohabits with parents and contributes to the household budget, etc.). At the same time, politicians spoke about the responsibility of individuals when discussing problems of predatory lending and inadequate legal protection. They usually invoked subject categories such as consumers or clients and almost never used the terms family and household, although some of them did refer to the effects of over-indebtedness falling hard especially on certain categories, such as elderly people or single-income households with children. This difference shows that the CNB and the MoF are locked in a specific discourse on the household economy that does not differentiate between individuals and households/families (as if they had roughly the same economic position and social status), while the politicians ascribed multiple subjectivities to them in various contexts – political ("citizens"), economic ("consumers") and social ("single mothers", "seniors"). Therefore, although the politicians ultimately individualized the solutions for indebtedness, they were at least able to politicize the discussion to a certain degree, unlike the CNB and the MoF.

The first argument on the modes of subject categorization is directly linked to the second argument that concerns the normative character of discursive household financialization. The chapter has revealed the importance of the idea of household (self-) protection and the specific combination of paternalism – suspicion of household irresponsibility packed with the need for surveillance – and neoliberalism characterized by appeals for households to be responsible for their own self-surveillance (on neoliberal and paternalistic elements of financial expert discourse, see Pellandini-Simányi and Conte 2020). Protection has thus been given a double meaning of protecting households from predatory lending techniques as well as from themselves (their own irresponsible financial practices, ignorance etc.). The accent on protection was repeated across various sites of discourse and was linked to the threat to households represented by the Czech debt enforcement system with its maximized value extraction from debtors in default. This finding demonstrates the important role of public institutions and the state in the processes of debt collection (Mikuš 2020), not only through setting the legal framework but also through discursive practices that refer to debt collection in order to influence household behaviour. The key means for delivering the double protection according to politicians and public institutions was financial education and literacy, which individualized and potentially depoliticized the issue, similarly to the financialization of subjects/households in core countries (Türken et al. 2015). The chapter has further shown that the modes of ascribing responsibility are similar, with an important role for emotions such as fear (Deville 2015) and the moral principles of duty and loyalty (Lai and Tan 2015: 75) that public institutions mobilize to influence the attitudes and behaviour of households. In another similarity with Anglo-Saxon contexts, households are put into an ambivalent position in which they are required to be financially active yet also prudent in order to meet the criteria for morally correct financial subjects (Beggs et al. 2014: 988).

Nevertheless, there are also major differences between the Czech case and, for instance, the one of the United Kingdom, where, according to Hillig (2019), asset accumulation has become the standard strategy of households, or the United States, where the subjectivity of the entrepreneurial investor seems to have attained a particularly strong position (Joseph 2014). In comparison, the strong paternalist component of Czech discursive financialization marks particular kinds of subjects as unable to properly conduct such strategies and develop such subjectivities and thereby, potentially, limits the spread of those strategies and subjectivities. This is influenced by the structural conditions in which financialization takes place. Namely, the semi-peripheral nature of the Czech economy and its financial system has made a significant share of population reliant on low-wage jobs, as a result of which they lack savings for unexpected expenses and turn to subprime and predatory credit. This is directly linked to another specificity of the Czech context: the punitive debt enforcement system that enables the maximization of value extraction from over-indebted people. This contributes to a material setting conducive to a form of paternalistic/neoliberal discursive financialization that admonishes households to be more prudent, rational and responsible in light of a proliferation of highly extractive enforcement proceedings interpreted as an outcome of excessive loan-taking. Debt enforcement thus serves as a spectre for disciplining households, similarly to the spectre of evictions in countries hit by mortgage crises (Palomera 2014; Placas and Sabaté, this volume).

In the Czech consumer credit market, the main cause for debt enforcement is non-bank and predatory consumer loans rather than subprime or FX mortgages found in some other semi-peripheral Southern and Eastern European countries. This is linked also to the segmentation of the credit market, as a result of which mortgages are used by the (aspiring) middle class, whereas consumer loans, especially non-bank and predatory consumer loans, are accessed mostly by those who have insufficient incomes and no savings and assets. The paternalistic tendencies in the discursive artefacts produced by public institutions are thus targeted at the use of consumer credit and implicitly at low-income and less educated citizens; it is consumer loans that are depicted as problematic and their users as those in need of financial education in order to protect themselves. This is the case even though the CNB and the MoF do not explicitly differentiate households according to their socio-economic conditions. However, while warning against an excessive embrace of consumer credit, the discourse on household finance ultimately directs households towards the use of financial products, albeit in a responsible and reliable manner that enables the financialized national economy to run smoothly (Beggs et al. 2014: 987). The debates surrounding the new Consumer Credit Act thus ultimately cemented the discursive financialization of households by affirming a vision of reality in which the use of financial products is taken for granted as inevitable and as a structural condition not to be questioned by public actors.

Acknowledgements

This work was supported by the Grant Agency of the Czech Republic [grant no. GA20-04863S]. I would like to thank the editors Marek Mikuš and Petra Rodik for their valuable feedback, which has helped me significantly during the course of writing. For support and inspiring commentaries, I would like to thank Karina Hoření, my colleagues Anja Decker and Lucie Trlifajová, and people from the Critical Studies Seminar at Institute of International Relation Prague.

Notes

1 Bohle and Greskovits (2012) distinguish between semi-core and semi-periphery and classify the Czech Republic as the former, but I omit these nuances here due to space limitations.
2 It is important to note that there is no publicly available data linking households' incomes with their loan portfolios. The argument here is based on indirect evidence such as income requirements to qualify for the various kinds of loans.
3 The CCA was discussed and adopted by both chambers of the parliament in March-July 2016 and became effective in December 2016 (Parlament ČR 2016a). The CNB's website *Money on the Run* was published in October 2016.
4 All translations of excerpts are my own.

References

Becker, J., Jäger, J., Leubolt, B. & Weissenbacher, R. (2010) Peripheral financialization and vulnerability to crisis: a regulationist perspective. *Competition & Change* 14(3–4): 225–247. doi: 10.1179/102452910X12837703615337.

Beggs, M., Bryan, D. & Rafferty, M. (2014) Shoplifters of the world unite! Law and culture in financialized times. *Cultural Studies* 28(5): 976–996. doi: 10.1080/09502386.2014.886480.

Bertalot, L., Johnson, J., Westig, D. & Pérez, S. G., eds. (2019) *Hypostat 2019: a review of Europe's mortgage and housing markets*. Brussels: European Mortgage Federation, European Covered Bond Council.

Bohle, D. & Greskovits, B. (2012) *Capitalist diversity on Europe's periphery*. Ithaca: Cornell University Press.

Bryan, D. & Rafferty, M. (2014) Political economy and housing in the twenty-first century – from mobile homes to liquid housing? *Housing, Theory and Society* 31(4): 404–412. doi: 10.1080/14036096.2014.947080

Čada, K. (2018) "They seemed like super businessmen": financial instruments in social housing policy. *Critical Housing Analysis* 5(2): 56–67. doi: 10.13060/23362839.2018.5.2.443.

Clarke, C. (2015) Learning to fail: resilience and the empty promise of financial literacy education. *Consumption Markets and Culture* 18(3): 257–276. doi: 10.1080/10253866.2014.1000315.

CNB (2016a). Rodina. Available from: https://www.penizenauteku.cz/zivotni-udalosti/rodina/ [Accessed 7 October 2020].

CNB (2016b). Bydlení. Available from: https://www.penizenauteku.cz/zivotni-udalosti/bydleni/ [Accessed 7 October 2020].

CNB (2020) Non-performing clients loans (ARAD data series system). Available from: https://www.cnb.cz/cnb/STAT.ARADY_PKG.VYSTUP?p_period=1&p_sort=2&p_des=50&p_sestuid=22023&p_uka=1%2C2%2C3%2C4%2C5%2C6%2C7%2C8%2C9%2C10%2C11%2C12%2C13%2C14%2C15%2C16%2C17%2C18%2C19%2C20%2C21%2C22%2C23%2C24%2C25%2C26%2C27%2C28%2C29%2C30%2C31%2C32%2C33%2C34%2C35%2C36%2C37%2C38%2C39%2C40%2C41%2C42%2C43%2C44%2C45%2C46%2C47%2C48%2C49%2C50%2C51%2C52%2C53%2C54%2C55%2C56%2C57%2C58%2C59%2C60&p_strid=AABBAE&p_od=200201&p_do=202008&p_lang=EN&p_format=0&p_decsep= [Accessed 7 October 2020].

Crouch, C. (2009) Privatised Keynesianism: an unacknowledged policy regime. *The British Journal of Politics and International Relations* 11(3): 382–399. doi: 10.1111/j.1467-856X.2009.00377.x.

De Goede, M. D. (2005) *Virtue, fortune, and faith: a genealogy of finance*. Minneapolis: University of Minnesota Press.

Deville, J. (2015) *Lived economies of default: consumer credit, debt collection and the capture of affect*. London: Routledge.

Doling, J. & Ronald, R. (2010) Home ownership and asset-based welfare. *Journal of Housing and the Built Environment* 25(2): 165–173. doi: 10.1007/s10901-009-9177-6.

Finlayson, A. (2009) Financialisation, financial literacy and asset-based welfare. *The British Journal of Politics and International Relations* 11(3): 400–421. doi: 10.1111/j.1467-856X.2009.00378.x.

Fligstein, N. & Goldstein, A. (2015) The emergence of a finance culture in American households, 1989–2007. *Socio-Economic Review* 13(3): 575–601. doi: 10.1093/ser/mwu035.

Forrest, R. & Hirayama, Y. (2015) The financialisation of the social project: embedded liberalism, neoliberalism and home ownership. *Urban Studies* 52(2): 233–244. doi: 10.1177/0042098014528394.

French, S. & Kneale, J. (2009) Excessive financialisation: insuring lifestyles, enlivening subjects, and everyday spaces of biosocial excess. *Environment and Planning D: Society and Space* 27(6): 1030–1053. doi: 10.1068/d7607.

Gabor, D. (2011) *Central banking and financialization: a Romanian account of how Eastern Europe became subprime*. Basingstoke: Palgrave Macmillan.

García-Lamarca, M. & Kaika, M. (2016) "Mortgaged lives": the biopolitics of debt and housing financialisation. *Transactions of the Institute of British Geographers* 41(3): 313–327. doi: 10.1111/tran.12126.

Hájek, M. (2014) *Čtenář a stroj: vybrané metody sociálně vědní analýzy textů*. Praha: Slon.

Hájek, M., Šrám, K., Kolomoiets, M. & Cuker, I. (2020) Uneasy neoliberal governance in a low-trust society: barriers to responsibilisation in the Czech Republic. *Sociological Research Online* 25(2): 201–218. doi: 10.1177/1360780419866464.

Halawa, M. (2015) In new Warsaw. *Cultural Studies* 29(5–6): 707–732. doi: 10.1080/09502386.2015.1017141.

Halawa, M. & Olcoń-Kubicka, M. (2018) Digital householding: calculating and moralizing domestic life through homemade spreadsheets. *Journal of Cultural Economy* 11(6): 514–534. doi: 10.1080/17530350.2018.1486728.

Hanna, P., Cunningham, L. & Walker, C. (2015) The indebted individual: dominant discourses and alternative understandings of personal debt in the UK. In: Değirmencioğlu, S. M. & Walker, C. (eds.) *Social and psychological dimensions of personal debt and the debt industry*. Basingstoke: Palgrave Macmillan, pp. 203–221.

Hillig, A. (2019) Everyday financialization: the case of UK households. *Environment and Planning A: Economy and Space* 51(7): 1460–1478. doi: 10.1177/0308518X19843920.

Joseph, M. (2014) *Debt to society: accounting for life under capitalism*. Minneapolis: University of Minnesota Press.

Kear, M. (2013) Governing *homo subprimicus*: beyond financial citizenship, exclusion, and rights. *Antipode* 45(4): 926–946. doi: 10.1111/j.1467-8330.2012.01045.x.

Lai, K. P. Y. (2017) Unpacking financial subjectivities: intimacies, governance and socioeconomic practices in financialisation. *Environment and Planning D: Society and Space* 35(5): 913–932. doi: 10.1177/0263775817696500.

Lai, K. P. Y & Tan, C. H. (2015) "Neighbours first, bankers second": mobilising financial citizenship in Singapore. *Geoforum* 64: 65–77. doi: 10.1016/j.geoforum.2015.05.023.

Langley, P. (2007) Uncertain subjects of Anglo-American financialization. *Cultural Critique* 65(1): 67–91. doi: 10.1353/cul.2007.0009.

Langley, P. (2008) *The everyday life of global finance: saving and borrowing in Anglo-America*. Oxford: Oxford University Press.

Langley, P. (2009) Debt, discipline, and government: foreclosure and forbearance in the subprime mortgage crisis. *Environment and Planning A: Economy and Space* 41(6): 1404–1419. doi: 10.1068/a41322.

Langley, P. & Leyshon, A. (2012) Guest editors' introduction. Financial subjects: culture and materiality. *Journal of Cultural Economy* 5(4): 369–373. doi: 10.1080/17530350.2012.703146.

Lazarus, J. (2017) About the universality of a concept: is there a financialization of daily life in France? *Civitas-Revista de Ciências Sociais* 17(1): 26–42. doi: 10.15448/1984-7289.2017.1.25942.

Maman, D. & Rosenhek, Z. (2020) Facing future uncertainties and risks through personal finance: conventions in financial education. *Journal of Cultural Economy* 13(3): 303–317. doi: 10.1080/17530350.2019.1574865.

Martin, R. (2002) *Financialization of daily life*. Philadelphia: Temple University Press.

Mikuš, M. (2019) Contesting household debt in Croatia: the double movement of financialization and the fetishism of money in Eastern European peripheries. *Dialectical Anthropology* 43(3): 295–315. doi: 10.1007/s10624-019-09551-8.

Mikuš, M. (2020) Making debt work: debating and devising debt collection in Croatia. In: Hann, C. & Kalb, D. (eds.) *Financialization: relational approaches*. New York: Berghahn Books, pp. 241–265.

MoF (2019) Vánoce na úvěr? Available from: https://financnigramotnost.mfcr.cz/cs/tipy-navody/tipy-a-navody-financni-vzdelavani/blog/2019/vanoce-na-uver-3188 [Accessed 7 October 2020].

Montgomerie, J. & Büdenbender, M. (2015) Round the houses: homeownership and failures of asset-based welfare in the United Kingdom. *New Political Economy* 20(3): 386–405. doi: 10.1080/13563467.2014.951429.

Montgomerie, J. & Tepe-Belfrage, D. (2019) Spaces of debt resistance and the contemporary politics of financialised capitalism. *Geoforum* 98: 309–317. doi: 10.1016/j.geoforum.2018.05.012.

Olcoń-Kubicka, M. (2020) Pursuit of fairness in household financial arrangements among young middle-class couples in Poland. *Journal of Consumer Culture* 20(2): 156–174. doi: 10.1177/1469540519891272.

Ošťádlová, Š. (2017) *Systémy a formy oddlužení v Evropě: srovnávací analýza*. Praha: Ekumenická Akademie.

Otevřená společnost & Ekumenická akademie (2019) Mapa exekucí. Available from: http://mapaexekuci.cz/index.php/mapa-2/ [Accessed 7 October 2020].

Palomera, J. (2014) How did finance capital infiltrate the world of the urban poor? Homeownership and social fragmentation in a Spanish neighbourhood. *International Journal of Urban and Regional Research* 38(1): 218–235. doi: 10.1111/1468-2427.12055.

Parlament ČR (2016a). Sněmovní tisk 679: Vl.n.z. o spotřebitelském úvěru - EU. Available from https://www.psp.cz/sqw/historie.sqw?o=7&t=679 [Accessed 11 November 2020].

Parlament ČR (2016b). Vládní návrh zákona o spotřebitelském úvěru /sněmovní tisk 679/ - druhé čtení. Available from https://www.psp.cz/eknih/2013ps/stenprot/044schuz/bqbs/b17502101.htm [Accessed 11 November 2020].

Parlament ČR (2016c). Vládní návrh zákona o spotřebitelském úvěru /sněmovní tisk 679/ - třetí čtení. Available from https://www.psp.cz/eknih/2013ps/stenprot/047schuz/bqbs/b17616001.htm [Accessed 11 November 2020].

Pellandini-Simányi, L. (2020) The financialization of everyday life. In: Borch, C. & Wosnitzer, R. (eds.) *The Routledge handbook of critical finance studies*. New York: Routledge, pp. 278–299.

Pellandini-Simányi, L. & Banai, A. (2020) Reluctant financialisaton: financialisation without financialised subjectivities in Hungary and the United States. *Environment and Planning A: Economy and Space*. doi: 10.1177/0308518X20960740.

Pellandini-Simányi, L. & Conte, L. (2020) Consumer de-responsibilization: changing notions of consumer subjects and market moralities after the 2008–9 financial crisis. *Consumption Markets & Culture*. doi: 10.1080/10253866.2020.1781099.

Pellandini-Simányi, L., Hammer, F. & Vargha, Z. (2015) The financialization of everyday life or the domestication of finance? How mortgages engage with borrowers' temporal horizons, relationships and rationality in Hungary. *Cultural Studies* 29(5–6): 733–759. doi: 10.1080/09502386.2015.1017142.

Pósfai, Z. (2018) Reproducing uneven development on the Hungarian housing market. PhD thesis, University of Szeged.

Prokop, D. (2018) Exekuce v Česku: zkušenosti poloviny chudých Čechů a dopady exekucí. Praha: Median.

Reid, C. K. (2017) Financialization and the subprime subject: the experiences of homeowners during California's housing boom. *Housing Studies* 32(6): 793–815. doi: 10.1080/02673037.2016.1240760.

Rodik, P. (2015) The impact of the Swiss franc loans crisis on Croatian households. In: Değirmencioğlu, S. M. & Walker, C. (eds.) *Social and psychological dimensions of personal debt and the debt industry.* Basingstoke: Palgrave Macmillan, pp. 61–83.

Rodik, P. & Žitko, M. (2015) Financialization, household debt and new vulnerabilities in post-socialist societies. In: Radošević, D. & Cvijanović, V. (eds.) *Financialisation and financial crisis in South-Eastern European countries.* Frankfurt am Main: Peter Lang, pp. 49–70.

Samec, T. (2018) Performing housing debt attachments: forming semi-financialised subjects. *Journal of Cultural Economy* 11(6): 549–564. doi: 10.1080/17530350.2018.1493611.

Samec, T. (2020) Normalization of mortgages in media discourse through affects and instructions. *Housing, Theory and Society* 37(2): 180–197. doi: 10.1080/14036096.2019.1584584.

Soederberg, S. (2014) *Debtfare states and the poverty industry: money, discipline and the surplus population.* London: Routledge.

Stenning, A., Smith, A., Rochovská, A. & Świątek, D. (2010) Credit, debt, and everyday financial practices: low-income households in two postsocialist cities. *Economic Geography* 86(2): 119–145. doi: 10.1111/j.1944-8287.2009.01066.x.

Szénássy, E., Kňapová, K. & Dvořáková, T. (2017) *Jak zůstat člověkem v síti dluhů: kvalitativní výzkum.* Praha: Ekumenická akademie.

Trlifajová, L. & Hurrle, J. (2019) Work must pay: does it? Precarious employment and employment motivation for low-income households. *Journal of European Social Policy* 29(3): 376–395. doi: 10.1177/0958928718805870.

Trumbull, G. (2012) Credit access and social welfare: the rise of consumer lending in the United States and France. *Politics and Society* 40(1): 9–34. doi: 10.1177/0032329211434688.

Türken, S., Carlquist, E. & Allen, H. (2015) Chasing happiness through personal debt: an example of neoliberal influence in Norwegian society. In: Değirmencioğlu, S. M. & Walker, C. (eds.) *Social and psychological dimensions of personal debt and the debt industry.* Basingstoke: Palgrave Macmillan, pp. 160–179.

Van der Zwan, N. (2014) Making sense of financialization. *Socio-Economic Review* 12(1): 99–129. doi: 10.1093/ser/mwt020.

Watson, M. (2010) House price Keynesianism and the contradictions of the modern investor subject. *Housing Studies* 25(3): 413–426. doi: 10.1080/02673031003711550.

Afterword

Jeanne Lazarus

Introduction

In Europe and North America, the withdrawal of the welfare state, the "risk shift", the growth of household debt and the increasing inequalities put in question the possibility of maintaining a middle class. A number of political signs attest to this concern: support for populist parties; protest movements such as the yellow vests (*gilets jaunes*) in France; and increased demands for protection against "others" (i.e. immigrants) and against the economic turmoil experienced by working people, many of whom suffer a downgrading of their socio-economic status and come to expect worse still for their children. The twentieth-century promise of stable work, collective protections and steady improvements in education and health that would bring general comfort and security and ensure smooth social reproduction is hardly fulfilled. This is undoubtedly one of the greatest political, social, economic and ideological challenges that societies in rich countries are facing today.

Financialization is often pointed to as one of the culprits for all these harms. The concept of the "financialization of daily life" arose during the early 2000s to describe how lifestyles have been disrupted by the uncertainties of a future increasingly dependent on financial market processes (Martin 2002). Individual subjectivities have been also altered: definitions of oneself, one's place in the society, one's family and one's children have become increasingly mediated by financial tools. Credit scores and investments in retirement savings or college education testify to households' success or failure (Fourcade and Healy 2013; Langley 2008; Langley and Leaver 2012; Zaloom 2019).

However, the literature on the financialization of daily life has initially developed in the context of the US whose characteristics are, of course, not shared by the entire world. Indeed, financialization of daily life is more pronounced in the US for several reasons. First, credit has been used already since the nineteenth century as a tool for the economic and social development of the country and a means of protecting its citizens against instability and economic shocks (Hyman 2011; Prasad 2012; Quinn 2019). Second, collective protections, even at times when they were relatively substantial, have never been as extensive in the US as in the European countries with the most generous welfare state regimes (Esping-Andersen 1989; Skocpol 2000). In the US, private pensions plans have long been the dominant form of pension insurance; health insurance is plural, very unequal and frequently insufficient, depending on one's occupation; and the education system is particularly expensive. The risk shift described by Jacob Hacker (2006) or Gerald Davis (2009), to the extent that it can be detected elsewhere, is first and foremost a transformation of US household finance. While analyses of the financialization of lifestyles and subjectivity soon developed elsewhere than in the US, notably in the UK, each country presents its own financial landscape and its own system of social protection, which are also embedded in a distinct labour market and local social structures. The amplitude, modalities and consequences of financialization on the economy and daily life must be described in detail in each context (Lazarus 2017). Such approach can enhance the understanding of the process, which no longer appears as a *deus ex machina* but as a social and historical phenomenon, enabled by concrete decisions, institutions and actors.

This volume, edited by Marek Mikuš and Petra Rodik, makes a major contribution to the understanding of these phenomena: observing the processes of financialization and their effects on households in countries that are rarely examined in international publications not only documents supplementary cases but, by shifting the viewpoint, also opens up new questions. As I will develop in what follows, the first major contribution of the collection lies in analysing financialization through household practices: such practices enable the financialization of the economy, which requires households to adopt financial tools for their reproduction. The chapters highlight the conditions of possibility of this adoption and its consequences for households, especially when economic crisis strikes. In addition to this main theme, a second theme is running through the chapters: protection. In Eastern and Southern Europe, over the last 20 years, households have been exposed to unprecedented financial risk without any accompanying system of protection. The collection invites the reader to wonder why such protection does not exist and to what extent it would be feasible.

Financialization and household practices

To understand the effects of financialization on societies, it is necessary to take a closer look at practices. But which practices? What is the right level of analysis for comprehending the relevant economic practices? Social sciences know that individuals are embedded in social spaces. Their economic practices are most often recorded at the level of the household, according to statistical definitions that associate the household with the place of residence. While contracts with financial institutions are signed by either individuals or couples, they are backed by the commitment of other people with whom they have family or friendship ties. The chapters of this collection address this question with a pragmatic approach: to understand who is attached to financial practices, be it daily expenses, investments, loans, informal money exchange or a contract between a bank and its client, researchers must comprehend the functioning of social and family ties in a given society but also within different social groups in the same society. At the same time, as Lofranco reminds us in the Bosnian case, we must avoid a culturalist view as these ties are also made of constraints: when the welfare state is insufficient, the extended family provides a safety net through money transfers or in-kind assistance including housing; when banks ask for guarantors, borrowers are forced to call on their entourage; when the law says that both spouses are committed by the signature of either one, people may inherit debts they have not signed up for and so on.

Given the many external links involved in its composition, this book demonstrates that the extremely complex and variable notion of the household is a constructed, yet essential, category. The household does not exist, but it is an indispensable fiction. Research then consists of defining its contours instead of taking it for granted and looking at how the financial industry itself participates in its definition. Why is this useful? The literature on household finance is constantly entangled in a contradiction between studying money in detail, in order to understand how it circulates, and categorizing it, in order not to simply describe but to go up towards generalization. Tracking money in finance, however, can very quickly lead up to categories as huge and hard to manipulate as financial markets, capitalism and (neo)liberalism. Individuals are then often presented as passive in the face of these large forces, as subject to them and having their own subjectivity colonized by finance. Looking at practices offers more complex narratives: individuals are more heterogeneous; other attachments and constraints appear; even if individuals cannot always resist the forces of finance, they regain agency. But is this not an illusion, one that arises simply due to the angle from which we observe these practices? Can social and economic domination be perceived by looking only at individuals? This is where choosing the appropriate methodology is crucial, as the contributors to this collection show: it is necessary to observe not only what individuals do but also their social integration and their interactions with institutions, including financial institutions. Economic ethnography in a financialized world must consider the multiple spaces of money in which people circulate.

The notion of juggling (Guérin et al. 2014) is very useful here. Developed by researchers working on countries of the Global South, it describes situations in which users of financial products not only master different spaces of economic calculation but use them in parallel to respond to different layers of obligations they encounter. Juggling is particularly visible between formal and informal forms of finance. This dichotomy is an object of debate: these categories, coming in particular from international institutions that promote the "formal" economy and discredit the "informal" economy associated with precariousness as well as with a lack of state control, illegal work and tax evasion, are both simplifying and overly judgemental. Informality is made of formalities, contracts and real commitments, and, conversely, the formal economy has many informal dimensions. Nevertheless, financial practices related to the financial industry operate differently from those that take place in families or networks of social acquaintances. One of the essential contributions of this book is to depict how households juggle at least four types of social spaces: the formal economy of lenders belonging to the world of finance, regulated to a greater or lesser extent by the state; the functioning of the labour market and the guarantees that may or may not be associated with it, depending on the welfare state regime; economic exchanges with relatives and other social contacts; and their domestic space, where they try to preserve a certain degree of autonomy and intimacy in relation to the three other spaces. Household finance draws on its knowledge of this intimacy: interacting with banks requires self-reporting on one's personal and professional situation; moreover social ties are integrated into loans through social collateral and credit scoring systems that consider the borrower's professional status as well as personal stability. In addition, insurance puts one's health condition on the table.

Do social ties and informality play a particular role in the financial practices of households in semi-peripheral countries in Southern and Eastern Europe? An evolutionary view would suggest that these countries are, in terms of financial development, more advanced than those of the Global South but not fully modern compared to the core countries and that they have retained social models that give a central place to the family as both a safety net and a means of pooling resources to participate in the formal economy. We must beware of the teleological narrative that assumes that each country needs to experience the same stages of development to ultimately reach an advanced stage of financialization of household monetary practices. Consequently, if financialization is less advanced in a given country, the latter is described as lagging behind. Yet the level of financialization of households differs between countries depending on political choices and the balance of power between financial markets and regulators. Moreover, its unfolding was not the same everywhere. Core countries experienced a much slower pace of financialization, which was preceded by massive bankarization controlled by governments and adapted to the socio-economic conditions of the population. The advanced stage of this process of financialization was characterized by, at least partial, withdrawal of the bank as an intermediary between household finance and market finance. In the countries examined in this book, financialization was much more brutal because it was not preceded by a developed and solid banking system as in Sweden or France, for instance (Husz 2018; Lazarus 2012). The history of these countries provides an explanation: in the 1960s and 1970s, Eastern Europe was under Communist rule, Yugoslavia experimented with self-managing market socialism, while Southern Europe was struggling with political crises, dictatorships and very fragile economic situations. The increase in the average standard of living came with the European Union and the opening of markets, especially banking markets, to foreign financial institutions. This took place in countries where states had relatively little leeway and in a period of economic history characterized by the triumph of liberalism, which appeared as the path to prosperity. This may explain the feeling that emerges from reading the chapters of the book – one of a careless exposure of the populations of these countries to predatory finance without providing adequate public protection. As the chapter on Hungary by Ágnes Gagyi and her co-authors puts it, some households have been "over-included" in finance, placing them in a highly risky situation.

For this book does not only discuss finance and households. It also discusses a major crisis, the 2007–2008 Global Financial Crisis, which occurred at the very time when many of the countries studied here have been accelerating the liberalization of their financial markets and the risk shift by withdrawing collective protections and replacing them with individual protections provided by the financial industry. When the crisis came at the height of this transformation, states and households were extremely vulnerable because old protections had been dismantled and new ones revealed their deficiency, or worse, turned out to be a source of risk themselves. Two interrelated problems emerged: mass-distributed loans became unrepayable as a result of the collapse of the labour market; and middle-class lifestyles that were promised could not be achieved. The value of autonomy, promoted by financialization, was shaken at its core.

The cases presented in this volume show that national laws frequently offered insolvent debtors in semi-peripheral countries poor protection. While countries where bankarization preceded financialization have been able to build personal bankruptcy and debt mediation systems (Ramsay 2017), households in the countries presented in this collection were often left to deal with the financial industry on their own. In many cases, not only did borrowers have to continue paying when their home had been foreclosed and even if the property developer had gone bankrupt before even completing the construction of the real estate for which people got indebted, but guarantors were solicited, leading to a generalized contagion of debt in societies as Irene Sabaté and Natalia Buier show for the Spanish case. Similarly, in the case of Bosnia and Herzegovina exposed by Zaira Lofranco, when the crisis occurred, the mobilization of family ties that had served to create the "fictional individual of financial contract" came to light. Greece and the Czech Republic, as respectively described by Aimee Placas and Tomáš Hoření Samec, tried to create protections for insolvent debtors, although the task was arduous during times of crisis: their states were in a weak position vis-à-vis financial markets, and the fledgling institutions were overwhelmed by the demands.

How to protect others and oneself?

Most of all, this volume addresses the issue of protection: the ethnographic approach reveals how individuals, households and families struggle to survive economically and safeguard their reproduction in the turmoil created by a rapid, poorly regulated financialization, exacerbated by the crisis. The analyses reveal four partly complementary, partly competing logics of protection in response to household financialization in semi-peripheral settings. First, one of the promises of financialization is that finance will become a protective tool. Insurance, investments and credit will provide the means to build up wealth, stabilize it and later allow for its transmission. If households, with the help of financial education, make good use of finance, they will succeed in protecting themselves in an autonomous way without being dependent on the state or on family and friendship ties. This is why financial educators in Bosnia and Herzegovina, in combating the public "guarantors' issue", advocate autonomy, itself at the heart of the "fiction" of the responsible consumer (Zaloom 2018). Therefore, protecting oneself, in this perspective, means breaking with family ties as the second form of protection in order to decide on rational and controlled budget decisions. Such "centripetal" tendencies, as Sabaté dubs them, have been visible in Bosnia but also in Spain and Greece. During the credit boom, the financial industry had integrated into its operations the strong ties that characterize families in these countries. When the crisis arose, these ties became dangerous for individuals, and these most traditional tools of protection have been called into question. Yet, at the same time, most of the chapters in this book also document a resilience of collective protection models based on family ties. They are the last safety nets, not without difficulties in societies where the standard of autonomy has risen sharply. The third form of protection can be found in the politicization of household finance, as seen, for example, in Spain. Collective organization among debtors became the force of resistance against finance when the state failed to play this role.

Finally, the fourth form of protection that can emerge from this politicization is public regulation. Depending on national histories of the construction of the consumer financial market, such regulation may coincide with the exposure of the population to financial tools or be built in response to financial crises. It can develop in two broad domains: as consumer protection, verifying the quality of the product sold and the process of its marketing (e.g. the information provided, the withdrawal period or the mandatory information that have to be collected), and as support for over-indebted borrowers through debt mediation or bankruptcy laws. However, in the countries examined in this collection, this regulation has mostly come late and remained weak.

Shifts

By presenting a series of in-depth analyses of the links between financialization and households in the semi-peripheral countries of Europe, this fascinating collection accomplishes a series of shifts from the now classic work on financialization. First, of course, a geographical shift: like many other subjects, household financialization has been extensively analysed in wealthy, especially English-speaking, core countries. These are influential countries in political and economic terms as well as in the academic world, in the sense that they are the geographic spaces that concentrate leading journals, accumulated and cutting-edge knowledge, and so on. In comparison, the rest of the world always appears "local". In English-language publications on a country other than the US or the UK, one routinely encounters, at one point or another, a section explaining differences with core countries – often in response to requests of reviewers originating from those countries. By undertaking to write about countries purely for their own sake and not to show differences with better-known models, the book shows that the financialization of a society may only occur if it is inscribed in a national history since it takes place within legal institutions, a specific labour market and a specific banking market. From this, it can be inferred that the financialization of everyday life portrayed in the "classic" literature is but one possible version of this process, which was shaped by the local conditions of Anglo-American countries and as such is by no means natural.

Finance strives to get rid of borders, but these remain important: when national cases are put alongside one another, the determinants of the financial landscape emerge. Law and regulation are crucial: the imagination of the financial industry can be more or less unbridled depending on the possibilities offered in a given country. For example, while the Czech Republic did not ban foreign-currency lending to households, policies that secured low inflation, low interest rates on the domestic currency and subsidies for mortgage lending in the domestic currency created an environment in which it was practically non-existent. Conversely, in other countries, "exploitative loans to all exploitable borrowers" (Aalbers 2016: 52, as quoted by Mikuš and Rodik, this volume) have flourished. The strength of consumer protection varies and is reflected in the extent to which populations are exposed to risk. This is part of a set of political and geopolitical questions that the geographical shift proposed by this book opens up. The notions of periphery and semi-periphery invite us to look at these countries as parties to relationships of dependence and hierarchy vis-à-vis richer countries and the financial industry represented by firms that are often foreign, over which political power has even less control than elsewhere.

At the same time, legal and regulatory phenomena like consumer rights themselves exist in a particular economic and financial context: how do households live? Are jobs and incomes stable? How do banks consider local lifestyles? Do collective protections adequately address health problems, divorce or unemployment? Are economic resources derived solely from wage labour or can social and family ties provide them? This book highlights the ability of finance to hook into local ecosystems. Finance is powerful because financial products are exceptionally flexible and financial actors work hard to adjust them to the functioning of the societies in which they operate. The financialization of daily life therefore appears less as a steamroller than fine-tuned work carried out by experienced actors who know how to embrace social factors as varied as social stratification, family models, labour law or emotions. However, if the financial industry knows how to adapt, it also transforms the social spaces in which it settles. It alters the norms through which individuals conduct their lives and evaluate each other. If habits are finally transformed, it is because finance has succeeded in being adopted and penetrating domestic spaces. As Viviana Zelizer (2005) has shown, the economy and intimacy are not separated by a firewall. Far from it; economic activities cannot develop unless they are accepted in moral terms.

In the cases discussed in this collection, financialization has damaged households as it forced its logic into relationships that operated according to other norms. Zelizer (2005) reminds us that the idea of the separation of spheres is recent, dating from the nineteenth century, precisely when the growth of economic activity increased the circulation of money in households, while capitalism imposed the norm according to which the economic sphere follows solely instrumental logic. Since then, there is more money in households than ever before. But households try to domesticate money by imposing limits on it. When family ties intersect with finance, especially through the use of guarantees, the limits set by individuals are undermined. Thus, individuals are hurt not by the presence of money in their exchanges – this was already the case – but because this presence is no longer driven by the emotional and family ties that justified it in the first place. Finance is not external to social life. The work gathered here reveals the ways in which it is becoming pervasive and sometimes dangerous.

Finance appears within an already existing imaginary of the good life. The imaginary of Western middle-class lifestyle is not new in semi-peripheries. At least since the 1960s, in most of these countries, this lifestyle model was already known and often fantasized, not only through the media but also through the presence of tourists, as in Yugoslavia (Duda 2016). This imaginary has been further transformed by finance. This is reflected in all of the cases presented. In Greece, the multiplication of consumer credit has gone hand in hand with an upsurge in average consumption levels and the availability of goods due to the multiplication of shopping malls. In Spain and Bosnia, the real estate boom in combination with the availability of credit has reshaped the definition of a middle-class household's normal home. Budget-management habits are transformed, as well as the share of income that it seems normal to dedicate to debt repayment. While the degree to which it has transformed individuals into financial subjects is not obvious, the financialization of households in European semi-peripheries has provided material means, if precarious, for actualizing the pre-existing aspirations to the idealized middle-class lifestyle originating from the richer countries of Western Europe and North America. This lifestyle requires a high level of consumption by an autonomous nuclear family. In Southern Europe, this means breaking away from the extended family; in Eastern Europe, it additionally implies movement away from the collective way of life promoted by the earlier Communist regime. Consumer finance promises autonomy: borrowing money means not having to seek help from anyone; it presents itself in the form of a contract free of emotional ties or moral judgement. However, wherever banks developed credit, they learned how to "attach" their debtors through multiple non-financial links (Deville 2015). Emotional and moral aspects abound in consumers' ties with the formal economy.

Finally, the book achieves also a methodological shift when compared to approaches to financialization that tend to limit themselves to a single layer of analysis. The chapters analyse neither "high" nor "low" finance but rather the circulation between the different "layers" (Deville et al. 2016): households in their diversity, notably specifying how modalities of financialization differ according to social groups; organizations such as banks and public institutions mandated to assist debtors or implement welfare measures; and the level of public policies, geopolitical relations between states, and strategies of global companies. Household financialization cannot be understood without considering all these layers. Escaping an overly narrow particularism and linking the described processes to large-scale economic and social issues require not only dexterity in description but also a method that deliberately acknowledges these different layers and is capable of reconstructing, in any particular case, the economic and political history of the country, the banking and financial market, the welfare regime, the functioning of family and social ties, the consumption patterns, the differences between social groups, and the actual practices of indebtedness, investment and payment.

The amount of work required indicates that international knowledge of financialization is a collective effort. This volume demonstrates that joining forces with researchers from different backgrounds and countries not only produces an incredible amount of knowledge but also advances our understanding of the processes that put household economies at risk as finance penetrated them while the protections that existed in the twentieth century, whether from the welfare state or family ties, deteriorated without being replaced.

References

Aalbers, M. B. (2016) *The financialization of housing: a political economy approach.* London: Routledge.

Davis, G. F. (2009) *Managed by the markets: how finance re-shaped America.* Oxford: Oxford University Press.

Deville, J. (2015) *Lived economies of default: consumer credit, debt collection and the capture of affect.* London: Routledge.

Deville, J., Lazarus, J., Luzzi, M. & Ossandón, J. (2016) *Domesticizing financial economies: studying finance in between market devices, everyday calculation and government.* SASE 28th Annual Conference: Moral Economies, Economic Moralities. University of California – Berkeley.

Duda, I. (2016) When capitalism and socialism get along best: tourism, consumer culture and the idea of progress in Malo misto. In: Archer, R., Duda, I. & Stubbs, P. (eds.) *Social inequalities and discontent in Yugoslav socialism*. London: Routledge, pp. 185–204.

Esping-Andersen, G. (1989) *The three worlds of welfare capitalism*. Cambridge: Polity.

Fourcade, M. & Healy, K. (2013) Classification situations: life-chances in the neoliberal era. *Accounting, Organizations and Society* 38(8): 559–572.

Guérin, I., Morvant-Roux, S. & Villarreal, M. (2014) *Microfinance, debt and over-indebtedness: juggling with money*. Abingdon: Routledge.

Hacker, J. S. (2006) *The great risk shift: the new economic insecurity and the decline of the American Dream*. Oxford: Oxford University Press.

Husz, O. (2018) Bank identity: banks, ID cards, and the emergence of a financial identification society in Sweden. *Enterprise & Society* 19(2): 1–39.

Hyman, L. (2011) *Debtor nation: the history of America in red ink*. Princeton: Princeton University Press.

Langley, P. (2008) *The everyday life of global finance: saving and borrowing in Anglo-America*. Oxford: Oxford University Press.

Langley, P. & Leaver, A. (2012) Remaking retirement investors. *Journal of Cultural Economy* 5(4): 473–488.

Lazarus, J. (2012) *L'épreuve de l'argent: banques banquiers clients*. Paris: Calmann-Lévy.

Lazarus, J. (2017) About the universality of a concept: is there a financialization of daily life in France? *Civitas* 17(1): 26–42.

Martin, R. (2002) *Financialization of daily life*. Philadelphia: Temple University Press.

Prasad, M. (2012) *The land of too much: American abundance and the paradox of poverty*. Cambridge: Harvard University Press.

Quinn, S. (2019) *American bonds: how credit markets shaped a nation*. Princeton: Princeton University Press.

Ramsay, I. (2017) *Personal insolvency in the 21st century: a comparative analysis of the US and Europe*. Oxford: Hart.

Skocpol, T. (2000) *The missing middle: working families and the future of American social policy*. New York: W. W. Norton.

Zaloom, C. (2018) How will we pay? Projective fictions and regimes of foresight in US college finance. *HAU: Journal of Ethnographic Theory* 8(1–2): 239–251.

Zaloom, C. (2019) *Indebted: how families make college work at any cost*. Princeton: Princeton University Press.

Zelizer, V. (2005) *The purchase of intimacy*. Princeton: Princeton University Press.

Index

Note: Page numbers followed by "n" denote endnotes.

www.ingramcontent.com/pod-product-compliance
Lightning Source LLC
LaVergne TN
LVHW021128300926
849160LV00010B/919